3/23/09

A History of the Heart

A History of the Heart

Ole M. Høystad

REAKTION BOOKS

For Sigrid, Gudrun and Torgeir

Published by Reaktion Books Ltd
33 Great Sutton Street
London EC1V 0DX
www.reaktionbooks.co.uk

First published in English 2007

This book was first published in 2003 by Spartacus forlag, Oslo, under
the title *Hjertets kulturhistorie, frå antikken til vår tid* by Ole M. Høystad
© Spartacus forlag

English-language translation © Reaktion Books 2007

This translation has been published with the financial support of NORLA Non-fiction

English translation by John Irons

Printed in China

British Library Cataloguing in Publication Data
  Hoystad, Ole
    A history of the heart
    1. Heart in art 2. Heart in literature 3. Heart – Mythology
    4. Body, Human, in popular culture
    I. Title
    306.4

    ISBN-13: 9-781-86189-311-6
    ISBN-10: 1-86189-311-6

Contents

Preface

Down through the ages, important books have been written because their authors have experienced so strong an urge to communicate something that they have embarked on their venture, despite the difficulties and obstacles in their path. The history of intellectual life and of civilization has to a great extent to do with the fate of books. And books continue to be read because they can touch our hearts, involve us, move us emotionally and intellectually, in our attitudes and actions, individually and collectively.

The subject of this book is this restless heart – the Augustinian *cor inquietum* – that seeks for something else, something better, and therefore strives to uncover the internal and external reasons for this restlessness. The book does not only deal with what touches people's hearts and moves them but also with all that the heart represents and symbolizes in our own Western and other closely related cultures. These creative forces have been the driving force behind my research within this field.

Even though the heart is the main symbol of what it means to be a human being, there are few specialist books on the heart in world literature. Some do exist, however, especially in German, as is apparent from the bibliography. To them I owe a debt of gratitude. My presentation differs from other books on the heart in including not only material from cultural history but also a particular anthropological and updating perspective that seeks to offer a more systematic, anthropological positioning of the representations of the heart in a disenchanted age. Furthermore, I also stress the importance of Islam and of Persian and Arabic poetry, normally conspicuous by its absence in histories of the heart, emphasizing the mutual influence and dependence that exists between Christian-European and Islamic-Arabic culture. For this, my approach is interdisciplinary. Alongside sources from the history of religion, culture and ideas I build on paradigmatic literary works seen from a cultural, historical and anthropological perspective.

To prevent the presentation, with its various perspectives, from drowning in references to the sources on which I base my argument, quotations and references have been reduced to a minimum. In a broad presentation such as this one, communicating with the reader must have pride of place. I hope that this has resulted in a book which is both readable and worth reading for more than just specialists – who in this particular instance are all of us, each and every one who is in contact with his or her own heart and wishes to learn its innermost secrets.

Without a proficient translator, this book – a revised and expanded version of the Norwegian original – could not appear in English. For a writer who comes from a small language community it has been a special pleasure to cooperate with John Irons, a translator sensitive to the stylistic nuances of minority Neo-Norwegian, who has translated the book as congenially as he has cordially. Thanks also to the staff at NORLA (Norwegian Literature Abroad), who with imaginative flair have assisted in the rebirth of this book.

Introduction

> The heart has its reasons,
> which reason knows not of.
>
> Pascal

Since the dawn of human cultural history, the magical pulsating heart within our breast has been the great enigma and mystery of human life. As early as the oldest written sources, those of Mesopotamia, about 3,000 BC, the heart has been at the centre, whatever fate had in store. The heart is a matter of life and death, not only physically but also mentally. What will happen after death is in most religions and views of life also a question of the personal and moral qualities possessed by the heart – and everything it stands for.

When the Sumer-Babylonian hero Gilgamesh (c. 2,000 BC), finds himself at the most critical and dramatic point in his life, he offers a heart to the gods. Why does he do that? When the ancient Egyptians embalmed a corpse, the heart was the only internal organ that was replaced in the chest cavity before it was sealed again and the body wrapped in a linen cloth. Why did the Egyptians take such special care of the heart?

While the Egyptians made sure that the dead person had his heart with him when entering the realm of the dead, the Aztecs in Mesoamerica took the heart *out* of thousands of living people, cutting it out of the chest with a flint knife and offering it, still beating, to the gods. The attitude of the Egyptians and the Aztecs demonstrates that the heart represents something very different in various cultures, that the heart may just as well divide as unite people. For Christians and humanist Westerners there is a special reason for asking why the Aztecs could be so heartless – if that is what they were.

Questions like these will be addressed in this book: how the heart has been perceived; what it represents symbolically in some central civilizations and how our own Western heart with its various figurative forms and functions has emerged via a long historical development. To limit the length of the account, this cultural history will only include the major cultures that in various ways, directly and indirectly, are part of our own European and Western history during a long period of development. This means that the Middle East will also be given a central position, since Judaism was a prerequisite for European Christianity coming into existence via an interaction of loans and influences from other local cultures. Special emphasis will be placed on the Sumer-Babylonian and ancient Egyptian cultures, against which the Jews often defined themselves in order to present an identity that was distinctive from that of their neighbours. This also applies to the heart, which has a completely different content for Judaism than it had for the Babylonians and Egyptians.

Even though the New Testament builds on the conception of the heart found in the Old Testament, the heart has a different content in Christianity than in Judaism. This has to do with the sufferings of Christ and the place that blood has in Christianity. The dramatic life of Jesus and the connection between his blood and heart provide ample scope for interpretations and symbolic presentations that function as a kind of engine and foundation for what in the course of the medieval period assumes the form of a European culture. This history is full of paradoxes.

One of these is the influence from Islamic-Arabic culture, which is often portrayed in opposition to the Christian-European. By focusing on the conception of the heart in the two cultures not only are differences revealed but also an Arab influence which in many ways – at variance with basic Christian thought – has shaped our European heart from the Middle Ages to the present day. My assertion is that the modern European is a product of the influence on European culture of Islamic-Arabic culture during the High Middle Ages. That is why the Islamic-Arabic conception of the heart is given a key position in this presentation.

According to the standard conception, European culture has two main roots: one originating from the Jewish-Biblical arsenal of ideas, the other from Greek Antiquity. While our religious faith dates back to an Arabic-Semitic tradition as recorded in the Bible, our art and rationality in the form of philosophy and science are to a great extent inspired by Greek culture. But the oldest Greek, as known to us from Homer's portrayals from about 700 BC, is perhaps very different from the European. Basing ourselves on the conception of the heart we meet in Homer – to the extent that his literary figures have a heart in our sense of the word – we therefore intend to examine whether there is anything that is constant in man, whether there exists anything universally human that links us to pre-Christian Homeric man. I will ask the same question of my genetic ancestors – the Vikings.

My Norse forefathers were not soft-hearted. They went berserk and made sacrifices – sometimes human ones. Their god of the hanged, Odin, sacrificed himself to himself, hanging himself in the holy tree. But whether in order to jump out of his skin (as a Shamanistic berserk) or to solve the mystery of life is unclear. The Norse heart is in many ways still an enigma to us. As is the Aztec heart.

The Aztecs have been given a chapter in this book because the heart in their culture has a spectacular place in a history so bloody and gruesome that it is defies comprehension. That the frightful can be a culture-creating aspect, as it is in Mesoamerican culture, where human sacrifice was widespread, can be difficult to understand. That is why the Spanish conquistadors regarded it as their duty to eradicate that culture. This they did with great efficiency – and with the blessing of the Christian Church. In the course of just a few years, the Europeans annihilated the Aztec and other Mesoamerican civilizations and plundered their treasures in a form of organized state theft on a scale not previously witnessed. During the sixteenth century, the population of Mexico dropped from about 25 million to about one million. Who were the heartless – the unchristian Aztecs or we humanist Westerners? It seems that the heart can be full of all kinds of emotions, sometimes creative, at other times destructive. This raises the question as to what sort of being a human is. The second part of this book tries to answer that question by following the development of the metaphorics of the heart in modern Western culture.

This focus on the European and our Western view of humanity in the second part of the book explains why there is no room for other cultures than those just mentioned. This means that some of the most outstanding achievements in the history of ideas fall outside the range of this presentation. This applies to the entire Asian tradition, the ancient Indian and ancient Chinese traditions, Hinduism, Buddhism and Taoism – to mention but a few. Nor is there any room for African cultures. For reasons of space and to maintain the central thread of the account, these traditions have had to be omitted, even though their view of man is no less important than the Christian European when it comes to creative and noble qualities. Compared with Buddhist requirements regarding composure, contemplation and inner harmony as antidotes to all kinds of desire, we Europeans would seem to be target-obsessed status-seekers, primitive power-seekers and egoistic materialists. But this alternative history we must let lie in order to deal in depth with the history of the Western heart.

It is, however, not easy to decide what the heart stands for, since it is first and foremost an image and a symbol that has to be interpreted. The heart is not simply an organ of the body, a blood pump. It has also been made the seat of our conscience, since bad conscience is experienced as a stab or sudden pain in the heart. For that reason, the soul is placed in the heart – conscience and soul being two sides of the same coin. Love and various types of feelings, though, are also often placed in the heart, since suffering for love, compassion and other emotions are experienced in a purely corporeal, sensory way in the heart, which thus becomes an image of these emotions. It does so because it also reacts sympathetically or symptomatically to something that takes place outside it – socially or personally. In rhetoric, such an image is called *metonymy*, where the part that houses a phenomenon is used instead of the whole phenomenon. Metonymy is thus able to contain both the physical and the mental aspect in one expression, the literal and the figurative in one word. These two sides of the heart perhaps explain why it has become the prime symbol in our culture, even though we otherwise cultivate the intellect of the brain. The brain is a fact, not an image. The heart is both.

The spoken language is full of metonymic and metaphorical heart expressions. We talk about being light-hearted, being sick at heart, not having the heart to do something, of losing our heart (which can be a source of joy). It is an ideal to listen to what one's heart says and to be faithful to one's heart. Out of the abundance of the heart the mouth speaks, though in Scandinavian languages one says to talk 'straight from the liver', which derives from an archaic, pre-Christian anthropology. What comes from the heart is honestly meant – and can reveal the dishonest person, since his heart is often on his sleeve and not in the right place. A kind-hearted person has a big heart; we can find something heart-breaking and have our heart in our mouths; the heart can be squeezed, broken or crushed because we have been struck to the heart, etc. And that the heart has something to do with the intellect can be seen from the expression 'to learn by heart'.

Many of the heart metaphors say something about personal qualities and in daily life reveal what sort of person we are dealing with – and what kind of personal and moral qualities we and our fellow human beings have. We talk about being good-hearted or heartless, of being hard-hearted or soft-hearted, of having a warm or a cold heart. Our kindness of heart and ability to feel compassion say who we are. For that reason it is necessary to search one's heart, even though it can be both painful and embarrass-ing when the qualities of the heart are revealed, so we can be down-hearted when others reveal that their heart fails them. Subsequently it can be tempting to say, along with Henrik Ibsen's Peer Gynt (who is quoting from the Bible), that it is not our job *to search the reins and heart*. That, though, is precisely the aim of this book – formulated as a divine com-mand in Greek Antiquity, with the inscription above the entrance to the temple of Apollo in Delphi: *Know thyself!*

The qualities of the heart are much more than something theoretical. This does not of course mean that reflection or theoretical clarification of what the heart is and stands for are not important in so-called real life. It is one of the great paradoxes of human life that words are not just words, but are proactive. Words create what they name. There is magic in words in some way or other. This also applies in relation to the heart, which in itself demonstrates the strange double relationship between language and what language refers to. The 'heart' is also a word and a concept, an important word for an image with a rich, composite content. When we talk about the 'heart', we do not always know if we are talking about the heart as something substantial linked to the mystery that beats with its steady rhythm within our chest, or something else that refers to the symbolic values, attitudes and personal qualities of various kinds for which the heart is a metaphorical expression. If the reference for the word is of the one kind or the other, both the 'real' and the 'symbolic' heart are shaped by the language we used to talk about them. There is an indissoluble link between the emotions of the heart and the words and concepts we have for them. For that reason, this book will just as much be a study of the heart of language as of the language of the heart.

The indissoluble link between the heart as something given or innate on the one hand and as an image or symbol on the other is expressed in the well-known quotation concerning human hearts from the Nobel Prize Winner of Literature, Sigrid Undset. At the end of her *Tales of King Arthur and the Knights of the Round Table* (1915) she writes: 'For customs and practices change considerably as times pass and people's beliefs change and they think differently about a great many things. But human hearts do not change one bit with the passing of time.' In this quotation, the heart is a metaphor for the emotions and for love, erotic passion in particular, since this sentence comes at the end of a work that deals with erotic passion in the age of chivalry – a historical period that to a great extent has shaped our Western heart. Of these emotions, erotic love and passion, Sigrid Undset makes the claim that they do not change but are the same at all times in all places. If that is true, man has a given or fixed being. Many people are convinced that this is not the case.

Many people feel that from birth a human being is an open and unfinished being that via learning and artificial or conscious shaping must be formed throughout life. In that case, man is not simply the most malleable of all beings on this earth, but also the most unstable and unpredictable of all beings. The instability and uncertainty to which man is exposed releases the wish and desire to seek to find something constant, something that represents a fixed or irreducible core in man against which all the relative leaps away from the core can be measured. This is where the heart presents itself as a worthy candidate as the seat of or image of love, the mind and the conscience. The heart has, at any rate, had such a function in our European culture since it emerged on the basis of Christianity several centuries after the birth of Christ.

It is, however, problematic to turn the heart into a moral norm, if we take Sigrid Undset's heart metaphor as our point of departure, as emotions and erotic passion often clash with what is morally right. Nor is it exactly an optimistic view of human nature Sigrid Undset is expressing here. It goes against the core of our Western humanist tradition, which definitely assumes that man is both freely capable of and responsible for shaping and forming himself. It is the education of the heart that is at stake here, and the heart and a possible change of attitude that is the main issue in our Christian tradition as well. But then we are told that the heart is an image of something emotional and erotic and yet, according to Sigrid Undset, something constant and unchanging – almost a natural law. If not something worse. For the assertion about human hearts implies on the basis of its context that man has always been at the mercy of his passions. If that is true, it is even more frighteningly topical in our age, since individuals, groups and societies have such weapons of mass destruction at their disposal that our democracy, our civilization and our species can be placed at risk if they fall into the hands of people who are literally at the mercy of their passions – no matter whether that passion is of a political, religious or erotic nature.

Sigrid Undset's claim that man is at the mercy of his passions applies only to one side of the human heart, the heart of darkness. The other side of the coin is the positive creative forces represented by Pascal's well-known phrase 'the heart has its reasons, which reason knows not of'. These two sides have been investigated in a number of civilizations and are the goal of many seekers after truth, e.g. of Sufis and Christian mystics. It is these creative sources that Romanticism seeks when it places the emotions above reason.

Since the heart, despite all its differences, would seem to be central in many cultures, it perhaps represents something that is common to all mankind. Perhaps the heart can build bridges between cultures that otherwise have problems in understanding each other? Perhaps there is a common language of the heart for all cultures, that enables people to understand each other instinctively across all language boundaries and all religious disparities and cultural differences?

Or maybe it is simply a cliché to say that heart speaks to heart? The encounter between the conquistadors and the Aztecs would seem to point in that direction. As does the relation between Jews and Palestinians in the present-day Middle East. But precisely because there can be abysses and fundamental differences of attitude between people of different cultures, it is even more important to understand the nature of these abysses, schisms and differences – not only to understand 'the other ones' – the aliens – but to understand ourselves as well. For it would seem that we need someone to compare ourselves with in order to understand our own identity. Differences and breaks are just as important for understanding as similarities and connections. The same applies to understanding our own age. We cannot understand the present age and know where we ought to be heading without understanding our past and the discontinuous leaps in cultural development. In order to understand the complexity of modern Western culture we have to know about the complexity of Western history. Similarities and differences are always necessary where any kind of understanding is involved. Comparative cultural studies, however, are difficult, simply because we cannot avoid looking at and understanding *the other* and *the others* with our own eyes. From such a familiar perspective one can soon end up making what is dissimilar similar and what is similar dissimilar. Form and function for instance are being mixed, as we forget that similar forms in dissimilar cultures can have dissimilar functions and meaning – and vice versa. We begin this story of differences and similarities, of breaks and connections, where it all started.

PART ONE

The Heart in Different Cultures

And now good morrow to our waking souls,
Which watch not one another out of fear;
For love, all love of other sights controls,
And makes one little room, an everywhere.
Let sea-discoverers to new worlds have gone,
Let maps to other, worlds on worlds have shown,
Let us possess one world, each hath one, and is one.
My face in thine eye, thine in mine appears,
And true plain hearts do in the faces rest;
Where can we find two better hemispheres,
Without sharp north, without declining west?
Whatever dies, was not mix'd equally;
If our two loves be one, or, thou and I
Love so alike, that none do slacken, none can die.
                    John Donne, 'The Good Morrow'

CHAPTER 1

The World of Gilgamesh

The known drama of the heart begins in Mesopotamia, the land between the rivers, where the cultural history of man has its origin. The oldest literary sources go back more than 5,000 years. The so-called Ishtar epics are among the most ancient, some probably written down about 3,100 BC. They speak of the goddess who was the most worshipped there, the goddess of love and war, Inanna, or Ishtar as she is called in Accadic, the language of the Semitic people, the Accadians, who arrived early on in Sumer. The Accadians were assimilated by the original people of Sumer, and took over the social structures of Sumer as well as the myths. The pattern for new invaders and conquerors during the following centuries was the regular one of assimilation, in some sort of relay of inheritances, loans and transformations. Also part of this tradition of Inanna is the best-known Sumer-Babylonian epic, about Gilgamesh, probably written down around 2,000 BC.

In the *Epic of Gilgamesh* we meet a heart that shows many similarities with the qualities it was to have throughout cultural history right up to the present day. *Gilgamesh* has to do with the power of the heart and the arts of love, with elementary life forces and the mystery of death, and the struggle between nature and culture. In this great epic the fundamental opposites of life are gathered together in one thematic artifice, in the friendship between Enkidu, the child of nature, and the lord of civilization, Gilgamesh, the Sumer king of Uruk. Initially, though, the relationship between nature and culture is turned on its head, since it is the savage Enkidu who represents the good and the peaceful, while Gilgamesh is a despot who violates the women of Uruk and oppresses his people. The gods create Enkidu in order to tame Gilgamesh.

Enkidu is the first noble savage, a child of nature who lives in a paradise-like state of harmony with animals and wild plants, outside and uninfluenced by civilization (the concepts of both paradise and the flood were borrowed by the Jews who wrote the Old Testament from their more ancient neighbours in Mesopotamia). Enkidu is the hero of all ecologically minded conservationists of nature, for he only eats grass and wild herbs, lives together with the wild animals, destroys hunting nets and uncovers the traps the hunters have dug. This leads to the hunters complaining about him to Gilgamesh, who is a great hunter himself, asking for his help. Gilgamesh knows what to do. He will tame Enkidu not by means of arms but with the power of the heart over the mind and with sophisticated arts of love.

A *hetaera*, a priestess trained in the arts of love from the temple of the goddess of love Ishtar/Inanna, is given the task of visiting and seducing Enkidu. She succeeds. They make love for six days and six nights. But Ishtar's priestess knows that erotic satisfaction is not enough to win Enkidu for ever. Therefore she also tempts him with all the material advantages of civilization. She offers him the tastiest of spices, intoxicating wine, beautiful clothes and fragrant ointments. And Enkidu knows how to make use of these expensive commodities. He eats and drinks and enjoys all of them. His heart is filled with joy and his face lit up with enthusiasm.

But on the seventh day, Enkidu's conscience troubles him and he wishes to return to the animals and lead a natural life. Now, though, he has become a different person and a stranger, and the animals do not want to have anything to do with him. This ancient insight is worth our attention even today: the very first civilization already knew that it is not simply reactionary but also impossible for man as a cultural being to get *back to nature*, as certain Romantics believe.

The *hetaera* is more than successful and is able to take Enkidu to Gilgamesh in the stronghold of civilization, Uruk. Here the two heroes test each other's strength. Gilgamesh wins the close-quarter encounter, but at the same time recognizes Enkidu as his equal because of his personal qualities, which bring about a transformation in Gilgamesh. Before then, he had vices – now, with his new virtues, he carries out heroic deeds. All of this is the result of their divine friendship. Heart speaks to heart and creates a change of character in Gilgamesh, placing an obligation on him to exercise the values and virtues that the friendship represents. Together, the two friends are invincible. Together they fell the dangerous tree and monster Humbaba in the great forest, in the threatening nature that had once been home to Enkidu. Thanks to Enkidu and his knowledge and strength, the monster is overcome.

However, Enkidu's fate is sealed after the goddess Ishtar has seen Gilgamesh's feat. She falls in love with the hero and asks him to become her husband and lover. But Gilgamesh rejects her, for he knows that she devours all her lovers when they have satisfied her. He has to pay for this rejection, for she sends the ox of the sky against him and Enkidu. With their gigantic strength they manage to kill the ox of the sky and thus pit their strength against that of the gods. For the supreme attribute of a god in these most ancient cultures is the ox and its horns. After having killed the bull of the sky, which comes with bolts of thunder, Gilgamesh and Enkidu cut out its heart and sacrifice it to the sun god Shamash. The first heart sacrifice in cultural history takes place. It is a proxy heart that is sacrificed. With the holy heart of the ox they bind the gods to their own heart. The fact that it is the heart that the heroes sacrifice tells us how important a place it occupied in Sumerian culture. The heart is in the real sense of the word a sympathetic organ, binding Gilgamesh and Enkidu together in compassion. Therefore man should praise the gods for having a heart – with all it represents. But Ishtar grows even more furious after the loss of the sky bull and Enkidu's slight of throwing a leg of the bull to her as if she were a dog. Since Gilgamesh is invulnerable, she strikes Enkidu down with a mortal illness, by means of which she can get at Gilgamesh. Suffering, compassion and love belong together in man as a cultural being from the very outset.

When Enkidu dies, Gilgamesh not only loses his friend and everything that the deep friendship represents, he also meets a new problem and a new challenge that he is to spend the rest of his life trying to solve – that of death. When Gilgamesh reads the fear of death in Enkidu's eyes, he also knows it in his own heart. He meets his *memento mori – remember that you will die!* For even if Gilgamesh is two-thirds a god, he is not immortal. Therefore, having seen how Enkidu decays and rots, he sets out on a new journey with new challenges (actually, ritualistic trials of initiation) to find the meaning of life or the life elixir that can make him immortal.

As the first person in history, Gilgamesh is the symbol of the restless heart (anticipating St Augustine's *cor inquietum*), one who cannot find rest until he has found an answer to the enigma of life and death that he can reconcile himself to. 'Why did you give Gilgamesh a restless heart?' the narrator asks the creator. Gilgamesh wanders alone in the desert, through valleys and over mountains; his helpers lead him above and below ground. All the time he is exposed to new trials. Some he successfully deals with, but a number of decisive trials he fails to resolve. He also finds the plant that can make him immortal, but does not take good enough care of it, allowing the snake (there it is already!) to swallow it and become immortal instead. That Gilgamesh does not manage to solve all the trials proves that he is not a god but a mortal. This is the wisdom he gains from the trials he is exposed to. He learns something of life's rough conditions. His wanderings and searchings have done something to Gilgamesh – they make him wise and earn him the name 'he who has seen everything'.

The answer to the enigma of life he gets from the Sumerian Noah, Utnapsihtim, who has survived the Flood and been made divine, is not all that uplifting, only definite. He learns that everything is transient, and everything external in vain. This also is what the Babylonian poems of wisdom teach – that justice is not always of this world: evil triumphs, nothing comes from praying, the gods are indifferent to what happens to humanity. Man wishes to determine his own fate, but is controlled by divine laws that govern the entire world. The closest man can get to happiness is to acknowledge his mortal nature and obey these laws – which the heart senses in its deep wisdom. That is why Gilgamesh asked Enkidu: 'Who in Uruk has such wisdom as you? Who gave your heart such remarkable insight?' Now Gilgamesh himself has gained such insight, he who dreamed of heroic exploits and great deeds when he set out on his journey, and 'who returned full of vulnerable wisdom and wrote of his travels on stone'.

The question of life after death and of the realm of the dead is one of the contributions the Sumerians have made to the history of mankind. It is especially in the myths concerning Ishtar that we meet the idea of the realm of the dead and the journey to the underworld. Once again, the heart is central. The epic of Inanna describes how the gods inflict diseases of the heart on each other in order to hurt each other. The gods are also rivals (different generations with different historical and ethnic origins compete against each other) for the right to control various parts of the earth and the world. Ishtar rules over life on earth and war, while Ereshigal rules over the realm of the dead. Chaos arises when Ishtar travels to the realm of the dead to defeat death. In doing so she goes beyond a boundary that cannot be exceeded. On her journey she is gradually stripped of her clothes until, naked, she is struck and turned into stone by the hateful gaze of death, her sister. In the Sumerian version, Ishtar is allowed to return to life and the light of day if someone is prepared to take her place in the realm of the dead (suffering by proxy is thus older that Christ's death and suffering on the cross). In the Accadian version, the sun god sends a singer to the realm of the dead, because life and growth ceased on earth when Ishtar disappeared into the underworld. The singer is to give Ishtar's heart new courage to face life and to force the evil sister and the realm of the dead to release her (cf. the Greek Orpheus myth). His song reverses the emotions in the hearts of the two rivals. Ishtar no longer feels any pain in her heart, while Ereshigal suddenly feels it and exclaims: 'Do not break my heart with your song!' The image of the broken heart, the heart in pieces, that we meet in a modern form in Shakespeare and contemporary pop songs can be traced back 5,000 years.

There are various aspects of the Sumerian conception of the heart which are interesting from a modern perspective. For puritan Westerners it is scary that *ecstasy* can have such a central place in a civilization like the Sumerian. Ecstasy, or intoxication, was part of the feast to the gods for fertility and a good crop. Especially for Ishtar/Inanna, who was the goddess of infatuation, love and eroticism more than that of mother earth and good crops. Ritual sexual intercourse between the king, in the god's stead (actually the shepherd Dumuzi/Tammus) and one of the temple priestesses (in Ishtar's stead) was a confirmation of the spark of life and the divine origin of joy in life as praised in the Ishtar poems:[1]

> My high priest is ready for the holy loins.
> She called for the bed that rejoices the heart.
> She called for the bed that sweetens the loins.
> He shaped my loins with his fair hands.
> The shepherd Dumuzi filled my lap with cream and milk.
> He stroked my pubic hair,
> He watered my womb.
> He laid his hands on my holy vulva.
> He laid me down on the fragrant honey-bed.
> My sweet love, lying by my heart.

The Jewish priests distanced themselves from this life vitality with a female goddess at the centre when, after their captivity in Babylon, they rewrote their holy scriptures in the sixth century BC and made Yahweh the only God and Lord (the male ruler) and the high defender of the patriarchy. It is edited out that Yahweh originally had a wife by the name of Ashera. For now the Jews wanted to establish their own identity, one that differed from the religions of fertility common in the Middle East at the time (which the Song of Solomon is a memory of in the Old Testament). With Yahweh's wife, ecstasy also disappeared as part of the Judaeo-Christian religion.

The main organ in Babylonian culture is the liver. Nor is the heart a strong organ of action for the Sumers. It is the compassionate organ and thus extremely vulnerable. In war and enmity between humans as well as gods the parties try to strike each other in the heart. That is why the pragmatic Sumers do not make the heart the centre of life but go instead for the large, blood-filled liver as the source of the life-force. No other culture gives the liver such pride of place as the ancients in Mesopotamia. It was, for example, the liver in which the secrets of the future were hidden and that was used for foretelling the future. The sensitive, percipient heart was first and foremost the organ of feeling. It was from this facet of Sumeric anthropology that the Egyptians drew inspiration.

CHAPTER 2

Ancient Egypt

We have a tendency to take for granted that the thoughts expressed in the Bible are exclusively Jewish or Christian. But this is historically incorrect. The central place accorded the heart in, for example, Judaism, has been directly influenced by older religions in the area, not least by that of the pharaohs, even though this influence is sometimes paradoxical. The similarities are debatable. For what seems similar in form and expression can often conceal a diametrically opposed and essentially different content. The view of the heart that is hard or of *stone* in Egyptian (where it is positive) and Jewish culture (where it is negative) is evidence of this. Even though the actual similarity and difference do not by themselves prove an influence – by opposition – it is nevertheless not hard to show that certain Jewish conceptions derive from Egyptian culture.

When it is emphasized in the Old Testament that God can replace a person's stony heart with a warm heart of flesh, one can see this as part of an old tradition that dates back to the exile by the Nile, and a way of distancing oneself from the heathen Egyptians with their heart of stone. This is particularly noticeable in Exodus, but can also be found in 1 Samuel, VI: 6, where it is said: 'Wherefore then do ye harden your hearts, as the Egyptians and Pharaoh hardened their hearts?'

In addition to the role the heart played in religion, it also had an important role and symbolic meaning in Egyptian cosmology. Cosmology and myths of creation were in fact the core of theology. The heart of the individual is analogous both to the cosmic sun and the gods who maintained the world. Resurrection for the individual in the hereafter thus corresponds to the daily rising of the sun. The Egyptians had many gods, and there were many different versions of the various myths about them. The balance of power between them also varied in different periods and mythical traditions. In the following, we are basing ourselves on a kind of standard version. In all of the periods, it was the *heart* that was at the centre, both religiously and humanly. The basic conceptions were strikingly stable for more than 2,000 years in Egyptian culture.

The religious function the heart had for the Egyptians also explains why it was so important for them that it was in place both physically and mentally after death – for good, for all eternity. That was why they made every effort to find a technique that could preserve the physical heart and prevent it from rotting within the mummy. Many religious rituals, rites and words in *The Book of the Dead*, for example, had a corresponding function – to ensure eternal life. The Egyptians had a conception of the soul as something intimately linked to the physical heart, with which it was identified. The soul is further closely linked to a person's *ba*, his spirit, which is also equipped with wings. This is why the heart was taken special care of and embalmed along with the body after death. The heart was the only inner organ to be replaced in the body after embalming. The rest were placed in jars and laid next to the mummy in the grave. The brain was seen as unimportant and was thrown away.

Models of the heart were also made that had a ritual function as well as small heart coffins, placed next to the mummy.

In order to ensure a good heart that could testify for the dead on the Day of Judgement, the Egyptians developed their own cult of the heart. This led from the embalming of the heart to a special heart symbol that acquired an increasingly magical function. There are two heart symbols which are predominant: a heart stone (formed like a vessel) and the 'heart-beetle' (scarab), which symbolized the rebirth of the heart and thereby of its owner in the beyond. The heart-beetle had its predecessor in zoology – the large dark-blue and indigo scarab, with a protective shell over its wings. A carefully made model of this beetle was placed on the chest of the embalmed person. The heart/soul could then rise from the dead, open its wings and fly into the beyond. Thousands of heart-beetles have been found in Egyptian mummies and graves, made of ceramic, stone or precious metal – some exceedingly beautiful, not least when the beetle has spread its wings in a lovely gilt mosaic.

Egyptian culture is an aesthetic one, composed of images and symbols. Even its writing uses images. Ancient Egyptian culture makes it clear that man lives in an artificial universe of symbols. In this universe the heart with its many images is just one of many symbols, all of which have to be interpreted. And our interpretations will never coincide completely with the meaning the image had at the time of the Pharaohs. The solution to many of the mysteries we face in their cultural history, the Egyptians took with them to the grave. This applies quite literally to the heart.

The close connection between heart, life and sun in ancient Egyptian mythology is often represented by the (heart-)beetle pushing a sun-ball in front of it. This symbol, by the way, has a profane ecological basis. For the beetle stores small pellets of dung in which it lays its eggs and protects them by rolling them in front of it, pushing with its horns. Just as the sun rises from earth each day, the beetle is born, so to speak, out of dung, since the beetles emerge from the dung when the eggs hatch. This is part of the natural explanation for why the beetle and the sun were the most widespread incarnation symbol in Egypt. The red pellet of dung the beetle pushes in front of it is analogous to the one various gods wear on their heads, and the one that Nut (the goddess of the heavens) extinguishes every evening.

That the Egyptian envisaged the heart as hard and cold has to do with their conception of the role of the heart at the transition to the other world. The heart as the central inner organ is both the cause and witness of everything that a man has done in the way of good and evil when alive. It knows everything, for it is equipped with memory (intelligence) and after death it will answer for the dead person. On the Day of Judgement, the heart is the dead person's companion and will stand at his side to testify *for* him – not *against* him. On that day, the heart (symbolized by the heart-stone/stone-beetle) will be placed on one side of a pair of scales and weighed, with the symbol of Maat, goddess of Justice, on the other side. If the heart balances with the weight of Maat, the dead person will live in harmonious balance in the other world. In this critical situation, a stone heart was an advantage against the natural and unreliable heart of flesh and blood, with all the vices it bore within it. The hard heart was a symbol of self-control and sober-minded behaviour. The inscriptions under the symbolic images are of an incantatory nature, indicating that the Egyptians were not entirely sure about their hearts. It therefore had to be exhorted to act correctly by means of magic words under the stone, such as 'My heart, do not rise up and testify against me!'

Other inscriptions on the heart-beetles bring out the double form the heart possessed, both as something given from birth ('My heart from my mother') and as something formed ('My heart of my upbringing'). In relation to death, the two main aspects of the heart find expression in both secular and religious literature: on the one hand, the heart is something given, divine or inherited, on the other, something society and the individual himself is responsible for forming according to given norms and ideals. In particular, the heart must be taught and formed according to the principles for which Maat (*ma'at*) stands.

Ma'at represents world-order, which is true, right and just, because the deity Maat created it as such from the beginning, so man must act in accordance with it. For a person to behave in a true and correct way, he therefore has to learn the nature of the divine order of the world. And it is with the heart that man recognizes this order and learns how to be formed by it by forming his own heart. 'You are to encourage your heart to follow Maat,' the formula says. To lack this formative influence is being heartless in a literal sense. Subsequently, the dogma is: 'Do not be a heartless man who lacks education.' To be 'educated' means to be able to hear the divine word (*ma'at*) in one's heart, that is, to recognize and acknowledge god. 'You have created my heart; I did not become wise by my own doing.' For the heart is also the seat of the divine in man. The conception of 'the hearing heart' comes from the Egyptians. And what the heart is especially able to hear is god and his will, so that he can live in accordance with the world-order.

The best source we have concerning how the Egyptians conceived death and life after death is the so-called *Book of the Dead*. It is not really *one* book but a collection of words of a religious nature – proverbs or words of wisdom that go right back to the Old Kingdom of about 3,000 BC, to which alterations and additions were made up until Roman times. These were proverbs and incantatory verses to help the dead person on his transition to the other world and to ensure that the resurrection in that world was successful, i.e. that they could rise again in flesh and blood and participate in a paradisial life along with all the just persons from other ages. The *Book of the Dead* itself comes from the New Kingdom, but certain verses can be traced all the way back to the *Pyramid Texts* of the Old Kingdom and the *Sarcophagus Texts* of the Middle Kingdom, thus recording a 2,500-year-old tradition. In this source the heart occupies a central position, for rising from the dead to a good or bad life in the beyond depends on the qualities of the heart.

The belief in man's resurrection in the religion of the ancient Egyptians is anchored in a cosmology where the sun is at the centre. The resurrection of man is analogous to the re-birth and re-rising of the sun. The Egyptians knew that just as human life depends on the heart with its regular beat, all life on earth is dependent on the sun. So it was dramatic when the sun set in the sea and darkness behind the horizon every evening. Would it rise again the following day? This question also lay behind the Aztec cult of the sun. In both cultures it was regarded as a gift from the gods when the sun rose the following day. Osiris was therefore praised. He had the sun in his care in the underworld at night. But the underworld was not simply negative as far as the Egyptians were concerned, as the sun also gained nourishment and new strength when in the underworld, enabling it to cross the heavens the following day. Thus the sun is reborn every day. The crocodile that lives in the water out of which life arises (directly and literally for the Egyptians on the banks of the Nile) can therefore assume the nature of a sun-god, with the characteristic red sun-disc on its head. So both Osiris and the sun-god Re are gods of life, as was Nut.

It is the goddess of heaven, Nut, who gives birth to the sun. Every evening she extinguishes the sun, which travels through her body in the course of the night. In the morning, Nut gives birth to the sun as a child. In the burial chamber Nut is therefore often portrayed as a firmament bending down over the dead person's coffin or mummy. She can also be depicted inside the mummy or sarcophagus. When the dead person was mummified and placed in the coffin, this was seen as entering the body of Nut in order to be reborn the following day like the sun. Man is made divine after death by sharing the fate of the sun-god Re, extinguished by Nut every evening and reborn every morning. To become like Re, the highest divinity, was the goal of the deceased in the other world. This goal was attained when the deceased's birdlike *ba* (more his spirit than his soul) undertook the cosmic journey together with Re and was reunited with his body to complete the daily resurrection to life. The connection between heart, Re and reincarnation is expressed in, for example, proverb 15 of *The Book of the Dead*, where it says: 'You [Re] journey across the entire firmament of heaven in the full width of your heart.' When this doubly central part of man, with the flying beetle or *ba* as its symbol, is reunited with the body, man once more becomes whole. Re (and not only with the meaning 'sun') can be recognized by man, because it is the same divine fire that burns within man as that in the heavens. And it is the heart with its glow that by analogy can recognize this cosmic glow of the sun and its divine origin. This is the basis for the heart in a double sense having been the central organ of the body in Egyptian anthropology.

ANTHROPOLOGY

On the basis of the so-called *Ebers* and *Smith* papyri, we know that ancient Egyptian doctors were well aware of the biological function of the heart. Among other things, they were able to take a person's pulse and they knew this was a function of the heart. This physiological insight was also the basis of the central place the Egyptians gave the heart. For the classical Egyptian conception of the heart had crystallized as early as around 2,000 BC: it is the centre and inner core of man. It is the centre of thought and all intellectual activity. Compared to our modern conception, the main difference is that the Egyptians believe they think and judge with the heart. An old source can subsequently make the following statement about a king: 'What my heart thought, my hand brought about', i.e. he carried out what his heart thought. Especially close is the relationship between heart and tongue, between thought and speech. Heart and tongue also have power over all other limbs, since the heart thinks everything that it wants, and the tongue commands everything the heart wants. Consequently, all other limbs also obey the will of the heart. The senses perceive what happens in the outer world, but it is the heart as the thinking instance that evaluates what is sensed, while the tongue communicates the will of the heart – and the other limbs act accordingly.

The heart (spirit) and tongue (words) are of the same divine origin. The heart is so central in Egyptian anthropology that it occurs as something in its own right, as opposed to everything else a human being is, which means that a kind of duality can arise between the heart and (the rest of) the individual. The heart is both the person's ego and alter ego. It can even be a conversation partner for anyone who is lonely. The Egyptian can thus consult his heart (as Odysseus did).

Since the heart is the seat of the intellect, a heartless person must therefore be a fool, a dimwit and a confused nincompoop, not a callous, unmerciful person, which is what we associate with the term. That the heart is intelligent also explains why Egyptians have a (stone) heart as an ideal. For the hard heart is also cold, stable and sober-minded. And the heart must be that since it has to pass the test on the Day of Judgement and participate in the good life in the divine world beyond this one.

The ancient Egyptians, like so many other civilized nations, had a composite, diverse conception of the human personality. This is borne out by the inscriptions on their graves, which list all the good qualities the dead person had to help him complete the journey to the other world. This diversity of characteristics is held together by the heart as the centre and the organizing central instance in man. It holds individuality together and provides both personal and moral integrity. The heart is so important that it alone can replace all other characteristics an individual has and be the personal nature of the individual and the spokesman of the personality. Faced with the changing nature of the individual and the outside world, it is therefore a special challenge and task for the Egyptian to give the heart its firm, concrete anchorage at the very centre of the individual. If the heart is not in its right place, the individual is literally beside himself. And when the heart is not in its right place, the individual also becomes tired. There are many proverbs that testify to these different moods and schisms for which the heart may be the cause, as at this point in the *Book of the Dead*:

> Look. My heart has stolen away,
> it is hastening to the place it knows . . .
> But I, I sit at home and wait for my heart . . .
> I watch, but my heart sleeps,
> my heart, which is not in my body.

The heart was also symptom-bearer of various forms of evil, and if important values were violated, it would say so. Then the heart became weak, tired or physically taxed. The best thing a wise man can wish a friend is thus an even heart. An even heart is a sign of mental balance and rest. An even heart is also a whole heart, one that has its moral and mental integrity intact. The heart and the personal integrity also belong together for the Egyptians. The whole person is affected concretely and bodily by evil, it strikes him to the heart, where his soul lives. Such suffering will paralyse the individual, making it impossible for him to live as a spiritual being. So a standard piece of advice wise men give their disciples is to avoid useless strife, also strife for the sake of doctrine. For, despite everything, the latter is not for the many and cannot be imposed on anyone. In accordance with such a fundamental attitude, proverb 13 in the *Book of the Dead* says: 'Morning star, make my path clear to me, so that in peace I can enter the beautiful West.'

It is not always sufficient, however, for the Egyptian to maintain his integrity in order to avoid mental suffering, for evil and suffering can come from without. To relieve one's heart and get rid of this suffering which the heart knows and bears is the greatest wish an Egyptian can have fulfilled, according to certain sources. In a text from the third millennium BC we can read these words of wisdom: 'A person bearing something bad wishes his heart to be relieved of it more than to have what he himself has requested fulfilled'.[1] Thus the Egyptian also feels compassion in his heart. To feel compassion for somebody is expressed by the set phrase *to incline one's heart to someone*.

Even though the ideal is a hard, firm heart, all ancient Egyptian literature to do with doctrine and wisdom is based on the idea that the heart is workable and plastic. Therefore, a teacher can exhort his pupil to keep his heart firm: 'Do not let your heart flutter like loose leaves in the wind.' At one and the same time, the heart is the weakest and strongest thing in the individual. It is also the most important and most problematic organ in the body. It is the centre of the individual and the force that organizes personal diversity. At the same time, it is the most vulnerable, being particularly exposed to impressions and influences from without and for desires from within.[2]

Since the heart is made up of many components, it cannot be perceived as given and unchanging but must be shaped and formed. This insight and the great care given the heart makes ancient Egyptian culture a culture of the heart where the aim is to prevent dissonance between the self and the heart. This schism is avoided by the Egyptian 'following his heart', as it is so often called. But this means something completely different to the Egyptian than it does to us. For it does not mean following one's conscience as a moral instance, the 'inner voice' as a kind of super-ego. The Egyptian does not have such a voice, for he does not live in a dualistic world that is split between the outer and the inner. For the Egyptian, 'following the heart' also means allowing society, i.e. the outer, its pound of flesh, so as to establish a balance with the inner.

Gradually, though, it becomes unsatisfactory for the tongue to say its piece on the Day of Judgement if the heart testifies to something else. Subsequently, an understanding emerges that there must actually be a correspondence between the outer and the inner, i.e. between what the tongue says and what the heart can recall from within and testify to in accordance with Maat's universal laws. Or, we could say, the tongue cannot lie at this stage of Egyptian civilization without coming into conflict with itself and the heart. In order to overcome this new schism the Egyptians in the Middle Kingdom (2050–1650 BC) develop a new ideal of 'following the heart'. This opens the path to giving the inner pride of place. Running parallel is the development of 'the hearing heart', a concept later found in Judaism. Following the heart is at this stage of development a personal matter, whereas the heart in the Old Kingdom (2650–2150 BC) followed the will of the pharaoh.

In the New Kingdom (from 1550 BC), the deepening of the inner dimension continues. Now the heart is to follow god's will and orientate itself more towards the other world. And there it is not a far cry to saying 'to love god with all one's heart', a conception found in several religions and cultures in the Middle East, not only in the Old Testament. 'The hearing heart', which is able to hear the laws of God, paves the way for the command to love God *with all one's heart*. Without an inner space having been created that is distinct from the outer, it would be impossible to make an appeal to this type of love.

This distinction between the outer and the inner that gradually develops in Egyptian culture is in accordance with a mental development in all civilizations in the Middle East and around the Mediterranean. It is absolutely fundamental to European culture and its cast of thought, culminating in a dualism that in terms of the history of ideas has been made responsible for some of the most destructive aspects of European culture – not least ecologically and anthropologically. To understand how our European heart is cleft in twain, we have to go back to the preconditions for this in Greek Antiquity, one of the main sources of European culture. While Egyptian culture was an aesthetic culture of images, Greek culture was very much a written culture. In many ways, the ancient Egyptians remain something of a mystery to us; we do not know how they actually experienced life. It is by no means certain, however, that the ancient Greeks, as depicted by Homer, are any less enigmatic. Greek Antiquity is especially important in our particular context because this is where we meet a conception of the heart that is completely different from the Christian – presupposing that the Greeks, to our way of thinking, had any kind of heart at all.

CHAPTER 3

The Complex Man of Antiquity

O Eros, the conqueror in every fight, . . .
no immortal god escapes from you,
nor any man, who lives but for a day.
And the one whom you possess goes mad.
Even in good men you twist their minds,
perverting them to their own ruin . . .
for there the goddess Aphrodite works her will,
whose ways are irresistible

Sophocles, *Antigone*

For us Westerners, it is obvious that soul (*psyche*) and heart belong together so intimately that the metaphor of the heart has been synonymous with soul. But that is not the case in all cultures. Not even when we seek for the roots of our own culture in Greek Antiquity do we find a coincidence of soul and heart. The ancient Greeks did not have a heart in our sense of the word. For them, the psyche (that we have to translate here with soul) meant something completely different to the soul of Christian Europe. And the liver and the lungs were far more spiritual than the heart for ancient Greeks. So we do not even need to go outside our own cultural history to have confirmed that there is nothing human that is constant and general or universal. It is perhaps not simply the image of man but man himself that has changed since Antiquity.

Greek Antiquity gives us unique source material for studying the cultural history of the heart, since we are here dealing with works that cover a long time-span, with various phases in the development of the concept of the mind. The oldest sources, represented by Homer (*c.* 700 BC) have roots in an oral culture. At the same time, Homer's works are of such a quality, both thematically and artistically, that they are the common reference point for a whole culture, from the time the *Iliad* and the *Odyssey* were written down until the great Greek tragedians, until classical Greek

Antiquity peaks with the philosophy of Socrates and Plato around 400 BC. During this period there is not only a cultural development of gigantic proportions in art, philosophy and science but also changes in the perception of man and his self-understanding.

These profound changes in the perception of man are a result of writing and written culture. When Homer's works are written down for the first time – characterized as a transition from *mythos* to *logos* (from myth to rationality), it represents a decisive, epoch-making change in man's understanding of himself. Writing makes it easier for man to make himself the subject, or object, of reflection. The barrier-breaking feature of this change is that man discovers that self-understanding and reflection have a reactive effect on what man actually is. In this process, it is the *psyche* in particular that is processed and reshaped in accordance with the principle of reason, while Homeric man was subject to the body and all it represented.

In the age after Homer, especially around 400 BC, the Greeks start to use the *psyche* as a kind of catalyst or mediator in their self-understanding. Consequently, it is quite reasonable to say that *psyche*, the human soul, is invented. But a precondition for such an invention is that man discovers he is living in an animate universe and has the ability to think something about something, also about himself. Therefore, it can be claimed that the spirit is discovered when man begins to acknowledge that he is the subject of thoughts, on a par with bodily impulses. This is the reason why Bruno Snell, one of the cultural historians who first provided an account of this turn in the view of man at the transition from Homer to Plato, called his classic work *Die Entdeckung des Geistes* (*The Discovery of the Spirit*, 1946). The spiritual is something that comes to man from without, while the *psyche* is something within that man himself invents, or constructs, in order to govern himself and control the forces that rage inside himself and to collect his thoughts and composure via *sophrosyne*, as it is called in Socrates and Plato, and as early as the *Odyssey*. With this decisive leap in the history of ideas (*Geistesgeschichte*), emotions also change in nature.

The discovery of the spirit and invention of the soul has a downside, one that has lain in the shadow of the predominant view of man and anthropological development. The German phenomenologist Hermann Schmitz has tried to tell this forgotten and repressed history via his philosophical work *Der Leib* (*The Body*, 1965). When man discovered the spirit and made himself the subject of reflection, this led to a covering of the body, because the body was not perceived as being something meaningful or a source of knowledge any longer. Schmitz therefore drily characterizes the history of mental development advanced by Bruno Snell as discovering the mind means covering the body. This repression and downgrading of the body also leads in the long term to a dualism between body and mind, between reason and emotions, that gradually spreads throughout Greek, Hellenistic and Western culture with great consequences for life and morals, for self-perception and ways of life.

For Schmitz, it is important to show what is lost in terms of human resources, not least intellectually and emotionally, when attempts are made to cover and conceal something as important as the human body via redefinition. To make his contribution to releasing these creative resources and make the bodily potential whole once more, he goes back to the period prior to the discovery of the spirit, before the transition from *mythos* to *logos*, i.e. to the Homeric period, before writing and the writing-down of Homer's epic. Only one whole, comprehensive literary testimony exists from that period, namely the *Iliad*, which derives from an oral culture. In the second work attributed to Homer, the *Odyssey*, we can already see in the figure of Odysseus the contours of a new kind of man, with self-awareness and a capacity for self-reflection.

HOMERIC MAN

Man as portrayed by Homer in the *Iliad* lacks the hierarchy with the rational soul uppermost that is later to emerge, based on Plato's teachings in the fourth century BC. Nor was Homeric man 'rational' in our sense of the term, since he had not developed a consciousness of his own reason, which we now take for granted exists in all human beings. Homeric man is at the mercy of immediate impressions, physical emotions, impulses, spontaneous thoughts, physical urges and passions in a way that perhaps is incomprehensible to us. For the Homeric heroes did *not* interpret all kinds of emotional impulses and passions as subjective states of the soul but as outer powers and divine impulses which seized them from without – something outside their own control. To imagine that Homeric heroes can actually stop the impulses that invade them by the exercising of rational reason, free will or conscious choice is to impute things that in many ways are irrelevant in relation to their self-understanding.

Homeric man can be seen as a symphony of impulses and 'voices' with different physical origins. He does not experience his body as a unity, as we do, but as a composite, divergent entity with various sovereign powers. Homeric man has no body in our sense but many individual body parts and limbs, according to both Snell and Schmitz. When Achilles and other Homeric heroes carry on a dialogue with themselves, it is the various parts of the body, the various centres of impulses in the diaphragm and heart region, and what these represent in the way of conceptions, emotions and urges – as sovereign partners to the I-figure. Homeric man is rather like an open force-field, maybe even battlefield, of various emotions and passions, impulses, thoughts and ideas. This is also the point of departure for the 'struggle of competences' that takes place in the individual between the various impulses of various bodily origins.

Just how Homeric man experienced what we would call a mental struggle can perhaps be illustrated via a modern parodic counterpart, *Jeppe on the Hill* (1722–3) by Danish-Norwegian author Ludvig Holberg. When Jeppe is on his way to market with money in his hand in order to buy soap for his wife, Nille, a struggle takes place between the various parts of his body which take over control from his will and his conscious self. His stomach wants to go to the inn to quench its thirst for liquor, and his back wants to go to the market in order to avoid a pain (Nille's beating), which is just as great as the thirst his stomach experiences. In this dilemma, Jeppe (Act 1, scene 5) is torn between the demands of these parts of his body:

> Quick legs! The devil will split you apart if you don't get moving! No, the rogues simply refuse. They would be off to the inn again. My limbs are at war with each other: My stomach and legs want to go to the inn, and my back to the town. Get moving, you curs! You beasts! You poseurs! No, the devil take them – they want to be off to the inn again.

For us, this scene is a figurative or personified presentation of what is taking place in Jeppe's vacillating mind. It is inconceivable for us today that parts of the body or inner organs have any real autonomy and that they are capable of carrying on a dialogue with each other, as was the case at the time of Homer. For us, everything decided by a conscious choice takes place in our central 'mental life', understood either as something moral or intellectual. We see conscious reason and morality as being of a higher order than basic urges, which are pre-verbal and preconscious. But in Homer, consciousness of one's own consciousness is *not* separate from what consciousness is conscious of. Homer makes no distinction between the outer and the inner, the physical and the mental, as we do – with all the implications that has for the life of the emotions.

The Greek word for body, *soma*, means 'corpse' in Homer. *Soma* is what is left lying on the field when the battle is over and the *psyche* has left the dead person. Only when the *psyche* is gone does *soma* appear to be something different from it, and vice versa. But even if Homeric man did not have an overall concept for the body in our sense, that does not mean that the body was downgraded in relation to, for example, the mind. On the contrary. It is as with primitive peoples that do not have an overall concept for nature but a great many words and expressions for natural phenomena. A standard example is all the words for snow in Inuit languages, which also lack a single word for the concept 'snow' (even though this has been disproved, the example may work as an illustration). If one is to think of Greek culture and pre-Socratic anthropology, one has to think in physical terms, and try to forget our body-mind division to avoid projecting it onto the Homeric way of thinking. The body is the Self for Homeric man. The term the Greeks use for the whole body is *autos*, self.

In Homer's work there are several words for what we conceive as the bodily organ of the heart: *ker*, *etor* and *kradie* (cf. *kardia* and cardiology). But since there is more than one word for 'the same thing', there is reason to believe that we are not looking at the same thing but rather various force-fields in the heart region. The Homeric heart is composite. The Greeks have different words for 'the same thing' in order to differentiate the feelings and impulses that have their seat or origin in the region of the heart and the diaphragm. Just how wide a range of emotions we are dealing with, or rather how heterogeneous the Greek heart is, can be seen from the literal translations of these words, which can locate the emotions in different parts of the chest. But when Homer uses different words for heart, it is not simply something emotionally noticeable but also something physically noticeable – differentiated physical reactions rather than specific bodily organs.

In Homeric anthropology, it is impossible to distinguish and categorically separate between the emotional, sensory and intellectual and rational in the way we do. So there is no one word that means 'reason' in Homer. There are several organs or physical force-fields that can be 'rational'. The most used words to denote the intellect and rational assessment and will are *noos* and *thymos*. And these are located in the chest region. *Thymos* can also be full of anger and resentment – something irrational. The idea of *thymos* is central in Homer's psychology. The word has been translated by the term 'blood-mind' to convey this combination of the mental and physical. *Thymos* is not located in a particular inner organ, but is physically connected to the blood supply to the heart and muscles that particularly occurs in stressful situations.[1]

Phrenes (the diaphragm) is also rational. That the diaphragm or even the stomach should be rational is inconceivable to us. But impulses of thought for Homer could just as well come from the diaphragm as from the heart – and never from the brain or the head. *Phrenes* is also used for the lungs. That breathing has something to do with the spirit (*pneuma*) is old news. Otherwise, the main rule is that where the impulses are felt is where they have their seat and origin – which is the body. In many contexts, the 'words for reason' *noos* and *thymos* are translated into English as heart, as is often the case in translations of Homer's work, although in other contexts this translation will not do.

Light can be shed on just how the Homeric hero views thought, which is not his, and self-consciousness, which is lacking, from a group of pseudo-monologues or conversations with himself in the *Iliad*. This applies in particular to a number of well-known situations with their standard phrases when the heroes talk and discuss with their 'great-hearted *thymos* ', i.e. it is really *thymos* that talks to the hero. In the *Iliad* Odysseus in particular is the one who conducts such a dialogue, e.g. in Song 11, verse 403 ff., where he is standing on the battlefield:

> Then mightily moved he spake unto his own great-hearted
> 　spirit [*thymos*]:
> 'Woe is me; what is to befall me? Great evil were it if I flee,
> 　seized with fear
> of the throng; yet this were a worse thing, if I be taken all alone,
> 　for the rest of the Danaans hath the son of Cronos scattered
> 　in flight.
> But why doth my heart thus hold converse with me?'

Elsewhere (Song 17, verse 90), it is the son of Atreus, Menelaus, the husband of beautiful Helen, who, 'sore troubled . . . spake to his own great-hearted spirit [*thymos*]'. Such episodes end with the hero breaking off the 'vain' dialogue with himself: 'But why doth my heart thus hold converse with me?' (verse 97).

The later ideal, from Plato to the present day, i.e. self-reflection and consideration (*sophrosyne*), is seen by the Homeric hero as a waste of time, empty words. And this is not because of a battle situation but because no functional space of meaning has been cleared for conscious self-reflection as long as man perceives himself as controlled either by god-issued decrees or by impulses and physical urges whose origin lies outside the self-control of the I-figure. Homeric characters do not really think for themselves, 'there is thinking in them', i.e. a physical impulse, especially from the *thymos*, rises up in them and takes the initiative from them. The exception is Odysseus. But his growing self-awareness and reflection is given low status in the *Iliad*, where Achilles, driven by his furious anger, is the ideal of the world of heroes. That is why Odysseus is called *cunning* and *crafty*.

Homer, however, ends his work by showing in the *Odyssey* how the new type of man is emerging, gaining control over both his mind and his desires by means of reflection, by entering into a dialogue with his heart and thereby inhibiting the urge for revenge and his emotional impulses to act. This occurs when Odysseus, after 20 years of absence, returns to Ithaca and discovers how the brazen female slaves are amusing themselves with the impudent suitors who are wooing his faithful Penelope. His heart boils and heaves within his chest in wrath at this shamelessness (Song 20, verses 17–22):

> but he smote his breast, and rebuked his heart, saying:
> 'Endure, my heart [*kradié*]; a worse thing even than this
>   didst thou once endure.' . . .
> So he spoke, chiding the heart in his breast, and his heart
>   remained bound within him to endure steadfastly.

This self-reflection marks the beginning of a split between body and mind. But it is still a long way forward to the Platonic teachings concerning the inner man. *Psyche* in Homer and Plato belongs to two different views of man. Nor is there anything that corresponds to the Christian 'soul' in Homer, even though he also uses the term *psyche*. Since Homeric man does not experience his body as a single quality, he does not view the soul, *psyche*, as one either – one that can be contrasted with the body. One is the prerequisite of the other. That is why Homer does not really have a proper word for 'soul' or 'spirit'. *Psyche*, the word for mind in later Greek, did not originally have anything to do with the thinking and feeling mind.[2]

In Homer the *psyche* is a principle of life, what animates and keeps man alive. It is the breath of life that leaves the body when it dies, the pale shadow of the body that goes to Hades. Homer does not say anything about how the psyche works in a living person, for it is integrated in the body. A 'body' that the *psyche* has left is no longer a body but a corpse (*soma*). To be a *psyche* is thus to be dead, since *psyche* does not show itself as a shadow of the body until it dies.

It is not the heart that is able to animate the body in Homer, but the blood. In the *Odyssey* he portrays how Odysseus finds out from Circe how he can get the pale souls in Hades to recall life on earth and regain the breath of life. This is achieved by drinking the sacrificial blood of a ewe that Odysseus offers them. Odysseus' deceased mother also drinks 'the black, steaming blood' and immediately recognizes her son and begins to talk to him. The widespread blood-magic is the basis in the history of religion of the place Christ's blood is given in Christianity.

The physical conglomerate of instances that prompt impulses and actions is the core of the Homeric view of man. Or rather, he does not have any core or single centre. Many of the concepts we find important and necessary in our Western view of man are lacking in Homer, including words for individual, person and personality, identity and self – with their present meanings. The same applies to words for self-consciousness, ethic responsibility and personal guilt as something internal and mental. There is no sharp boundary in Homeric man between an ego and a non-ego. Man is a force-field where it is difficult to distinguish between what is a person's own and the alien that invades him from without. Nor is there any boundary between emotion and behaviour. Fear resembles what one fears. Emotion is not a mental state, but *exists* in the action and the impulse that releases the passion. Homeric man manifests himself as unity in a concrete diversity. The situation dictates whether a person manifests himself in his arms, his stomach, his heart, his eyes, etc.[3]

When the individual is determined by forces that invade him from without, morality must also be an outer morality, i.e. persons are judged according to their outer social status and proficiency or skill (*areté*) in external actions. Such a yardstick is honour. And when one's honour is violated, the individual experiences shame, which can only be removed by an action that re-establishes one's honour. This is a morality of shame and honour – the aim is honour and posthumous reputation, something decided by external actions. This is the basis of the Trojan War. Prince Paris of Troy has dishonoured Menelaus by seducing and abducting his wife; that is why the Greeks go to war against Troy. The *Iliad* depicts the tenth and final year of the war, when King Agamemnon has dishonoured Achilles by stealing the spoils of war from him, his beautiful mistress Briseis. For that reason, Achilles refuses to take part in the battle until the Trojan hero Hector kills his best friend Patroclus and Odysseus asks him to be reconciled with Agamemnon. Achilles, jealous of his honour and revengeful, is the prototype of Homeric man – his self is first and foremost his body with its desire and anger. This is his *autos*, the scenario where the complementary forces of *eros* and *eris* (the battle) are enacted unrestrainedly.

What Homer has and we perhaps have lost is a large, rich vocabulary full of subtle distinctions concerning physical phenomena and physical reactions of all kinds in an external world of action. The basis for understanding Homeric man is also clear – linguistic expressions in a literary work. In other words, we have to understand Homer's language if we are to understand his view of man, as language and reality belong together. His 'body vocabulary' tells us something about what actually went on inside humans at the time of Homer and how they perceived themselves. And this vocabulary included words for the phenomenon later to be suppressed in the Christian era – divine laughter.

Just how different the relationship is between the body and reason in Homeric man and the modern Westerner becomes obvious when we turn to *laughter*. We like to see laughter as an intellectual phenomenon emanating from the brain, especially in the form of irony and satire. We laugh at what is stupid. Homeric unstoppable laughter, *asbestos gelos*, on the other hand, comes from the stomach. This kind of deep laughter, rediscovered by Friedrich Nietzsche (1844–1900), contains insights into and a perspective on the world that only it can give. It precedes all conscious reflection and is of divine origin. Unlike the solemn Christian God, the gods on Olympus laugh heartily, e.g. when they surprise 'shameless Ares' with his trousers down in unfaithful Aphrodite's bed, both of them caught in the cunning net of her deceived husband, Hephaistos the smith: 'Then the blessed gods burst out laughing'. For in relation to Aphrodite and everything she represents, all morality is irrelevant. Laughter reconciles, and the 'sinners' go free, and the deceived husband recovers his honour by finding apposite words when the laughter has died down.

Normally, though, it is Dionysus who is the god of laughter in Antiquity. At his ecstatic feasts, laughter and lust meet in transcending the body. The Dionysian popular feast survived Antiquity via the theatre, especially via comedy, which was originally dedicated to Dionysus. The Greeks were the first to define man as the only being capable of laughter. Laughter is also connected to lust and desire, represented by the libidinous satyrs who accompany Dionysus.

Along with the other active force-fields in the body, the erotic and sexual forces illustrate dramatically how archaic and Homeric man was the subject of passions of various origins. For the Greeks, eroticism was a quintessential principle of divine origin that manifested itself in a divine, a human and an animal form. Aphrodite and her companion, small Eros with his bow, represented divine and divinely inspired erotic love. Eros has a bow – a dangerous weapon – not merely to 'light the fire' but also to wound and make someone a victim. Erotic love is always vulnerable or wounding. Pan is responsible for wild, animal eroticism. He had a different domain from the closely related god Dionysus, who, apart from being the god of fertility, was also the god of wine, feasting and drama, the one who releases physical, erotic and aesthetic pleasure. All of these functions found expression during the Dionysian games that Greek drama became. Greek tragedies deal not least with what misfortunes arise when erotic passion takes over human beings. But the presentation of eroticism differs from one period of Antiquity to the next. In this process of mental change, it is eroticism that forces man to adopt a conscious relation to himself, as it gradually becomes a problem and therefore also a question of ethics.

One of the great gifts the Greeks bestowed on mankind is eroticism. They turn it into an art that stages the most important and finest, the most frightful and destructive in man without judging morally the sexual desire it all starts with. In their myths and epics, poems and drama people can find illustrative material for the joys and problems all of us meet as lovers and loved ones, when happy and unhappy. Homer, though, is silent when it comes to love, for it has not yet been invented and conceptualized. On the other hand he has a great many words for the various passions that invade his heroes and rage in their hearts when they seek their erotic ends and fight for beautiful Helen.

Just how the Greeks originally imagined the encounter with primitive eroticism has survived in language for thousands of years via the term *panic*, which the maidens/nymphs/maenads were stricken with when 'horny' lascivious Pan, with animal-like urges, wanted to take them. The word *panic*, derived from Pan, testifies eloquently to the emotional life of a distant past. The same applies to the word *fascinating* (from the Latin word for an erect penis, *fascinus*). The words also tell a long, old history of transformation regarding the connection between feelings and language. That is why such words as panic are important. Through them we have gained other ways of working out what people thought and felt in such situations at a time pre-dating written sources of such information.[4] Etymology tells its own history of mentalities and is an important supplement to the oldest written recordings of oral and mythical traditions.

The transition from Pan to panic also tells us something about a major change of mentality in cultural history – the transition from the outer to the inner, which will be referred to as internalization. From being external phenomena or objective forces that people experienced completely concretely on their bodies, they become internal and mental, and thus subjective, states and thereby more accessible to language and to be expressed in language.

A corresponding internalization takes place in the relationship between Pan and Psyche, who in pre-Hellenistic times were opposites and external antagonists, but who in the course of Hellenism are portrayed as a pair, as two complementary sides of the same thing. When Pan and Psyche are used after this change of mind-set, after internalization, the usage is purely metaphorical or allegorical – for mental states and impulses as part of a dualism. This accords with a general tendency as regards consciousness. Originally, the gods were part of a religion, cult and religious ritual. They then became part of a mythology, as in Homer's work. In the third phase, they became mythological forces used in a literary way in Greek drama as figurative representations of something completely human, something mental. The godlike becomes human, the outer something inner. Seen from the outside, we are left once more with merely linguistic reminiscences of an archaic world that could accommodate other forces that man's own. What is finally left of Pan, Eros, Aphrodite and Dionysus is a series of metaphorical and allegorical expressions or, to use Nietzsche's words, 'a moving army of metaphors, metonyms and anthropomorphisms'. At the time of Homer, these phenomena still represented outer realities. At the time of the last major tragedian, Euripides, they have become purely literary images of inner mental states.

The connection between the various bodily organs, the emotions and thought tells us a great deal about how different Homeric man was from the twentieth-century Westerner. As mentioned, the human heart in Homer did not even reside in the heart. Even so, Homer's language concerning the emotions still speaks to us. We are, however, in the presence of language and words and not the emotions and passions themselves. We experience something different when *we* read Homer's two epic poems than contemporary listeners did or those of later Antiquity, and we interpret the depicted passions in a different way. In many ways, it is a mystery to us how Homeric man, the Vikings and medieval man actually felt and experienced themselves, each other and life. There is perhaps a wide chasm between the language of the heart and the heart of language that language can never bridge.

We do not, however, have any other form of access to the language of the heart than language if we wish to look at it in depth and understand how it has developed in time and space. That is why the transition from Homeric to Platonic man is an important period from an anthropological point of view. This transition is not least one of how the body is perceived. Plato breaks so radically with the 'body culture' that had previously been predominant that we are perhaps unable to understand how pre-Socratic people felt and thought, e.g. when they behaved in a 'Dionysian' way.

THE DIONYSIAN AND THE APOLLONIAN

One of those who has attempted to comprehend pre-Socratic man and his complex origins is Nietzsche. He uses both an anthropological and a historical approach in trying to understand what generates Greek culture. He operates with a view of man that is stratified. The various layers of this anthropology can be illustrated by their literary cornerstones, Homer and Archilochos.

Archilochos, born on Paros in the early seventh century BC, is considered to be the first to write 'personal' lyrical poetry: his poetry is detached from the function lyrical poetry had in cult plays with choruses, in dances and cult festivals with eulogies, etc. Instead, there is a new, more self-conscious and personal 'I-figure' who expresses his subjective feelings in this lyric work, where the heart acquires something of the function it later has in poetry. Alongside Archilochos, Sappho from Lesbos is the best-known writer in this new genre. Archilochos is of more interest to us here, since he represents a brutishness, a direct disillusion and an apparently primitive vitalism that we find difficult to understand. He represents a stratum in anthropology that modern man has little contact with – 'the Dionysian'.

In his classic work *The Birth of Tragedy* (1871), Nietzsche stresses the difference between Homer and Archilochos on the basis of two complementary principles, the Apollonian and the Dionysian, which are the primordial urges fundamental to the world and still active inside man. The Apollonian stands for dream and vision, harmonious order, an organizing and delimiting principle (ethics and knowledge, visual and epic art). The Dionysian stands for everything that is driven by undivided passion, intoxication and ecstasy, creative and lyric art (in connection with the Muses and rhythm). In the Dionysian rapture the boundaries of Apollonian individuality dissolve, and the ecstatically elated person feels one with the creative principle of the world, lust for life and joy in life, as these forces were experienced during the Dionysian feasts and plays, although they did not end in life-destroying orgies because of the Apollonian counterweight.

Homer is Apollonian (he creates order), while warlike Archilochos is Dionysian in his brutishness. 'Precisely this Archilochos frightens us when placed alongside Homer, with his hateful, scornful cries, with his drunken outbursts of desire'.[5] This deep, personal voice that sings out from the Dionysian, Nietzsche sees as the great mystery in both Greek culture and the development of art. For without the vital energy and passions that the Dionysian unleashes, art and culture would dry out. And that is precisely what has happened to Western culture, in Nietzsche's opinion, where Socratic-Platonic-Christian moralism and contempt of the world have suppressed and crippled the life-asserting passions, which means that we have lost contact with the creative forces in the deep layer of the body that upholds life and art. That is why we no longer understand Archilochos and consign him to 'subjective' lyricism instead of viewing him as a voice from our anthropological underground – the Dionysian.

Nietzsche sees the Apollonian as something that emerges from the Dionysian in a formative process. The mystery is why 'the Dionysian

Greek had to become Apollonian . . . i.e. allow his will to the monstrous, complex, uncertain, abominable be converted into one to moderation, order, the simple, to conforming in rule and concept.[6]

This Apollonian will to moderation, restraint and order is the culture-creating exterior of the Greeks. Nietzsche emphasizes that the struggle with the forces of chaos in order to create the beautiful is not given but acquired. Art – like logic – is conquered, willed and struggled for. Beauty is the victory of Greek culture. This is the main point in our context, for this process of Apollonian formation, in the form of Platonism, leads in the long term to the body and everything for which it stands as a Dionysian principle being suppressed. It becomes too demanding to live in with the awkward tension between high and low, rationality and vitality, the Apollonian and the Dionysian. This means that the passions and the emotions also undergo change in Greek culture.

The 'personal' lyricists further the development of consciousness heralded by Odysseus and completed by Plato by suppressing the Dionysian. They stand on the threshold between the Dionysian and the Apollonian, between the *autos* of the body and the self-conscious *psyche* of reason, between passion and the general concept of it, between lyricism as a collective and individual phenomenon, between language as speech (*mythos*) and as writing (*logos*). The written language does not only provide a new view of man but also a new man, first completed in the view of man found in the writings of the scholar Plato.

The struggle for the new view of man passes via the body and its unruly passions. In this history of the body, homosexuality occupies a central place – and a strange intermediate position between the apparently natural and the artificially formed. The transition from early personal lyric writing and Sappho from Lesbos to Plato with their respective views of humanity is also one from lesbian and, in particular, homosexual love between a man and a youth to a general 'bodiless' love, with the love between a man and a youth as the axis around which both the emotions and knowledge revolve.

HOMOSEXUALITY IN ANTIQUITY

Homosexuality is the classic example of how emotional life in its various forms is determined by time and place. Cultural history and anthropology have long documented the fact that homosexuality in many cultures is or has been viewed as something 'sick', madness, a perversity or abnormality, a moral flaw or the expression of an insatiable sexual desire, as conventionally perceived in our Christian culture until the end of the twentieth century. The standard example of homosexuality not only being socially accepted but actually a characteristic of a social and intellectual upper class is that of Greek Antiquity.

In various city states and certain social strata homosexuality was widespread. Greek homosexuality was always a relationship between a man and a youth, one under 18. It other words, we are dealing here with *pederasti*, from *pais*, youth, and *erastés*, lover. It was also a pedagogical, or teacher–pupil, relationship. Elite troops, as in Thebes north of Athens, were assigned younger warriors who were to learn the art of war from them. Especially among the Dorians, pederasty was a pedagogical institution. In Sparta it was more of a social duty for the man to train children for other men, with pederasty as the institution for this. And the relationship between teacher and pupil as well as between philosopher and disciple in various schools in classical Antiquity was in various degrees a homosexual relationship.

Homosexuality in classical Greek society was not the same as homosexuality in the West nowadays. It was deeply anchored in the culture. The Greek gods unblushingly entered into homosexual relationships. There is also an inner connection between Greek homosexuality and the Homeric ethics of *areté*, with its praising of the art of war. It was not until his bosom-friend Patroclus, with whom he shared a tent, had been killed that Achilles entered the battle and decided Troy's fate – though it was the fight for a woman that set the whole thing in motion.

The Greeks and the Athenians in particular did not view any form of love as 'sinful' in our sense of the word. But in the classical period the erotic relationship with the highest status was that between men. It was seen as both more beautiful and manly than that between a man and a woman. The purpose of marriage was to continue the line and to guarantee that the husband was father of the wife's children. In addition to marriage with a woman for the sake of the family line and a homosexual relationship to a youth, Greeks had courtesans/*hetaeras* for their own pleasure and concubines for everyday needs, as the politician Demosthenes (384–322 BC) formulated it. While it was common for grown men/free citizens to have a homosexual relationship with a youth, homosexual relationships between women were less widespread, although pictures on vases and Sappho's poetry testify to the fact that they occurred.

Michel Foucault (1926–1984) has given a detailed account of the function homosexuality had in the classical period in *L'usage des plaisirs* (*The Use of Pleasure* 1984), volume II of *The History of Sexuality*, a never completed series. His interest in the history of sexuality is part of his investigation of the mechanisms of power and the 'games of truth' that decide how people perceive and stage themselves in various ages. It transpires that the understanding and regulation of sexuality and how individuals view themselves as sexual subjects in different societies become a kind of catalyst for man's self-understanding in different ages. This applies to a striking extent to Greek Antiquity, where Foucault is especially preoccupied by the Athenian city state (*polis*) and the highclassical period of 400–300 BC, Plato's dialogues in particular. Foucault sees sexuality and the systems of truth and knowledge that follow them as being the axis around which antique self-knowledge revolves and out of which comes the divine motto *Know thyself!*

Since homosexuality cannot guarantee procreation and the family, the focus in the relationship between the man and the boy was on the aesthetical dimension and pleasure, which could be difficult to legitimize morally and socially. The discussion was on the complex social relations in such a relationship and on the personal relationships between the two friends. Consequently a whole set of unwritten rules grew up for what was good conduct in such a relationship – something that placed the homosexual relationship under a cultural and moral overload. It was a question of giving the relation a beautiful, aesthetic and morally acceptable form. It is Foucault's project to show how Eros was redefined in the process: first from pleasure to utility, then from something impermanent to something that could continue after the youth had become a man and himself a lover. A way of legitimizing this is friendship – the *philia* relationship – which can be measured against Plato's idea of eternal friendship. Plato found the *universal* that Archilochos and Sappho had sought for to console themselves in their unhappy love. *Philia* stands between Eros and common love, pointing forwards towards equality between men and women. This completes the circle, since the point of departure for Greek homosexuality was part of man's struggle against the chaotic powers of nature and against the matriarchy via the establishment of the patriarchy and Greek male-dominated society.

In the well-known dialogue on the nature of love in the *Symposium*, Plato develops the new concept of friendship, which in terms of the history of ideas changes Greek eroticism. The focus shifts from love of youths and the art of moderation with the mastering of pleasure and a desire for the eternal being of love and friendship. Wooing and pleasure in the body are now torn out of their concrete contexts and legitimized on the basis of ideal concepts, or 'eternal' ideas. The discussion is conducted by Socrates and deals with true love understood as love (*eros*) of truth. The person who thus loves truth and wisdom is a *philosophos*, a friend of truth, as opposed to the Sophists, who used knowledge as a means to power in their rhetoric. For that reason, a 'philosopher' is now called such, rather than a Sophist. And Eros undergoes a series of transformations.

The goal of Eros changes from the youth (the sexual object) to the wise man, represented by Socrates (*philos*), who by virtue of his beautiful and rational soul is capable of contemplating the beautiful in itself beyond the firmament. Youth therefore seeks Socrates in order to participate in his insights. The goal of Eros is not primarily the beautiful body but a beautiful soul, a perceptive and wise soul. And by virtue of insight into beauty itself, the soul is also able to lift itself up, above all the ties represented by desire and physical pleasure. Socrates is programmatically informed about all these transformations and levels of cognition not by a man in love but by a woman, Diotima, as described in the *Symposium*:

> And the true order of going, or being led by another, to the things of love, is to begin from the beauties of earth and mount upwards for the sake of that other beauty, using these as steps only, and from one going on to two, and from two to all fair forms, and from fair forms to fair practices, and from fair practices to fair notions, until from fair notions he arrives at the notion of absolute beauty, and at last knows what the essence of beauty is. (211a)

In this way, Psyche wins over Eros as early as Antiquity by Eros as love of truth filling the soul. The beautiful body of the youth by comparison loses something of its glow, according to Diotima:

> 'This, my dear Socrates', said the stranger of Mantineia, 'is that life above all others which man should live, in the contemplation of beauty absolute; a beauty which if you once beheld, you would see not to be after the measure of gold, and garments, and fair boys and youths, whose presence now entrances you.'

The point for Socrates is that whoever has seen the good, beautiful and true in itself also becomes good, 'and to the extent that a human being can become immortal, he does so'. This link between love and soul, truth and eternal life is also the basis for Christianity's making use of Platonism in order to legitimize itself and downgrade sensual love of the body, and to conceal the true motives of humans, power and the exercise of power, with idealism.

The need to legitimize the love of youths with the changes it underwent, first via the concept of *philia* and later via Platonism, can in the long term be seen as the basis in terms of the history of ideas for our culture being unable to love without viewing love in one form or other as the expression of something universal and/or ideal. In that sense, all of us are Platonists. For if we love without being able to justify our erotic practice with universal ideas of one sort or other, we have a bad conscience. And when we intentionally infringe the prevailing social rules for sexual behaviour, we are also subject to certain general ideas – even though in conscious opposition. For there are ideas, notions and ideal expectations that control us and colour our emotions. As such we are highly controlled, even when we speak out as apologists for the body and proclaim spontaneity, sensual pleasure and free self-realization.

Our natural innocence has been lost for good. This is inevitable in a necessary development of consciousness where sexuality is a condition for the establishing of a moral subject. That is why eroticism and ethics are two sides of the same coin in the Socratic dialogue with oneself about oneself in order to know oneself. One of the reasons why the thoughts of Socrates have made such a profound impact on our culture is because of the images through which Plato has transmitted them in his philosophy. One of the images that has formed our Western heart is the Platonic soul.

THE PLATONIC VIEW OF MAN

The composite, body-bound view of man found in Homer is divided by the split between body and soul that first emerges in the work of the philosopher Democritus. The Orphics and later the Pythagoreans also distinguished between body and soul. So dualism is older than Plato. But it is Plato who further develops this dualistic tradition by constructing a model that later becomes the predominant view of man in our culture, where the rational soul is the centre of man. The first stage of this historical development is found in Odysseus' dialogues with himself in the *Odyssey*. The most important thing about the anthropological leap from the *Iliad* to the *Odyssey* is that conscious self-control is in the process of repressing unpredictability in the spontaneous ideas and divine impulses that permeate the human being. The rise of conscious self-control takes the form of a distancing of the person from forces supplying the impulses, enabling them to become objectivized and be placed in more foreseeable, general contexts.

The central feature of this consciousness-raising process is that the emotions become something subjective and internal that is linked to the formation of a personal, conscious ego. Just how this *internalization* of emotional impulses results in reflection can be seen in Odysseus' appeal to his nurse Eurycleia to restrain her joy and suppress her cries at the sight of the shameless wooers whom the returned hero has killed (in Song 22, verse 411): 'Rejoice in your heart, old one, but constrain your uncontrollable rejoicing.'

In this type of rejoinder the inner organs are in the process of becoming metaphors and thereby objects of consciousness. At this stage of consciousness, the re-interpretation into something internal of impulses that are felt externally is starting to take place, resulting in a usage similar to ours when, for example, we say that our heart is struck or moved. By means of such metaphors, the body is reinterpreted into something hidden, intimate, private and mental. The use of images is based on a similarity (not identity) between the corporeal and what is personal and emotional. That reactions felt by the body and inner organs are described metaphorically testifies not only to a particular perception of the emotions but also to a changed emotional life compared with the mythical Homeric. This line of internalization is completed in and with Plato. The rest is a legacy that has lasted right up to the present day – one that still influences the heart and emotional life of us Westerners.

In a double sense, the *psyche* is the central concept of Western anthropology. First, the rationally ordered *psyche* is the 'centre' of man in relation to which the other dimensions can be defined, because the soul in the post-Platonic tradition is identical with the capacity to think and the consciousness. Second, the *psyche* is the instance that gives man a personal or subjective identity or integrity. But it is not 'natural' for man to have such a centre, for the *psyche* to be this centre, or for personal identity, the self, to be inscribed in the *psyche*.

When Socrates is interested in the self, he talks about the *psyche*, which is no longer just the breath of life in the body. The *psyche*, then, is not a product of nature but a historical product of culture, an invention, the result of a process of formation where conscious control and the sublimation of desires and passions become a major task. Just what kind of emancipatory gain this process of formation has resulted in is more than clear when Socrates with his *sophrosyne* (self-reflection, self-restraint, temperance – the idea of 'nothing to excess') is compared with the endless struggle the Homeric heroes have with their unruly desires and impulses. But the price paid for this self-composure by the emotions is not perhaps fully realized until the twentieth century with Freud's psychoanalysis – and with Nietzsche as a transitional figure and discoverer of bodily spontaneity as a necessary precondition for free man.

The construction of the soul promotes centralization and leads to a limitation of experience. It is in particular the sensual, the emotions and the language of the body, that becomes restricted, downgraded or repressed in a normative image of the soul such as that of Plato. Plato saw the body as the grave of the soul. Just how negatively he viewed the physical and sensual as well as any literary rendering of it can be seen from his rejection of poetry. In his ideal state, Homer is the only writer allowed in.

And only one scrap of Homeric text gets past Plato's hostile scrutiny, where Odysseus beats his chest and asks his racing heart to calm down:

> So he spoke, chiding the heart in his breast, and his heart
> remained bound within him to endure steadfastly.

Thus does Odysseus regain control over his agitated body. This text is also referred to by Plato in the dialogue *Phaidon*, where Socrates attempts to convince Simmias that the soul is something independent that fights against the body 'in a thousand different matters' in order to gain control of it and not be controlled by it. If the soul is successful, an inner concord will arise between the components of the soul and all the other anthropological components with reason as its first part.

Plato operated with a tripartition of man, as expressed in the tripartition of the *psyche*. In the dialogue *Phaedrus*, and especially in the fourth book of *The State*, he presents his well-known teaching of the three parts of the soul, referred to by the allegory of the team of two horses. Plato sees desire as an evil power and calls it a monster. The rational part of the soul must gain control over it by forming an alliance with the will and with courage. 'All soul is immortal, for she is the source of all motion both in herself and in others. Her form may be described in a figure as a composite nature made up of a charioteer and a pair of winged steeds,' Plato says in *Phaedrus*, where the charioteer is the courageous will, and the two steeds are thought and desire. In Plato, courage, the will and reason have to be trained via upbringing and reflection in order to gain control over desire. It is only the rational part of the soul that is immortal and that thus enjoys a special position. The life-soul is located in the region of the heart, while the rational part, which is the supreme organ, is located in the head – with desire in the lower belly.

The fact that Plato divides the soul into three means that he cannot be so dualistic as he is represented in the history of ideas. It is perhaps mainly in terms of ethics that he is a dualist – not anthropologically and in his view of the world and nature. He has been made to appear more dualistic than he actually was by Plotinus (AD 205–70) and the neo-Platonists of late Antiquity. Plotinus also strengthened the ethical aim, to gain control over all bodily impulses and sensual pleasures, so that the soul with the aid of reason can free itself from the body and matter and reach the beyond, the One from whom man also emanates. While both Plato and Plotinus sought for the very source of existence in the beyond, Aristotle firmly placed it active in the here and now.

While Plato, historically speaking, has formed our moralistic super-ego, Aristotle (384–322 BC) has to a greater extent formed our ego via the rational and in particular the realistic part of the psyche, providing us with rhetoric as a means of shaping it. Aristotle, to a greater extent than Plato, has furthermore influenced the history of knowledge, especially that of the natural sciences, whereas Plato has enriched our metaphysics and study of the human mind. The fact is often ignored, however, that it was Aristotle's teachings concerning the soul and the mind that were prevalent in the High Middle Ages, when Thomas Aquinas developed his monism (in opposition to the dualism of the time) under the influence of Aristotelian holism (where everything belongs together but has various forms and functions). William Harvey and the study of anatomy in the Renaissance were likewise inspired by him, as were the alchemists in their conception of the human heart.

Aristotle was the philosopher of the heart in Antiquity. He championed the heart's pride of place in his natural philosophy and anatomy. The heart is the origin of the other organs in the development of the body. Aristotle, then, retains a pre-Platonic principle of creation. The heart is the basis for the production of blood. All organs filled with blood grew out of the heart, the seed or germ out of which the whole body developed. Therefore the soul's sensitivity and capacity to grow must reside in the heart. The *psyche* or soul controls the body from the heart. Soul and heart are thus intimately interconnected in Aristotle. The reason why it can be the centre of life is because the soul is located there.

Like Plato, Aristotle also operated with a tripartition of man. This also underlies the rhetoric that Aristotle develops, which was the basis for general education in Western culture until the Romantic period. It can be claimed that rhetoric is a result of the Greek's attempt to master passion without suppressing it. Rhetoric enables the Greeks to make use of the insights they have gained concerning human nature in order to know how they are to convey their thoughts in an effective way. If people are to fully understand the message of the speaker and teacher, it must not only instruct (via *logos*) but also please by means of its confidence-inspiring attitude (*ethos*) and move people's hearts or arouse their enthusiasm and passion (*pathos*). To the three functions of rhetoric – logos, ethos and pathos – correspond the three main dimensions or levels of man that both Plato and Aristotle operate with in their anthropologies. For both of them, pathos is the problem – both as erotic passion, wrath and anger. Cultural history also deals with how unrestrained anger is to be controlled and sublimated. In rhetoric, pathos is defined as the strong single-stringed and single-tuned emotion that has no room for the reflected *divided* emotion, ethos, from which ethics is derived. This is why passion and ethics cannot normally be combined, even though holy wrath and anger can in themselves motivate ethical involvement and reflection.

With his holism and psychosomatic way of thinking, Aristotle also comes to emphasize the interaction between mind and body. If the mental state changes, so does the body and its movements. Here, he is able to expand the ideas of Hippocrates, who developed his Four Humours, analogous to the four elements of Empedocles the Elder (*c.* 483–423 BC). He claimed that man could sense and perceive the world because he himself was made up of the same four basic elements as the rest of the universe. In line with this, Empedocles claimed that thought resides in the blood round the heart, since the blood can absorb and actively convey all the basic elements or elementary bodily liquids to the rest of the body.

In the struggle for predominance between the liver, heart and brain, Aristotle's upgrading of the heart was an important reason for its retaining the central position almost into the modern age. In a number of other cultures, the heart has to compete with the liver as the most important organ. Many ethnologists and archaeologists believe that originally people everywhere considered the liver to be the seat of life and that it was not until later that the heart contended for this place of honour. This applies in particular to the Sumer-Mesopotamian tradition, but to the pre-Socratic Greek tradition as well. It is not only in Mesopotamia, for example, that the liver is used to foretell the future. In the Promethean myth, one of the oldest in Greek culture, it is the liver that suffers when the eagle hacks away every day at the bound body of Prometheus as a punishment for his having stolen fire from Zeus and the gods and given it to man.

However, as early as the fifth century BC, the liver and the heart – or rather the region of the heart – began to be challenged for pride of place by the brain. This is a result of the first scientific dissections we know of in Antiquity, carried out by the Pythagorean physician Alkmaion. He claimed that both the senses and reason reside in the brain. The greatest physician and teacher of medicine, Hippocrates (460–*c.*370) also proposed that the capacity to think, *nous*, lies in that strange, motionless, grey mass of matter. That started a medical discussion and a philosophical dispute as to whether reason and consciousness resided in the heart and blood (Greek *haima/hemo*) or in the head and brain (Greek *enkephalos*). This dispute lasted throughout Antiquity, the Middle Ages, the Renaissance and well into our own age.

The school of medicine in Alexandria and Galen (AD *c.* 131–200) marked a climax and a conclusion for the medicine of Antiquity. Galen developed Hippocrates' theory of the four humours further, on how the balance between blood, gall and slime, or phlegm, kept the body healthy. Blood did not only have a positive role. That was one of the reasons why Galen, after Hippocrates, recommended collecting blood, or bloodletting, which was an important 'treatment' well into the modern period. Galen's 'new ground' was his direct linking of the physical balance of humours to a person's mental balance by developing the theory of the four temperaments: the sanguine, phlegmatic, choleric and melancholic. This precursor of modern psychology came to predominate the scientific view of the inner man until the modern age. Galen's teaching concerning the heart enjoyed a monopoly for just as long a time – as a matter of fact until Harvey.

It is striking just how Galen's conception of the heart managed to predominate from late Antiquity, through the entire medieval period and up to the late Renaissance, in Western as well as in Arab culture. It also illustrates the power of habitual thinking in the sciences, how a logically attractive system of thought and the power of language via established patterns and metaphors can prevent new insights being made. Galen regarded the heart as a source of heat created by the bloodstream from the liver to the heart, during which the blood comes into contact with air from the lungs. This interaction between element and organ creates a biological melting furnace that heats, purifies and animates the blood with the spirit (*pneuma*) that air represents. From the heart the vital forces from this spirit are transported via the arteries to the other parts of the body, including the brain, where they are transformed into natural or animal spirits that are responsible for the transformation into outer action. The essence of this conception of the heart is, then, heat that is produced in the heart-furnace in the workshop of the body. The metaphors Galen uses for the heart correspond to the development of production and working life at the time. Pumps had not yet been developed for production, so Galen did not conceive the heart as a pump.

Considering the fact that the heart that constantly and regularly beats in our breast is one of the first mysteries that man has attempted to understand, it is also striking how tenacious Galen's theory has proved to be. But his spiritualization of the blood and heart corresponded to and supported the spiritual position the blood and heart of Christ were later to occupy in Christianity. This is perhaps a partial explanation why the theory managed to survive, since the problem had actually been solved by the Chinese, with a long medical tradition that was a possible alternative to the Western one. As early as 2,000 BC the Chinese had discovered that the heart was a pump that pumped blood round the body, which accounted for the human pulse. In *The Yellow Emperor's Classic of Internal Medicine*,

Chinese physicians could distinguish between 28 types of pulse. The explanation of how the Chinese solved the mystery is, among other things, that they are pragmatically oriented through experience, whereas we Westerners, after Plato, are more bound to hierarchical abstract systems of thought.

THE PLATONIC LEGACY

It is reason's pride of place and the often suppressive and regimented control over the sensual and the emotional aspects of human nature that are the most fundamental and widespread influence exerted by the Platonic view of man on Western culture. It is a logical consequence of a hierarchical model that what constitutes the lower ranks is downgraded and thought to be of lesser value. This results in dualism. When the rational soul reigns supreme, everything else in the body is standardized and reduced to something inner and mental. Everything emotional is reduced to something that belongs to the inner world, and all the sovereign and spontaneous manifestations of life that have a physical or sensory origin other than that coming from conscious, universal reason are lumped together and called the *psyche*, which reason must keep wary eye on so that the dangerous and destructive forces (Plato's 'monster') do not escape and take over control.

Reason's control of the emotions does not only change the conception of them in theory but the very emotions and passions themselves. In short, human resources are decimated or stunted. Alternative sources of perception dry out, and people feel and experience their emotions in a different way than before. And when that happens, man (Western man) has really become something else than he was prior to the Platonic impoverishment of emotional life.

Not only are the emotions reduced in terms of quantity and quality within Platonism, they are no longer an end in themselves but easily become a means for reason, which can use them instrumentally for purposes and interests that lie outside itself. Thereby, however, reason too becomes a means, a means for a form of control that is not questioned. And this opens the door to power, enabling political, economic and in particular institutional power to exploit both reason and emotions for its own purposes and interests. Rationalism becomes technical instrumentalism.

Francis Bacon aptly sums up this instrumental ideal in the seventeenth century: 'Knowledge is power', power to remodel nature – also human nature – to serve external means and ends. Platonic self-control has become control and exploitation of nature and the whole world. Bacon gives people the go-ahead to seize power for themselves and change self-control into control of the world. This is the basis in terms of the history of ideas for commercial forces during the so-called free (actually unrestrained) market forces of the twentieth and twenty-first centuries being able to exploit the emotions by linking them to material commodities that have a large value of fascination, or to strong sense-impressions such as those provided by present-day audio-visual mass media, if we agree with Hermann Schmitz and other historians of ideas who have assessed the Platonic legacy. The father of the modern History of Ideas as an academic discipline, Arthur O. Lovejoy, in his classical work *The Great Chain of Being* (1936) places special emphasis on the fact that Platonism as well as Christian theology are preconditions for the downgrading and exploitation of nature in our culture, since nature, as matter, has no soul. For the goal of the soul is precisely to free itself from matter and the body.

An important reason why Plato's psychology could have such a great impact on Christian theology is of course that he operated with an *immortal* soul, whose origin was elsewhere than this world, in the eternal and unchanging world to which it would return after the death of the body. This is Christianity reduced to a philosophical formula (or vice versa), and it underlies why the doctrine of the soul has been pivotal in Christianity up to the present day. What status the soul has in the twenty-first century is a completely different story. But until now, the Platonic ideal – that the corporeal, emotional and sensual should be subordinate to the ethical, to will and to reason – has definitively shaped Western hearts. Even though Platonism in Western culture has been used to legitimize and justify Christianity theologically, the view of man and the metaphorics of the heart were originally different in the Bible from in Plato.

CHAPTER 4

The Heart in the Bible and
in Christianity

He who fights with monsters might take care
lest he thereby become a monster.
                                                    Nietzsche

Alongside the influence from the Platonic view of humanity in the history
of ideas the Bible and Christianity are the main sources of the most widespread conception of the heart and metaphorics of the heart in Western
culture. It can admittedly be quite difficult to determine what is originally
biblical and what is later theology and the result of the institutions and
practice of the church. Nor is Christianity something that is given once
and for all – it is also the result of interpretation.

Nor is the metaphorics of the heart in the Bible the expression of
anything homogeneous. In both testaments the heart is the seat of both
good and evil. In both the Old and the New Testament it is the heart that
tells us about man's relationship to the divine and the moral, while also
being the bearer of feelings and emotional impulses. The heart thus
becomes an image of individual human nature and disposition. If a person
is good, he or she has a good heart; if evil, an evil heart. This is where
the basis of much fundamentalism lies – with everything that it entails
socially and politically. Apart from that, the basic view in the New
Testament, as the basis of Christianity, is that good and evil reside in every
single individual. Intrinsically, the heart has no fixed qualities. These it
only acquires via the soul, as this concept and a corresponding new
anthropology are developed in Christianity on the basis of the New
Testament, in which the conception and the metaphorics of the heart
differ strikingly from that of the Old Testament.

The conception of the heart in the Old Testament is part of a long, unbroken tradition that goes all the way back to the exile of the Jewish people in Egypt – possibly even back to their origins in Mesopotamia, before this ethnic group migrated to Palestine. Among the Babylonians, the liver competed with the heart as the central internal organ with properties linked to the soul. Consequently, it was the liver, especially from sheep, that the wise men used in order to interpret and foretell the future. The Jews, however, consciously distanced themselves from their former kinsmen when they early on made the heart the seat of the soul. In that sense they are more closely related to the Egyptians. If the metaphorics of the heart is influenced in the Old Testament by the pharaonic, we are dealing with a conception of mankind that goes back several thousand years. The oldest Egyptians, however, make little distinction between the physical and the mental heart, whereas the Jews place little emphasis on the heart in the physical sense. They do not clearly recognize the heart as an organ that maintains life. In this respect the Jews can be called *pneumaticians* (from the Greek *pneuma*, breath). For them, the real sign of life is not the beating of the heart but breath, breathing. God does not create man by inserting a heart into the lump of clay that is to become Adam, but by blowing into his nostrils: 'And the LORD God formed man of the dust of the ground, and breathed into his nostrils the breath of life; and man became a living soul.' (Genesis II: 7). When man breathes his last, he also exhales his soul. The anatomical fact that the heart stops at the same time is not mentioned.

The heart is called either *leb* and *lebab*, or *lev* and *levav*. It is one of the most frequently used concepts in the Old Testament – the word occurs over 850 times. But it is not certain that the heart of the Old Testament is the seat of the emotions, as we normally conceive it. Nor is it correct to translate these two words with the English word heart. This leads to mis-understandings. There are several words in the Old Testament that border on the anthropological function and the metaphorical interpretations that modern Westerners give to the heart. *Nefes* (or *naefaes*) has to be mentioned, which is translated by soul, but which originally meant breath, breath of life (cf. Homer). The difference in relation to modern anthropology can be illustrated by the fact that *nefes* in terms of concrete anatomy means throat, breath, mouth – or even hunger – and is located in the area of the throat, breast or stomach. Life for the *nefes* is often thought to reside in the blood, *dam*, which has many of the meanings we ascribe to the heart (cf. Christ's blood). Passion is also linked to *nefes* – that which one is seized by or driven towards.

Just how complex and ambiguous man was inside for the ancient Jews is seen from all the concepts for internal organs and functions. Related to *lev* are – along with *nefes* – *neshamah* (breath, understanding from God) and, especially, *ruach*, the literal meaning of which is force, wind, breath, and which can be translated in anthropological terms by spirit or intellect. *Ruach*, however, transcends the anthropological dimension, since it is God who imbues this kind of spirit.

As in other ancient cultures, the concept of individuality and correspondingly the heart, the central bodily organ, is highly complex and ambiguous in Judaism. But the main tendency in the interpretation of *lev* goes in the direction of 'the inner man', the inside and the centre of the human being. Here too lies the source of the emotions, good and bad. The heart is also the seat of the will, wishes, language and desire, as well as lust – characteristics that are connected to conscious thought, planning and mental activity in general, both positive and negative. The heart is to keep God's commandments (Proverbs III: 1), and one's heart is to 'devise one's way' (Proverbs XVI: 9). But it is incorrect to translate heart with 'reason', for it is a deeper understanding and wisdom that reside in the heart: 'Behold, thou desirest truth in the inward parts: and in the hidden [part] thou shalt make me to know wisdom.' (Psalm LI: 6), and 'The wise in heart shall be called prudent' (Proverbs XVI: 21). The heart also hides the mystery of a man, and only God can see the depths of the human heart (Psalm XXXIII:15; XLIV: 21), since it is God's will, wisdom and law that are embodied in the heart. Readers of the Old Testament, however, probably did not make original sin and sin a physical phenomenon linked to the Fall of Adam, as does Augustine.

The heart does not only represent the most important emotions in man but also the most important aspects of existence and moral life. In the oldest parts of the Old Testament it is emphasized that the human heart is evil – man follows his base desires and it 'grieved Him at His heart', arousing God's anger and punishment (Pentateuch). The stony heart has to be replaced if man is to be able to receive God's commandments and words: 'And I will give them one heart, and I will put a new spirit within you; and I will take the stony heart out of their flesh, and will give them an heart of flesh', it says in Ezekiel II: 19. The central question, already in the Old Testament, is how the heart is linked to God's love. Deuteronomy, VI: 5–6 formulate what in a way is also the basic principle of the Christian metaphysics of the heart: 'And thou shalt love the LORD thy God with all thine heart, and with all thy soul, and with all thy might. And these words, which I command thee this day, shall be in thine heart.'

These words, with all that they represent, have left so profound a mark on the hearts of both Jews and Christian Europeans for the last two thousand years that the historical power of the words can hardly be exaggerated. The Bible makes love a commandment: you *shall* love and not other human beings first, but God first and last, who in return loves His people, i.e. His 'chosen people', the Jews – not other peoples and those of different beliefs. The love between God and the Jews is a covenant that has to be understood on the basis of the difficult political and ethnic situation in which the Jews found themselves in the Middle East during the various periods when the books later included in the Old Testament were written: if the Jews love Him, God will help them; if they do not obey His commandments, they will be punished. Therefore, they must also fear God. Love is maintained via dread, threats, fear of punishment and revenge. This God, who is a passionate and jealous God, makes use of strong measures to punish the disobedient and apostate: plague, disease, catastrophes and lean years. To our modern eyes, this is not love but an authoritarian exercising of power so as to maintain a particular regime, Jewish monotheism and the patriarchy – a male society. Woman is given a subordinate role. She is to love her husband, who is the 'god' of the family, give him children and thereby ensure the continuation of the race. If she is unfaithful, she is to be exterminated, something which did not apply to men in a similar position (a view with which Luther concurred).

The female aspect is not part of the Jewish deity, unlike the Greek, where women had a central place in the world of the gods. The original female deity of Jewish mythology was 'edited out' after the exile in Babylon. The role of women in the Old Testament is, via Eve, a negative one, that of the scapegoat – or 'fall guy' in a literal sense. It is she who is Satan's tool and temptress with her desirable sex – and as such responsible for the Fall. That is the basis for Christianity demonizing the female sex and making sexuality a sin, unlike Judaism, where sexuality was not a sin if entirely on the premises of the man and the patriarchy.

THE NEW TESTAMENT

The centuries separating the Old and the New Testament have not served the heart well. In the New Testament the heart is once more first and foremost the seat of evil. What was it the Authorized Version said: 'For the imagination of man's heart is evil from his youth'? (Genesis VIII: 21) On several occasions, Jesus complains about *people's hearts*, especially those of the academics and theoreticians of his time, the scribes and hypocritical Pharisees who, among other things, censure the young for not observing their regulations concerning acceptable food. This gives rise to Jesus's fulminations against the heart. It is the heart that is the central issue, not what one eats or does not eat:

> But those things which proceed out of the mouth come forth from the heart; and they defile the man. For out of the heart proceed evil thoughts, murders, adulteries, fornications, thefts, false witness, blasphemies (Matthew 15: 18–19, cf. also Mark 7: 18–23).

The import of such words is strictly anti-materialist. The physical and physiological are of no consequence, morally speaking. That which enters man from the outside, 'entereth not into the heart but into the belly, and goeth out into the draught' (Mark 7: 19). Here, Jesus formulates a heart-religion with a corresponding ethics, one of sentiment, which Kant in particular has expounded and legitimized philosophically. At the same time, the words have an anthropological and physiological meaning that imply that the heart (and the blood) are separate from the process of nutrition. This is a view that diverges from the Greek view of physiology, where the heart (*kardia, ker*) was closely linked to the stomach. Here, the influence of Egyptian thinking is more obvious. The well-known Biblical expression 'For out of the abundance of the heart the mouth speaketh' (Matthew 12: 34) corresponds to the Egyptian idea of the link between heart and tongue. The mouth and what the tongue speaks always reveal the heart. When the heart is so often evil, it cannot be any general symbol either for what is good and for love – whether it be sensual or suprasensual.

In what is thought of as being the Christian Song of Songs to love, Paul's Epistle to the Corinthians, there is not a single word about the heart: 'And now abideth faith, hope, charity, these three; but the greatest of these is charity.' (1 Corinthians 13: 13). Neither Jesus's nor Mary's heart are mentioned in the New Testament, although the heart is frequently mentioned – 160 times I think, which is roughly only a fifth of the frequency in the Old Testament. And it is the zealous Paul who most frequently uses heart metaphors. The heart thereby becomes a central Christian symbol, and the changing of the heart is a prerequisite for faith. In other words, the heart is plastic, a vessel that can have different contents. Compared to Sigrid Undset, who wrote about the unchanging nature of human hearts, Christianity has the exact opposite point of departure: human hearts are absolutely changeable. This is the basis of the Christian ethics of disposition. In Protestantism, man is saved via a change of disposition, faith being sufficient – a possible source of false security for many people (Catholics don't get off so easily – they must actively do penance for evil in both word and deed before they can obtain absolution).

The essential quality of the heart in Christianity is to serve as a dwelling for the soul (which thus acquires substance). The key to the mystery of life (and death), the most secret and irreducible, lies concealed in the human heart as a dwelling for the God-given soul, which does not follow the path of the flesh but which, under certain conditions, can be saved (or lost for good), the gleaming pearl that, at death's door, can roll over the threshold into eternal bliss. It is this doctrine of the soul that is developed in the New Testament, where God's love (from the Old Testament) is supplemented by and linked to the equally important 'love of one's neighbour' in *agape*, which also has its seat in the heart: 'Thou shalt love thy neighbour as thyself' (Matthew 22: 39). All other forms of love are subordinate and subject to these two forms. Furthermore, erotic or physical love becomes a source of sin and shame and cannot be combined with love. This finds expression in the Greek word Paul uses about love, *agape*, in distinction from – and in opposition to – the word used by the Greeks, namely *eros*.

In his classic work *Den kristna kärlekstanken* (*The Christian Concept of Love*, 1930) the Swedish theologian Anders Nygren gives *eros* a narrower interpretation, defining it as a motivated love, as human striving to reach God, the divine and the eternal (as does Plato). *Agape*, on the other hand, he sees as being divine love, particularly in the sense of God's love for mankind, despite man's sinful nature. This form of love is unmotivated and spontaneous, since it is God's being or nature that comprises everything: God *is* love. For that reason, man cannot do anything to motivate God's love. *Agape* is God's path to man, but there is no path from man to God. Even so, man is to love God by, for example, loving his neighbour as himself, as God loves man: in an unmotivated, spontaneous way, free of any ulterior motives and unconditionally. As God loves sinners, man is to love friend and foe alike. Love of one's neighbour is, then, anchored in religion and is something much more than 'just' altruism and sympathy for one's neighbour. Love of the self and egoism are overcome by love not being directed towards the self but towards one's neighbour and God. Apart from this, it is one of the bones of contention between Protestants and Catholics – whether *eros* and *agape* are reconcilable opposites. Catholics believe that they are not different in kind, whereas Martin Luther – along with Nygren – believes that they are.

Based on the content and function of the heart as depicted above, it can be said to be synonymous with the soul. The heart fleshes out the soul and is the incarnation of the divine in the human soul. The warm heart that characterizes the divine spark is also the basis for the distinction being made both in the Bible and in Christian theology between inanimate (and false) words and words that come from the heart, e.g. in Matthew 15: 8, which quotes Isaiah: 'This people draweth nigh unto me with their mouth, and honoureth me with their lips; but their heart is far from me.' For the heart can be both good and evil and know of the evil desire it has. This is the point of departure for the corporeal morality that Paul preaches, and that – quite literally – was branded on the hearts of Europeans for centuries.

PAUL

Paul has often been made a scapegoat for the strongly dualistic and anti-corporeal attitude that Christianity has practised through the ages. And not without good reason. He is in many ways the theologian among the apostles and has held a vice-like grip on both Christian theology and its view of humanity, which he conveyed with all the zeal of the newly converted. He was influenced by dualism in the popular Orphic tradition (the belief in two worlds) with its notions of a better life in the hereafter – a belief that was widespread among slaves and the oppressed in the Middle East and in the Hellenistic region in the time before and after the birth of Christ. Therefore his dualism cannot be unequivocally traced back to Plato's teaching. The same applies to his view of the body.

Hermann Schmitz (1965) has attempted to ignore Paul's view of the body as the seat of eroticism and desire, i.e. his corporeal morality, and to look purely anthropologically at it compared with the Homeric view of the body. Using this as his point of departure, Schmitz believes that he can find notions of the body in Paul that are more reminiscent of pre-Socratic than Platonic Antiquity. This means that bodily organs or limbs play an independent role or represent a force for which the individual is not personally responsible, although it is responsible for how it views these forces. Such an anthropology makes it understandable for Paul to start by accepting people as they are from nature's hand: 'And I, brethren, could not speak unto you as unto spiritual, but as unto carnal, even as unto babes in Christ' (1 Corinthians 3: 1). For Paul, sin is not something that takes place in the human soul but in the parts or limbs of the body, which do as they want by nature. From this perspective, Schmitz interprets the well-known words from the Epistle to the Romans (7: 19, 23):

> For the good that I would I do not: but the evil which I would not, that I do . . .
> But I see another law in my members, warring against the law of my mind, and bringing me into captivity to the law of sin which is in my members.

Paul is the first to depict this struggle between an autonomous body and its equally sovereign limbs – a struggle that the new Christian cast of mind must gain control over via good will. Paul's conception of the body, however, is not as one-sidedly dualistic as his morality. For, according to Schmitz, Pauline man does not have a soul to which it can withdraw and from which gain control over bodily impulses. This distinguishes him from Plato.

In Paul, *pneuma* (spirit) and *sarka/sarks* (flesh) would seem to have taken the place that the reasonable *psyche* and *soma* have in Plato, but they are not dualistically opposed. Paul often uses the word *soma*, but not as opposed to *psyche*. Human flesh is not something man is either to free himself from or give in to; the solution is for sinful flesh to be inspired by *pneuma*, by means of which God can 'quicken your mortal bodies by his spirit that dwelleth in you' (Romans 8: 11). Man in Paul is both *in* the spirit (*pneuma*) and *in* the flesh. Therefore, Paul (1 Corinthians 3: 16) can call the human body a temple in which the spirit dwells: 'Know ye not that ye are the temple of God and that the spirit of God dwelleth in you?'

There is apparently a quantum leap from Plato, who views the body as the grave of the soul, to Paul, who calls the body a temple of the spirit that lives in man. But, inspired by Plato, theologians are quick to define the body as being the prison of the soul, a cesspool of sin for sexual temptations, even though 'your body is the temple of the Holy Ghost', according to 1 Corinthians 6. In this chapter, Paul underlines the reciprocal relationship between body and spirit: 'The body is not for fornication but for the Lord; and the Lord for the body' (13), and he once more reminds the reader that the body is divine: 'Know ye not that your body is the temple of the Holy Ghost which is in you?' (19). Paul speaks of a *bodily* heart that is inspired, or animated, in all men, not of a pneumatic soul: 'And because ye are sons, God hath sent forth the spirit of his Son into your hearts, crying Abba, Father.' (Galatians 4: 6). The spiritual does not enter a soul but a body (cf. 1 Corinthians 6: 19 and 3: 16). Without the body, there is no spirit. The spirit dwells in man in a physical and sensory way. There can be no talk of freeing oneself from the body as from a grave or a piece of clothing that the soul can cast off, but of making the body come alive and freeing it from sin by the spirit (cf. Romans 8: 11).

Schmitz has attempted to understand Christianity from the inside, via what is in principle a positive view of the body, speaking purely anthropologically. In Paul, release comes by when the physical body with its sovereign urges is filled by the holy spirit, which is love. Baptism and the sacraments are a promise to the one who believes, not a promise of the body's life and death but of the resurrection of the body by means of Christ's suffering and God's grace. The body shall rise in the hereafter!

Resurrection of the flesh is the sweet carrot whose psychological function is to offset the frightful fear of hell that is used as a whip against all joys and pleasures of the body. This brings us to the other and historically most spectacular and effective aspect of the Christian view of the body. There, the words of Paul definitely did not fall on stony ground, but have branded themselves on the hearts of people for many centuries.

So there seem to be two highly different conceptions of the body in Christianity. One leads to an upgrading of the body (*sub specie aeternitatis*); the other to a downgrading of the sensual and corporeal (when alive). In fact, the entire Christian church as an institution is based on Paul's notion of the body, which claims that all Christians via their faith belong to one body – that of Christ. But this is a symbolic body. The suppressive and often suppressed Christian story of the body is painfully concrete. It has left profound, ugly wounds in human hearts in European culture since what were to have been glad tidings were announced for the first time. This story of suppression and crippling runs like a red, not to say bloody, thread through Christian history up to the present day. Blessed St Paul must also assume legitimate and illegitimate paternity for this rather uncourtly history of the sexes.

Paul takes over the Jewish patriarchal view of woman – even making her directly responsible for the Fall. For it was Eve, and not Adam – although both were tempted – who allowed herself to be deceived by Satan and to disobey God's command (1 Timothy 2: 14). Therefore, Paul believes that it is 'good for a man not to touch a woman' (1 Corinthians 7: 1). This can easily lead to his fall, even though *eros* in itself is not sinful in the gospels. For the lust of the flesh/body is 'Satan's work', his way of tempting away from the spirit, with which man is to be united. This leads to a demonization of the body, sex – especially the female sex – and sexuality, something the witch-trials are one historical manifestation of.

Paul, by the way, had little success in demonizing the body during the first centuries of the history of Christianity. It was not until well into the medieval period that Satan became a popular figure, especially from the twelfth century onwards. Conditions were better suited then for people to be more receptive to such a figure of fascination. Nor did Jesus himself ever express himself in such an anti-corporeal way as Paul; on the contrary, he blessed someone reputed to be a prostitute, a former sinner with whom his relationship was not totally Platonic. Mary Magdalene was one of Jesus's inner circle. She also assumes an utterly central role in the story of the resurrection, since she was the first person to find Jesus's tomb empty, and the first one to meet and hear Jesus's voice after the resurrection. But the fact that it was a woman Jesus first revealed himself to did not make Paul any more tolerant towards the female sex. On the contrary.

After having fulminated against prostitution and prostitutes in Corinth, Paul comes with his judgements concerning prostitution, whoredom and the lusts of the flesh. His vocabulary and imagery were most effective and have had a legacy that has exceeded not only his health programme in Corinth at the beginning of the Christian era but perhaps the core of the Christian love of one's neighbour:

> Know ye not that your bodies are the members of Christ? Shall I then take the members of Christ, and make them the members of an harlot? God forbid. What? Know ye not that he which is joined to an harlot is one body? For two, saith he, shall be one flesh. But he that is joined unto the Lord is one spirit. Flee fornication. Every sin that a man doeth is without the body; but he that committeth fornication sinneth against his own body (1 Corinthians 6: 15–18).

Paul, though, knows that the body and nature demand what is theirs; consequently he views marriage as a safety valve, where desire can be given plenty of rein, but in a controlled form:

> It is good for a man not to touch a woman. Nevertheless, to avoid fornication, let every man have his own wife, and let every woman have her own husband. Let the husband render unto the wife due benevolence: and likewise also the wife unto the husband. The wife hath not power of her own body, but the husband: and likewise also the husband hath not power of his own body, but the wife. Defraud ye not one the other, except it be with consent for a time, that ye may give yourselves to fasting and prayer; and come together again, that Satan tempt you not for your incontinency (1 Corinthians 7: 1–5).

Paul has made morality identical with sexual morality and laid the foundation for it to dominate not only the Church but people's everyday lives for 2,000 years. But Paul does not even make a virtue out of necessity (as Luther does with sexual needs). There is not much room for love in marriage for him – not at any rate for eroticism in married life. This view of sexuality and eroticism, divorced of all love, is almost improbably primitive and clumsy in Paul: time for a quick one, then, if carnal desire gains the upper hand! That was that – almost brutish. The art of erotic love and the sacred have been removed from Christian sexual life. The glad tidings have nothing to do with the pleasures of the body.

By condemning physical desire, Paul also condemns the desire to indulge in laughter and other forms of pleasure. Jesus's laughter is erased from the gospels, nor is there any room for laughter in the glad tidings, either. That life should be lived without laughter has truly shaped the view of the Western heart to just as great an extent as the downgrading of sexuality, to which laughter is inseparably linked. The no-laughter attitude has soured life for generations and made it unnecessarily hard to bear. For when laughter and humour are repressed, the 'oil' that prevents life from stiffening into mechanical motions and melancholy also disappears. When laughter is forbidden, power also has a free rein. For laughter is anti-authoritarian and liberating, capable of turning all power hierarchies upside-down. There is no room for divine laughter, the inextinguishable *asbestos gelos* with its deep insight, as cultivated by the Greeks, in Christianity. With Christianity clearly in mind, Nietzsche is thus able to state his aphorism: 'And may we deem every truth false that is not accompanied by laughter!'[1]

One of the deepest truths in life is suffering, which is the basis for the most important teaching of Christianity. Jesus is the first in history to link suffering and compassion, quite concretely. But the concrete circumstances of his suffering would seem to have been forgotten when the theologians make dogma out of it. The distinctive feature of this Christian dogma is that it is someone else, Jesus, who must suffer for us, in the sense that he is the one who must pay and atone for our misdeeds. And it is primarily ineradicable passion and original sin that make it necessary to have outside help in order to be saved. An alternative attitude to this dogma of 'surrogate suffering' is to view passion and suffering as conditions that mutually define each other – and personal compassion following the example of Jesus as an active model and not a pretext for doing nothing.

For Paul, it is impossible to see erotic love and religion as combining in a positive way – as actually having the same origin – even in Christianity, according to the myth of the Fall. 'Eroticism is what in human consciousness questions the nature of man's being,' claims the French thinker Georges Bataille.[2] Since Christianity rejects the idea that the origin of erotic love is religious and the erotic experience transcendental, the sacred in Christianity also becomes weakened, according to Bataille. In other world religions – as the history of religion makes clear – the erotic has a completely different and central place – as part of the divine mystery. In the cradle of our own culture, the Greece of Antiquity, erotic love was divinely inspired. Consequently, there is still good reason for us in the West to consider the long-lasting and often paradoxical consequences of Christianity's censorious view of sexuality. When eroticism is turned into something base and inferior, the way is open for sexuality to become precisely that – as seen in present-day pornography. In many ways, the pendulum around the year 2000 has swung back to what was the negative point of departure before Augustine's founding of the medieval church – to a body culture with more frivolity than respect for the most intimate in human life. What lies in between is just as much the work of Augustine as it is of Paul.

AUGUSTINE

Among the fathers of the church and in medieval theology the concept of the biblical heart was strongly influenced by the philosophy of Antiquity, especially by neo-Platonic Plotinism. Augustine (354–430) in particular sets this interpretation in motion. This takes place when *cor* (heart) becomes virtually synonymous with such terms as *anima, animus, mens, intellectus* and *ratio* – the Latin words for soul, spirit and reason. This is completely in accordance with Plato's understanding of the indivisible part of the *psyche* as something non-corporeal and immortal.

Augustine, the first great Christian theologian, developed his own theology of the heart. His main work is *Confessiones* (*c.* 400). There is probably no literary work (apart from the book of books) that has had so great an influence on emotional life and self-awareness in an entire culture as this, the first autobiographical work in our culture. For his *Confessions* are not only the introduction of a new literary genre but also of a new type of human being, with the focus on the inner self and self-awareness, even though many centuries were to pass before the new mentality made its mark on European culture. Augustine is also confessing to his fellow human beings:

> To whom do I narrate this? Not unto Thee, my God; but before Thee unto my own kind, even to that small part of the human race who may chance to light upon these my writings. And to what end? That I and all who read the same may reflect out of what depths we are to cry unto Thee. For what cometh nearer to Thine ears than a confessing heart and a life of faith?[3]

At the centre of his *Confessions* Augustine places the restless heart, *cor inquietum*. The heart is restless because it is divided between love of this world and love of God, and can, according to the well-known words in the first section of the confessions, only find rest once more in God: *et inquietum est cor nostrum, donec requiescat in te*. In order to find rest in the one great unity, man must first free himself from desire and will of the self and follow God's law. Augustine distinguishes between God's will and the law that is written in men's hearts, which is godlike. Since the human heart has been imbued with a divine spark by its Creator, man is able to know the unknowable divinity. Lit by God's word, the divine spark can flare up in a holy glow after becoming one with God and overcome the inner division. Augustine is driven by such a glow – therefore the flaming heart is his personal sign and, several centuries later, his icon in art.

What impels the awakened heart is love of God. In the key section of the second book, the repentant sinner expresses why he confesses, and what is vital in Christian soul-heart metaphorics, something that has applied to European culture throughout the Middle Ages and up to the present day:

> For what is closer to your ear than a confessing heart and a life out of belief . . . Theft is punished by Thy law, O Lord, and by the law written in men's hearts, which iniquity itself cannot blot out . . . Behold my heart, O my God; behold my heart, which Thou hadst pity upon when in the bottomless pit. Behold, now, let my heart tell Thee what it was seeking there, that I should be gratuitously wanton, having no inducement to evil but the evil itself . . . I loved to perish. I loved my own error . . . Base soul, falling from Thy firmament to utter destruction.[4]

With Augustine, the internalization of the emotions that Plato system-atized, and the moral downgrading of the corporeal and sensual that Plotinus carried further in late Antiquity, is transferred to a new culture and integrated into the Christian view of man. Seen in that light, Augustine represents a new view of man – at any rate in relation to the view of the body of Antiquity. The inner, mental and supernatural spiritual world now becomes the real one, and the heart becomes a dwelling-place for a soul whose sights are set on the hereafter. The punishing God up in heaven found in the Old Testament, 'Yahweh', becomes in Augustine something internal in the form of a strong sense of guilt and a conscious-ness of sin that make life a path of penance.

Augustine incorporates a synthesis between the Graeco-Roman and the biblical-Christian thought on which European culture is founded – although with the distinctive feature that he downgraded Greek Antiquity. Augustine himself was grounded in the Greek cultural tradi-tion and had been educated as a rhetorician. In his lifestyle, too, he was closer to a 'Greek' culture of the body, allowing it its natural place – not least when it came to the erotic. *Confessions* deals to a great extent with Augustine's erotic life – in a culture that was by no means anti-corporeal. The story of his conversion to Christianity is depicted as a struggle *with* and increasingly *against* the body, until, at the age of 32, he became a believing Christian and was baptized. Between the ages of 19 and 28, he had followed Manichaeism. The contempt for the world, *contemptus mundi*, found in the Middle Ages, was strongly influenced by such schools of thought as Manichaeism, which divided the world between good and evil, light and dark – something man was not really responsible for. For that reason, the erotic was not decisively moral, either. The soul and sex were separated in dualistic fashion. Plotinus' neo-Platonism, which was crucial to Augustine's transition to Christianity, is part of this tradition, with its moral downgrading of matter and the corporeal-sensual. In Plotinus, Augustine found assurance of the fact that there is something supra-sensual which is man's true goal – one that can be reached by liberating the soul from sinful matter.

An important element in the intensification of morality in Augustine's view of the body is the change in the relationship between reason and will, something that has enormous consequences for Western self-awareness. For in the struggle against physical impulses the human will, more or less free, is now given the place reason formerly occupied in Plato and Aristotle. By making *will* and free choice conditions for man to exist morally, Augustine makes man responsible not only for his actions but for his emotions and urges. Even impure, sensual thoughts become sinful as a result of everything being subject to personal responsibility. No matter how involuntary man's thoughts are, they can nevertheless lead to punishment and eternal damnation. It was both a theological and personal dilemma for Augustine that there was something in the body that was not dependent on the will, plaguing him with sexual dreams that refused to obey his will. However, the will is not free, and man can only be saved via God's mercy by love, a doctrine Luther took over when he made faith only (*sola fides*) a condition for salvation instead of and independently of good deeds, reason and the will, which is egoistically turned in on itself (*incurvatus in se*). Man is caught in an insoluble dilemma, for even if he could gain control over all thoughts, attitudes and actions, he is prone to perdition as a result of original sin. Augustine believed that desire (lust) had broken free of will at the 'Fall':

> At several points it seems as if Augustine believes that original sin is transferred to all mankind via the sinful lust of sexual intercourse, which leads him to consider sexuality itself as the source of infection.[5]

The pathological metaphorics come from Augustine: because of the Fall, sexuality is to be understood as a sexually transmitted disease. Lust is like a source of infection and is God's punishment for the sin committed by Adam and Eve. With Augustine, Christianity becomes completely Freudian in its idea that truth about the self is to be found in sexuality, with the important difference that the sexual side of the human personality has to be denied for the individual to be able to be saved.

THE AUGUSTINE LEGACY AND THE MIDDLE AGES

In addition to Augustine branding sexuality as the worst possible sin, medieval church institutions had a whole series of penalties and sanctions at their disposal that intensified fear and dread of both divine and satanic punishment for sins great and small. The most efficient means of internalizing fear in the struggle with and against bodily emotions and passions was the fear of punishment, of Hell and eternal torment there. It is hard for us today to imagine what the fear of Hell meant for Christians in the Middle Ages. Linked to ineradicable physical desire and all kinds of similar thoughts, which were reduced to morally pernicious 'temptations', the fear of Hell represented a constant pressure on the individual, his creative joy in life and his spontaneous personal development.

Hell's terrors were intensified by means of an invention that belongs to the Middle Ages: *purgatory*. The inventor was a French cleric by the eloquent name Pierre le Mangeur ('Peter Bookworm'). He was the first person to use the term Purgatory (which, strictly speaking, means 'cleansing', 'purification') as a noun, in the 1170s. Purgatory was seen as a stopping station and a temporary habitat before the deceased and his soul were finally sent to Heaven or Hell on the Day of Judgement. Sinners were able to gain a foretaste of both Purgatory and Hell while still alive in the stocks or, even worse, when tortured or burnt at the stake. During the Inquisition, not only did the Pope and the Church approve the use of torture, they encouraged it in order to extract confessions. The methods of torture that the Church developed and used are no less obnoxious that those used later by various terror regimes.

In Christianity, man is caught in a trap in both this life and the afterlife. In this life he is imprisoned in the passions and temptations of the body, and the afterlife constantly threatens with eternal damnation in a hell that offers suffering that only the most inventive imagination can visualize. The Church's condemnation of the body, hell-fire doctrine and other means of oppression not only gave rise to fear but to a constant bad conscience and feeling of guilt in whole hosts of people. Man is caught both logically and emotionally in a trap. For the struggle against the body is in vain, and the body is subject to Satan. Man has no choice but to obey

God's will. That gives rise to a paradox: man has free will, but this will is insufficient, for self-will does not choose the good and therefore has to be subject to God's will. But this exceeds man's will and reason; therefore man has to trust in God's mercy and be saved by something else, i.e. by Jesus's surrogate suffering.

The symbol both of Jesus's suffering and man's salvation that is especially developed in the Catholic high and late Middle Ages is *blood*. Later, in the art of the Renaissance and particularly of the Baroque, the heart takes over in a concentrated form much of what is represented by blood. Blood was the visible, dramatic expression of Jesus's suffering. Theology and art in the Middle Ages and the Renaissance depict a bloody Jesus. He bleeds when bearing his own cross, when flogged, when the crown of thorns is placed on his head, and especially when being nailed to the cross. And lastly when the Roman soldier pierces Jesus' side with a spear, with blood and water running from the wound. It is this blood that is collected in the cup, the chalice, and that people can drink at Holy Communion in the form of the consecrated wine. According to papal confirmation in 1215, the wine actually became the blood of Christ, and the bread really *was* the body of Christ – something Luther rejected as superstition. Faith alone, *sola fides*, was enough for him. Religious images (e.g. by Bernini) depict quite concretely how man is washed in the blood of Christ, in *fons pietatis* (the bath of cleansing). Only blood could cleanse man of his sinful nature and wash away all guilt and sin. The Sacrament, which everyone ought to receive at least once a year, was to ensure man's resurrection of the body in the hereafter – if man's frail flesh did not succumb to the cesspool of sin.

Eroticism is negatively charged in Christianity because love must first and foremost go to 'God' and 'one's neighbour'. Erotic love becomes not only a rival of love of God but a temptation that comes from God's real rival and enemy, Satan. That is why eroticism is demonized in the course of the medieval period. Gradually the Old Testament myth of the Fall, where woman was depicted as the tool of Satan and made responsible for original sin, was linked to Paul's view of woman. Woman thus became demonized. With her erotic desire, she is in league with the devil and responsible for the carnal lust and temptations. The female sex is where evil goes amok and spreads like a virus. It creates the demonic triad *woman-body-sexuality*, which has a downgrading and taboo-creating effect on all three.[6]

The demonization of woman is the basis for the witch trials, which, inspired by the Inquisition, grew in strength during the late Middle Ages to culminate in the seventeenth century. The trials, which continued right up to the period of the Enlightenment, not least in Protestant countries, were an expression of the fear earlier Christians felt regarding the punishment of both real and imaginary sins, making them an easy victim of popular superstition in alliance with those who exercised power. Initially, the Church regarded the belief in witches as a heathen superstition that ought to be eradicated. But the need of a scapegoat in order to gain mental and physical control of power, combined with the need to give the dread of punishment free rein, laid the foundation for the hunting of witches. To the great satisfaction of the Church, a papal bull of 1484 decreed that witches existed. The Reformation did not put a stop to witch trials – quite on the contrary in Scandinavia and other Protestant countries – an historical fact that Luther carries a heavy responsibility for by strengthening the belief in and teaching about witches, the Devil and Hell. Belief in witchcraft was combined with a belief in the Devil, one that Luther made even more scary by making hell much more unambiguous than the Catholics, with their many gradations of hell.

One of the most grotesque examples of the demonic linking of woman, gender and sexuality in the scare campaign of Christianity is 'The Hammer of Witches' (*Malleus Maleficarum*) written in 1486 by the Dominican monk Heinrich Kramer as a result of the bull of Pope Innocent VIII of 1484 against intercourse with devils, which could lead to all sorts of witchery and evil. The book became a bestseller. By 1669, it had been reissued 28 times and regularly updated. It formed the authoritative and legal basis for many witch trials and inquisitions during the next couple of centuries. Concerning woman, it stated, among other things:

> that she by nature is more of the flesh than man, as is obvious from her many bodily abominations . . . and the deadly desires that are insatiable in women . . . There are three things that are never satisfied – indeed, a fourth that never can have enough: the entrance to the womb. Which is why, to slake their desire, they seek intercourse even with devils.[7]

There is no other attitude that has literally branded the human heart in an entire culture in such a strong and stigmatizing way as the Christian condemnation of body, gender and sexuality.

The religion of sin and confession of which Bishop Augustine makes himself spokesman in confronting his earlier sensual life culminates in Pietism in the late seventeenth and early eighteenth century and in the popular religious revivals of the nineteenth and twentieth century. The censorious attitude to gender and sexuality in the spirit of Paul and Augustine held sway in our culture right up until the so-called sexual revolution of the twentieth century, with Sigmund Freud as the inspiring force. The similarity between Augustine and Freud is that both they view sexuality as the key to the truth about man and the explanation of man's inner life.

Augustine was ranked the supreme theologian throughout the Middle Ages. Even though Thomas Aquinas (1225–1274), the greatest theologian of the High Middle Ages, was not as dualistic in his view of the world as Augustine since he had the teachings of Aristotle rather than Plato and Plotinus as his point of departure – his image of the soul was not basically different from that of Augustine. But Thomas can be called a monist, because, among other things, he sees evil as being a lack, something mediocre, a form of degeneration. This means he dethrones Satan, who does not become an absolute being, merely an un-being lacking essence in himself. While Augustine did not appear to offer the restless heart peace and rest before the afterlife, Thomas emphasizes the idea that a change of a mind may take place, i.e. a change of heart in this life. For the heart is the seat of rebirth. Such a change of heart will involve a renewal of everything in regard to attitudes and actions: *Recedant vetera, nova sint omnia: et corda et voces et opera* (Let all the old depart, let everything be new: our hearts, our voices, and our works).

However, it is not Thomas's realism or monism but Augustine's conception of the body which derives from Plato, Plotinus and Paul that we Europeans have accepted as being that of Christianity. It has been forgotten that Platonic-Socratic virtue had reason as its end, while the means for liberating and developing reason was the controlling of passion. Christianity, however, made passion in the form of the command *fear and love* the cardinal virtue, a passion that is also split between two extremities, fear and love, i.e. two passions in one. This bipartite passion was linked to a tripartite God. Hardly surprising, then, if dreams of a punishing God associated him with the three-headed monster of folk tales.

In the main, the medieval view of man is confirmed by modern Christianity, with Luther as the castigator and inspirer behind Pietism. In many ways, Luther leads the process of individual internalization for which Plato and Augustine laid the foundations into individualistic modernism. For Luther makes guilt and responsibility for all sins, great and small, in word and deed, attitude and action, an exclusively private matter of conscience. The individual must answer for all his thoughts and deeds solely to God in his own conscience or on the Day of Judgement. The consequence of this constant bad conscience was often self-forgiveness in the recesses of one's heart, based on the principle 'your faith has redeemed you', with the outward blessing of the Church in addition.

Everything that is human is divided, usually into negative and positive. This also applies to Christianity. Positively, it represents a spiritual power that collectively could concentrate and release creative energy in a whole culture. Some of the greatest works of art in the history of the human race are the result of this creative force – with Augustine as the foremost theological source of inspiration.

The negative present-day evaluation of Augustine's view of sensual eroticism should not overshadow the fact that the core of the great man's theology is actively creating, compassionate love, *caritas*, that reconciles men – with each other and with God. Augustine's preoccupation with love as the core of God's being is also the basis of a *caritas* tradition and a contemplative mysticism in European culture, both of which were further strengthened and inspired by Bernard de Clairvaux in the High Middle Ages (cf. Part 2). The cordial *caritas* tradition runs like an unbroken thread through European culture from Augustine via Bernard and Luther to Hannah Arendt, who began her life-work with *Der Liebesbegriff bei Augustin* (The Concept of Love in Augustine 1928/2003), which inspired more than just the title of her main work, *The Human Condition* (1958), also known as *Vita Activa*, where Arendt puts forward publicly acting and openly discursive citizenship as an ideal.

From our historical and anthropological perspective, Augustine's *cor inquietum* thus exceeds the medieval theological framework and stands for something universally human: a deep feeling or intuition that there is something larger than oneself and social life, something it is possible to become a part of by opening oneself to what the heart is testifying, something that can inspire us to take care of what has been given us individually and culturally – and to realize the rich potential for a better world. Without this unrest, no peace on earth.

EUROPE'S GREATEST AND MOST BEAUTIFUL CREATION?

The art based on Christianity that was created in the High Middle Ages and the Renaissance is an expression of the essence of European culture, before science came to define the image of man and the world. Never has Europe created greater art than in the Renaissance. Only the High-Gothic, Baroque music and certain literary summits later on can seek to rival it. If we believe that the core of European culture is an innovation that follows two main tendencies – those of New Testament Christianity and Greek Antiquity – and wish to find the best and most valuable artistic expression that results from this basis, the love motif of Renaissance art would appear to be a worthy candidate. Love is the essence of Christianity ('The greatest of these is charity'), as the portrayal of passion in art in many ways was in Antiquity, from Homer to Sophocles. Art also reveals what transformation the conception of love has undergone since Antiquity.

The heart we meet in Christianity and the artists of the Renaissance is something else than that of Antiquity – something that a favourite motif of pictorial art in the Renaissance and the Baroque, Amor with his bow and arrow, bears witness to. We see it as perfectly obvious that love and *amor* have something to do with the heart. And people in Antiquity knew of course that the heart beat faster when one fell in love or in the case of erotic love – but they viewed things differently. Eros and the heart were not directly connected to each other in philosophy and art. A work as late as Plato's *Symposium*, which marks a high point in the history of love in Antiquity, does not mention the heart at all. Nor do the Graeco-Roman gods show any particular interest in the heart. Aphrodite seduces humans erotically, but she does not touch their heart, nor does her Roman counterpart, Venus. None of the ancient statues of love goddesses makes it clear that the heart is the organ of love. The youthful Eros, Amor in Roman mythology, is admittedly depicted with a bow, but it is not certain at all that he aims at the heart. This only happens definitively in the Renaissance and Baroque art (earlier in poetry).

The image of Eros with a bow, often in the company of Aphrodite, is especially widespread in the Hellenistic period. The visualization of the heart which we find in pictorial art in the late Middle Ages, the Renaissance and, in particular, the Baroque is also something new. It is a huge leap from capricious Aphrodite, who toyed with the fighting and loving Homeric heroes, to the well-known depiction of holy Theresa by the Baroque master G. L. Bernini (1598–1680), in which her heart is transfixed by the arrow from Jesus, in the form of Amor, and she swoons in holy ecstasy. Theresa herself has related how the arrow with its white-hot tip bores through her heart and pierces her stomach. In the same way, it is the arrow of God's or Jesus's love that pierces Augustine's heart, sets it on fire and lights the holy flames in the picture by Murillo (1618–1682), or in a similar picture by Rubens from 1620. A fourth painting that sums up the central aspects that the heart symbolizes in Western culture is Henry Holiday's *Dante and Beatrice* (1883). Dante involuntarily puts his hand to his heart when in the street he chances to meet Beatrice, unattainable on this earth. The only way in which he can be united with her is via a God-given love so great that it offers a hope that their souls can meet once more in the hereafter. The love of the heart is the divine inspiration that leads Dante to write a literary masterpiece of European culture, *The Divine Comedy*, with everything it represents allegorically with its metaphors of the heart. (Although reconciliation seems to give way to perdition among all the sinners Dante meets in his fictive hell.)

The link between the arrows of Eros or Amor in Antiquity and the arrow in Augustine's heart and that of holy Theresa is the spear thrust into Jesus's side when on the cross. As depicted in the Bible, Jesus is not pierced to the heart, but in the side or abdominal cavity (Greek *phrenes*). In fact, Jesus's heart is not mentioned in the Bible. This conception is reinterpreted in the high and late Middle Ages, the Renaissance, and especially the Baroque, when the symbolism of the heart culminates. Blood and heart have now become almost identical, a story to be told in later chapters. Christ suffers on the cross, but is saved by God's love and himself saves mankind by sacrificing himself for humanity in his divine love. And beneath the cross lie the women who love Jesus's body and soul respectively, the two Marys. For his mother it was prophesied shortly after her son's birth, thinking of Christ's lot: 'Yea, a sword shall pierce through thine own soul also' (Luke 2: 35). Here, the soul is presented as something substantial that resides in the heart. For this reason, suffering is also situated in the heart. The mother suffers out of compassion and motherly love for her son. Thus the heart, via a long historical process, became the image and symbol both of love and passion, suffering and compassion.

The heart also becomes an image of what love can do when it suffers with and for others – reconciliation and salvation. This is perhaps the right place to call to mind that theology (both as ethics and law) defines reconciliation as the restoration of a broken communion, whether it be with one's neighbour, with other people, with society and the social community, or in a religious sense with God. Human fellowship is also dependent on a person emotionally including others in it, even if one does not like or love them. This is Christianity's spiritual contribution to Western culture: a humanization via a breach of the morality of revenge. On the basis of this mind-set and view of mankind, much of the best of European art and culture came into being.

Alongside art, science and rational reflection, Christianity is one of the pillars on which European culture rests. Even though Christian (sexual) morality in many ways has crippled and corrupted lives, Christianity has also made a vital contribution to a more human society, with respect for other people. This is a historical effect of the command to love one's neighbour. Kant's moral philosophy, which impels the individual to act in a way that everyone else could have acted in a corresponding situation, is inconceivable without Christianity with its corresponding rule. 'And as ye would that men should do to you, do ye also to them likewise,' it says in Luke 6: 31. Respect for the individual and the other person, one's neighbour, is vital in Christianity for the individual's own salvation. The call to love one's neighbour as oneself and to turn the other cheek creates different attitudes between people from the Jews' primitive an eye for an eye and a tooth for a tooth, which to a Christian way of thinking is sinful and hardens one's feelings as well as being socially destructive in a vicious circle – something we can see demonstrated daily in the present-day Middle East.

Western individualism, for better or worse, is inconceivable without Christianity as a precondition in terms of culture and the history of ideas. What is important is the salvation of each individual. The way in which the Westerner (ideally) can show compassion towards and respect for the individual, and the way in which he places the social status of the individual and the rule of law (which is by definition for the individual) at the centre, distinguishes him from collectively oriented cultures such as the Chinese, for example. Typically enough, it was a Westerner who took the historic photo of the 'madman' (seen with Chinese eyes) who with his unChinese plastic bags stood alone in front of a column of tanks during the student unrest in Tianeman Square in Beijing in 1989, and who was taken care of by his own group and able to disappear into the masses after his one-man demonstration, avoiding being identified by the Chinese powers. In Europe, the identity of this symbolic figure would be known before the unrest was over, like that of the female student with the Tricolore in her hand who sat on the shoulders of a co-demonstrator during the student unrest in Paris in 1968. She individualized something collective, while Chinese culture collectivizes the individual. For in Chinese culture the heart lies in collective society, with us it beats in and for the individual.

The relation between the individual and the collective or common-cultural is of decisive importance for just how sustainable a culture is, and how capable of surviving. Western culture faced an apparent crisis or tragedy in the late twentieth century because common values were no longer able to hold individualism in check, with a resulting decline into egoism and materialism. That is why it is interesting to take a look at how Christianity's kindred spirit, Islam, is capable of integrating the individual into the overriding social and religious order, so that Islam and the holy book, the Koran, would appear in many Arab countries to be the most important spiritual force in society. This has, not least, something to do with the role of the heart in Islam.

CHAPTER 5

Islam's Culture of the Heart

I also gave Him life
by knowing Him in my heart.
Ibn Arabi on God

In Islam, the heart is so important emotionally, intellectually and in
particular spiritually that Islam and hence Arabic culture may be characterized as the foremost, perhaps the last surviving, heart culture. For in
Islam the heart is not only a metaphor but an objective organ for sensing,
intuition and cognition – not to mention inspiration, revelation and
divine insight. This distinguishes Islam from Christianity, where the heart
is totally subordinate to the soul and ends up providing only one of
several images for emotional life in general and for the soul.

Another important difference between Islam and Christianity may
help to explain why one religion is more vital and of current relevance
than the other: the relationship between the Creator and His creation. The
Christian God has created the world once and for all; His work of creation
is over, while in Islam it is still in progress, not least via the mediators that
are spiritually inspired by God. God in Islam may also be perceived as
participating in what has been created, i.e. in man. And it is specifically in
the heart, if man opens himself to the divine power it is endowed with,
that he can meet with God. That is why it is said that God is closer to the
individual than the individual is to himself, 'closer to you than your own
jugular vein!' as the Koran puts it (Sura 50, 16).

Within Arabic culture, it is especially Sufism that has developed the
concept of the heart into a separate doctrine and a particular intellectual
practice. But to understand Sufism it is necessary to be familiar with
certain main aspects of the life and teachings of Muhammad.

Islam is the only world religion that at the turn of the twenty-first century
is rapidly expanding in several continents, especially in Africa and large

parts of Asia, although also in Europe, mainly as the result of large-scale immigration from Muslim countries. Part of the historical explanation for Islamic expansion is political, now as at the time of Muhammad. Today, Islam can claim to be on the side of the oppressed, and thus to represent justice, legitimizing violent outbreaks of the holy wrath felt by many Arabs at the present-day political situation. For the one who follows his heart can claim to be following God's law, since the ardour of the heart is of divine origin, according to Islam. Whoever follows God's voice does not need any other form of legitimation. That the status of the emotions in Arabic culture may be one of the reasons why fundamentalism and religiously motivated violence is so widespread in our age is something that has not commanded much attention as yet.

The close connection – almost identity – between God and the heart assumes a different form in Islam than in Christianity, not least because of Sufism and Islamic mysticism. One striking aspect of Islam is that its mystics, spearheaded by the Sufis, through the ages have contributed to a revitalization and renewal of this religion and prevented its institutional fossilization, while the mystics of Christian institutions have been perceived as marginal eccentrics. That Sufism is partially marginalized and partly suppressed in the present-day Muslim world may be a sign of spiritual stagnation within Islam, of authoritarian closure and collective indoctrination.

The basis for the central position of the heart in Islam is the strong element of revelation, epiphany and theophany in the life and teaching of Muhammad. Islam is in several ways a religion of revelation, since it is founded directly on the revelations that Muhammad (c. 570–632) experienced over a number of years. This is why Muhammad is called a prophet. His prophetic mission began with a number of ecstatic experiences of a visionary and in particular an auditory nature. Prophets and angels, above all the Archangel Gabriel, revealed themselves to Muhammad. In a dream Muhammad was introduced to the Word of God by Gabriel, with the order to 'Read!', i.e. to tell and to preach the sacred Word. This revelation was to become the foundation of his teachings. When he awoke after the dream, it was as if something had been inscribed in his heart. This is why the heart is the messenger for God's word and spirit. But only after having such revelatory experiences over a three-year period and keeping them to himself did Muhammad in the year 612 begin to preach in public, after another revelation had ordered him to do so – with equal political and religious success.

Something was still lacking, however. Muhammad was now called upon to prove himself a true prophet by ascending to heaven and returning with a book of Holy Scripture, as when God appeared before Moses and presented him with the Tablets of the Law. This event took place during another ecstatic experience; riding his horse al-Buraq he reaches Heaven, where Gabriel leads him to Allah's throne. Here, Muhammad learns from the mouth of Allah that he is His elect, in preference to all other prophets. God then gives him the holy Koran containing the Law. In addition, he is granted an esoteric insight which he must not share, even with believers. Thus an opening is created for mystics and Sufis who can seek their esoteric knowledge without conflicting with Islam.

Islam has a simple message. Its creed says simply: 'There are no gods but Allah, and Muhammad is his prophet.' From the outset, monotheism was a major issue for Muhammad and was particularly directed against the polytheism found among the non-Christian and non-Jewish Arabs. Because of this monotheism, Muhammad initially hoped for support from the Jews, for many of his notions and mythical figures were taken directly from the Old Testament. Judaism is initially his main source of inspiration. Thus Abraham, together with his son Ishmael, is the founder of Ka'ba (also spelled Kaaba), the holiest of Muslim shrines in Mecca, chosen to be the centre of Islam after rejection by the Jews made Jerusalem impracticable. By this stroke of genius, Muhammad laid the foundation of Arab unity through Islam, since the Ka'ba was also a holy site in a polytheistic pre-Muhammadan society.

Literalists gained a strong position in Islam early on, a position they have retained to this day – as witnessed in certain Muslim regimes by *sharia* – secular criminal justice based on the letter of the Koran. Muhammad himself, however, opened up a wide range of interpretation in Islam. The Prophet himself contributed to this tendency, for example, by adjusting and 'correcting' his own revelatory experiences after the event. The oral tradition after the Prophet and his alleged sayings (*hadith*) have also provided a fertile ground for reinterpretation and conjecture. Sufis and chosen imams with divine insights and abilities can represent both Creation and Truth in a new form. This room given for creative reinterpretation and fresh divine revelations in Islam is lacking in Christian and Jewish dogmas of creation. Furthermore, Islam imposes no strict demands on its members, but promises a good life, in flesh and blood, with a wealth of earthly pleasures in the hereafter. To Muhammad this was more important than labouring the tortures of Hell. To suffer martyrdom, a possibility that many Islamic leaders offer on a lavish scale – through holy war, *jihad*, for example – is thus no misfortune for believers, who expect rewards for their efforts and sacrifices in the other world. In other respects, Muhammad himself preaches restraint and mercy.

As a state religion, Islam enjoyed spectacular success in political terms; in a few decades after the death of Muhammad, it conquered all of the Middle East and Northern Africa, gradually establishing itself all the way from India and Persia to southern Spain, from Central Asia to Turkey. This expansion also laid the foundation for a unique cultural development where art and poetry enjoyed a central position. In poetry, the encounter between the Persian language and ancient Persian traditions and the Arabic language and culture resulted in some of the finest creations of world literature, with poets such as Rumi, Hafis, Attar, Omar Khayyam, Sadi and Djami – to mention just a few. Islam possessed an expansive, vivid and creative language, while Christian Europe for centuries continued to write in dead Latin. The meeting place for religion and poetry in Islam is frequently to be found in Sufism, where the qualities of the heart are of crucial importance.

THE WISDOM OF THE HEART AND THE HEART OF WISDOM IN SUFISM

To describe a foreign culture's secret doctrine, such as that of Sufism, can be compared to asking a car mechanic to explain the nature of quantum mechanics. For internal reasons too it may be self-contradictory to make any pronouncements about Sufism. Strictly speaking, it is an esoteric (i.e. an exclusively internal) doctrine, and thus essentially alien to the exoteric (external). For Sufism is not a theory about the innermost depths, but a practice that takes place exclusively in those inner regions concerning the innermost of man, and thus impossible to describe in conventional language without becoming something else. The inner space is inaccessible to the uninitiated and the undeserving. This in fact applies to all mysticism, regardless of its cultural environment, but in mysticism inspired by Islam this esoteric and elitist exclusivity can be traced all the way back to Muhammad and acquires social legitimacy in his doctrine, in the esoteric insight he was granted directly from God. It is especially shi'ism, the Gnosis of Islam, that has emphasized the esoteric aspect of Muhammad's doctrine and the necessity of personal or inner interpretation. The main branch of Islam, *sunna*, has therefore accused the Sufis of being shi'ites. Sunna is based on the conventional interpretation of the Koran, not the individual and esoteric.

Muslims thus make no claim that their holy scripture contains the whole truth. There is a truth deeper than the truth proclaimed in the Koran. This inner and ultimate truth will subsume all other truths which the Sufis seek in lifelong study and refinement, in meditative self-communion and self-transcendence. No other religious movement seeks truth as uncompromisingly as Sufism. The Sufi may leave wife, children, house and home, if inspiration seizes him and he feels the call to seek the path to truth and salvation. Many Sufis are thus nomads.

The Sufi seeks both the (holy) places where the innermost may reveal itself to him and the chosen learned and wise person who, in conversation and discussion, meditation and prayer, song and dance, can grant him enlightenment and release the deepest insights that lie hidden behind veil upon veil in his own innermost depths, concealed in darkness like the Ka'ba behind its walls and veils in the cube-shaped shrine in Mecca. The Sufi seeks not only enlightenment, but the source of the light and the light itself, so as himself to become this light. His aim is not so much self-realization as de-realization, in order to re-emerge transformed at a higher level. What he wants to strengthen is not his ego in our individualistic sense, but the self beyond all self-interest, external needs and desires. The ego is the greatest obstacle to reaching that end. The Sufi seeks the life that sustains life and the self, the creative force that gives the self integrity, the overarching principle in which the self would be integrated and feels a self-effacing urge to be resolved and become one with – in a word: Love.

Love is not only the cosmic force that has created everything and thus a synonym for God. Love is also the innermost depths of the human being, that which illuminates darkness and existence and tells the Sufi about his primary and ultimate goal. Only love is an end in itself. For love is God, and God is love. Sufism thereby becomes an active relationship between a lover and the beloved. Only the one who loves, and loves love itself, can attain God, who reveals himself in the heart of the one who loves Him. Therefore the one who loves can become one with God. Unity with God is the aim; the path is love. The path goes inwards, since love is housed quite materially and physically in the heart. It is from here all emanations proceed, and communion and ascension begin.

The anthropological basis for Sufism would seem to be universal – that the heart speaks to the heart. This can also take place independently of words. But Sufis go deeper and seek 'the heart of hearts', i.e. unity with God. To develop this unity the Sufis elaborated a 'science of the heart'. Unity is the irreducible essence from which the visible world has emerged. This unity was also the starting point for Mansur al-Hallaj from the first classical period of Sufism, which stretches from the eighth to the tenth centuries.

Hallaj (867–922) was the first to emphasize love as the precondition for as well as the path towards the experience of God. He was also one of the first to preach publicly or exoterically the esoteric doctrine. This led him to fall foul of both the traditional Sufis and, soon afterwards, the legal and secular authorities. Some of his statements display similarities with late Antiquity and Plotinus. Both European and Arabian mysticism are of course both rooted in late Antiquity, when several ecstatic and mystic movements saw the light of day. Besides Plotinus' doctrine of *unio mystica*, Manichean tendencies were strong; these too had a mystical side, as did gnosticism. (It is worth noticing that St Augustine was influenced by this intellectual climate.) What they all share is a negative view of the body. For the neo-Platonists, it was the tomb of the soul, made of morally inferior matter. For many Arabian ascetics and mystics, the body was the earthly shell for the soul, i.e. something external and inferior to what was within, while Muhammad and the Koran present a less negative view of the body and of eroticism.

Hallaj calls the body his earthly shell, and his soul sought inner light in the darkness. In a state of ecstasy he pronounced the famous words, 'I am the Truth' (i.e. God). This was regarded as both blasphemous and heretical. Several years later, in 922, Al-Hallaj was arrested and executed. He was flogged, tortured, crucified and decapitated before being burnt. His martyrdom and uncompromising attitude made his doctrine even better known, although the Sufis subsequently sought to avoid offending official theology and jurisprudence. Many of the later Sufis built on al-Hallaj and his statements concerning the heart, e.g. the following verses:

> I saw my Lord with the eye of the heart.
> I asked: Who are You?
> He answered: Thy self.

Central in this mystic tradition proceeding and inspiring al-Hallaj was the Sufi poet Sumnum the Lover, well known for these verses:[1]

> I have separated my heart from this world –
> My heart and Thou are not separate.
> And when the slumber closes my eyes,
> I find Thee between the eye and the lid.

This unifying identification with God expresses that man is himself divine since love is instilled in him. God is therefore not exclusively otherworldly in Sufism and Islam. He is both in this world and the next, hidden behind veil upon veil in a darkness that only total and pure love can illuminate when the divine chooses to reveal itself – as love. And all this takes place in and through the heart. The heart is to a great extent synonymous with the soul. God reveals himself in the heart of the one who loves him. This explains why the heart is something objective and essential, not merely a metaphor, in Islam and in Sufism.

Even if the aim of Sufism is esoteric, it also developed an exoteric or an external, informative side. Sufism is basically a doctrine and a school where disciples with special gifts may be enrolled or elected, but not all Sufis founded or belonged to a school or a particular persuasion. In

Sufism techniques have been developed by means of which the path to God and unity with Him may be discovered and attained. These techniques are mainly based on concentration, meditation, *dhikr* with admonitions of God, prayer and the repetition of God's name and various kinds of formulas. Asceticism, vigils and fasting are practised by some, while others reject asceticism. The latter include Jalal al-Din Rumi from the second classical period of the twelfth and thirteenth centuries, who cultivated music, song and even dance. First and foremost, however, Rumi – like so many other Sufis – cultivated the poetic word. From the outset, poetry and literature were an important part of Islam and Sufism. Many come to Islam via Sufi, Persian and Arabic literature, not only through the Koran.

Since the ego with its egotism and external aims commonly obstructs the path towards God, it takes a change of mind-set, a conquest of the self, a new awareness or experience to make an individual turn towards God. The journey back to God begins when He looks into the heart of His servant and fills it with divine love. This instant of time is *tauba*, 'the turning of the heart'. The journey to find and become one with God is lifelong and painful, but also filled with ecstatic experiences and salvatory insights that leave no doubt about the journey's purpose and value.

The most famous description of the journey back to – or on towards – unity with God is *The Conference of the Birds* by Farid od-din Attar (*c.* 1120–1230?), which is not only a masterpiece of Persian mysticism but also of world literature. The allegory describes how a large flock of thousands of birds takes to the sky, flying through seven valleys, through desert and wilderness, facing all sorts of difficulties and obstacles in all kinds of weather, in order to find their king, the great Simurgh. Most of them perish on the way. Only 30 (*si*) birds (*murgh*) finally arrive. Having passed the test, they are allowed to experience peace, splendour and beauty in the royal palace, pervaded by a light that is reflected within them, making them incapable of distinguishing between the outer and inner, what is theirs and what is Simurgh's/God's. After their long journey, now that they finally get to see what is hidden behind Simurgh's thousand veils, they realize that the aim of the journey was to find the path to themselves, to discover that God and they are one:

> The sun of majesty sent forth his rays, and in the reflection of each other's faces these thirty birds (si-murgh) of the outer world, contemplated the face of the Simurgh of the inner world. This so astonished them that they did not know if they were still themselves or if they had become the Simurgh. At last, in a state of contemplation, they realized that they were the Simurgh and that

the Simurgh was the thirty birds. When they gazed at the Simurgh they saw that it was truly the Simurgh who was there, and when they turned their eyes towards themselves they saw that they themselves were the Simurgh. And perceiving both at once, themselves and Him, they realized that they and the Simurgh were one and the same being.[2]

In the Western world, it is in particular the Frenchman Henry Corbin (1903–1978) and the German-American professor at Harvard, Annemarie Schimmel (d. 2003), who have done much to remove the mind-blunting veil between the cultures and to provide insight into the creative core of Islam and Arabic art and culture. Schimmel's many worthy works include *Mystical Dimensions of Islam* (1975), *And Muhammed is His Messenger. The Veneration of the Prophet in Islamic Piety* (1985), and *The Triumphal Sun. A Study of the Works of Jalaloddin Rumi* (1978). Corbin is one of the great researchers into religion, who has done most to spread an understanding of the place occupied by the heart among Arabian intellectuals in Islamic art, religion and culture, e.g. in *Creative Imagination in the Sufism of Ibn Arabi* (1958).

A central idea in Ibn Arabi (1165–1240) is that the heart is the seat of inner creative power, the *imagination*, and consequently forms ideas in images. The heart is an organ of perception of a sensory and spiritual nature and cannot be distinguished from the physical heart:

In Ibn 'Arabi as in Sufism in general, the heart (qalb), is the organ which produces true knowledge, comprehensible intuition, the gnosis (ma'rifa) of God and the divine mysteries, in short, the organ of everything connoted by the term 'esoteric science' . . . the gnostic's heart is the 'eye', the organ by which God knows Himself, reveals Himself to Himself in the forms of His epiphanies.[3]

The source of this divine imaginative power is called *himma* in Arabic, a composite concept that may be translated as 'the heart's creative power'. What is special about the images from the heart's *himma* is that they cannot be reduced to something subjective or to 'mere images'. They are live images and may as such be compared to the voice of the *daimon* that attended Socrates, something objective that the specially qualified individual becomes a medium for. Once the *himma* has received and developed the images, they somehow exist outside the contemplative imagination that has transmitted them. What has been imagined cannot, therefore, be reduced to something subjective, but is perceived as real and objective images, that which makes the life of the spirit possible and vital. The heart's *himma* is a visionary or reflecting organ that mirrors and manifests the source of inspiration and the levels into which life is divided, from the material to the divine (cf. neo-Platonism and gnosticism).

It is impossible to talk about Sufism without mentioning Jalal al-Din Rumi (1207–1273), not just because he is the best known Sufi in the West, but because via his poetry he has exerted an enormous influence on Islamic and Arabic culture (even though he wrote in Persian), and has renewed and vitalized Islamism. He was a well-respected legal scholar in Konya in Asia Minor, with many pupils. One day, however, an event took place that changed his life. On 29 November 1244, a wandering dervish, Shams of Tabriz, arrived in Konya. The encounter with this more than 60-year-old man led to a conversion, and Rumi became his pupil. But Rumi's pupils were jealous of Shams, who was assassinated after a few years. Rumi was inconsolable, and eventually wrote a collection of mystical poems in his friend's name, *Divan-i Shams i Tabriz*. They deal with love and sorrow, and although they are apparently about earthly love, they are in fact a description of divine love. This is also the case in his main work, *Mathnavi* (Arabic 'couplet', or Persian *Mesnewî),* a huge mystical epic of some 26,000 lines. This deals with texts from the Koran and Islamic-Sufi traditions, along with fables, legends and motifs taken from popular narrative traditions in the Orient and the inner Mediterranean area, with strong elements from ancient Persian traditions.

Rumi was the leader of the 'Whirling Dervishes' (the Mevlevi-order), who early on became known in the West. He is part of a long Persian tradition, where ecstatic dance, sacred music and poetry had been practised within Sufism from the very outset. Particularly worthy of mention in this connection is how Rumi, with fiery passion and unrivalled poetic force, sings the praises of divine love – often with allusions to Hallaj: 'Without love the world would be lifeless'.[4] And to the question 'What makes the Sufi?' he replies simply: 'Purity of heart'.

Rumi lives in a stratified universe (influenced by Plato and the Neo-platonism of Plotinus), where man is to ascend from the material and vegetative to the animal and human – and hence to the rational and spiritual, reaching the divine and heavenly via an angelic level. The richness of his imagery also includes that of man merely being a drop in the world ocean (God). But when, as a drop, man dissolves in the ocean, he himself becomes the divine. Rumi, however, goes even further, asserting that man is a prerequisite for the divine:

> My image rests in the King's heart; the King's heart would have been ill without my image [i.e. he must mirror himself in it in order to become himself]. Light from all spiritual creatures emanates

from my thought; heaven was created on the basis of my original being.[5]

With poetry, song and dance to the reed flute he coaxes forth the ecstatic experience where he becomes one with his origin. He also uses the reed flute as an image, allowing it to tell of the sources of music and what kind of longings it has roused – as in the following well-known introduction to *Mathnavi*:[6]

> This plaint of the flute is fire, not mere air.
> Let him who lacks this fire be accounted dead!
> 'Tis the fire of love that inspires the flute,
> 'Tis the ferment of love that possesses the wine.
> The flute is the confidant of all unhappy lovers;
> Yea, its strains lay bare my inmost secrets . . .
> Hail to thee, then, o LOVE, sweet madness! . . .
> Love exalts our earthly bodies to heaven,
> And makes the very hills to dance with joy!
> Did my Beloved only touch me with his lips,
> I too, like the flute, would burst out in melody.
> But he who is parted from them that speak his tongue,
> Though he possess a hundred voices, is perforce dumb.
> When the rose has faded and the garden is withered,
> The song of the nightingale is no longer to be heard.
> The BELOVED is all in all, the lover only veils Him;
> The BELOVED is all that lives, the lover a dead thing.
> When the lover feels no longer LOVE's quickening,
> He becomes like a bird who has lost its wings . . .
> LOVE desires that this secret should be revealed,
> For if a mirror reflects not, of what use is it?
> Knowest thou why thy mirror [the heart] reflects not?
> Because the rust has not been scoured from its face.

Love and its fire are also praised in Rumi's many *ghazals* (love songs). There too it is the heart that is the microcosm that mirrors and mediates the macrocosm: 'I looked into the heart – it was a sea, a space of the worlds, a sea that moves in a thousand waves.'

That the heart should be insightful, reflective, thinking, and actively creative is hard for us in today's Western culture to conceive, for we see the brain as possessing these abilities and functions.

The insights and the images that the heart can provide are many and varied, depending on the culture and the context of their origin. The fact that different images can give rise to different parallel imaginary universes that can be equally true or valid in their own particular way ought to invite us to be tolerant. Ibn Arabi, the Andalusian mystic of the heart living in a multicultural Europe, is just the person to teach us, both Westerners and Muslim Arabs, something about this, in his well-known poem (after Schimmel 1975):

> My heart is capable of every form,
> a cloister of the monk, a temple for idols,
> a pasture for gazelles, the votary's Kaaba,
> the tables of the Thora, the Koran.
> Love is the creed I hold: wherever turn
> His camels, love is still my creed and faith.

To the extent that the human heart is an anthropological constant, as Sigrid Undset claims, it is so as an open channel of communication. Since, to use Ibn Arabi's words, the heart is open to all forms, it is also open to different ideological winds of fashion – religious as well as political – and can be full of prejudices and closed to all address from the other, the alien. The moment there no longer is any room for individual address and a personal reply to it, the heart dies, as does open dialogue, which is driven forward by an endless dialectic of question and answer. For it is only individuals who have heart, not groups or communities, which can create strong common feelings and single-minded passions that bind group-members together emotionally. But as the passion of the group is not open to address from outside and perhaps labels *the other* an enemy, there is no longer the inclusive divine glow that Ibn Arabi wrote about which fills the heart; instead, a fixated passion that confuses the secular matter with openly inclusive divine inspiration. Ibn Arabi's open attitude also represents an alternative voice in Arabic culture as well as a challenge to present-day Muslim communities in West and East that show a tendency to shut themselves in a collectivist one-track mentality.

In poetic form, Ibn Arabi expresses one of the main ideas of this book: the heart is an image or symbol of something between bodily emotions and language, one that can be filled with anything at all, so that everything human – also that which we perceive as divine – is the subject of human constructions. No culture knows better than Arabic culture that the divine in itself – hidden behind a thousand veils – is inaccessible to man and cannot be expressed. The moment we try to express the divine, there is something limited and human that finds expression. *Alles vergängliche is nur ein Gleichnis* (All that is transitory is but a parable), Goethe wrote, strongly influenced by the Arabic mode of thought. Political activists and fundamentalists who claim their war is holy and that they are dying the death of a martyr are basically blasphemers, for no one else than God (who exists or does not exist) can decide who will be saved and who not and will come to what we describe as heaven or hell – metaphors of archetypal ideas more than the notion of something that is totally alien to us humans, *totaliter aliter*, as it was called in the High Middle Ages.

These wise words from the Islamic thinker may serve as an appeal for tolerance in an age when strong forces are making communication between Western, Jewish and Arabic cultures more difficult. Dog eats dog, but humans need not eat each other. Against this background it is fitting to conclude this section with a reminder as to how deeply Arabic culture has influenced our own Western culture.

THE INFLUENCE OF ARABIC CULTURE ON WESTERN CULTURE

As is well known, it was the Arabs who after the fall of the Roman Empire took care of – and further developed – Greek philosophy and science. The great mediators and philosophers include Ibn Sina or Avicenna (980–1037) and Ibn Rushd with the Latinized name Averroës (1126–1198). Aristotle's position as the great philosopher of the Christian High Middle Ages, whose ideas Thomas Aquinas developed further, is mainly the result of Averroës' translations of Aristotle – as well as his commentaries.

Arabic culture was not only a mediator of the philosophy and science of Antiquity; it also made independent contributions to European culture. Arabic mysticism was also disseminated, as was alchemy. Various manifestations of this influence can be registered as late as the late Renaissance, where both alchemy and mysticism were a separate spiritual movement, usually connected with the *sophia* tradition. This tradition, with its roots in gnosticism and the mysticism of late Antiquity, maintained that knowledge, and thereby philosophy, literally had its origin in the heart. *Sophia*, wisdom, was allegorically depicted as a flower growing out of the heart, or as a spring streaming from the heart, which one could drink from. The rose and the flower were central images in Arabic and Sufi art.

Muslim southern Spain was an important station for the passage of traditions from Antiquity to Europe. Islamic culture had strong roots in southern Spain, or Andalusia, which was Muslim way into the thirteenth century, when the Moorish regime and its territory gradually diminished. But Arabian Granada, with flourishing arts and culture, continued to exist until the Sultan was forced to surrender to Isabella and Ferdinand in 1491. Arabian Andalusia represents a zenith not only of Islamic culture but European culture as well.

Cordoba, where Averroës also lived, probably had the richest intellectual life of all contemporary European cities. Greek Antiquity enjoyed a renaissance here a couple of centuries before the remainder of southern Europe. But not only impulses from Greek philosophy and science, mysticism and alchemy found their way to European culture via Andalusia. At least as important is the Arabic influence on European mentality and sensibility via the new ideals of love that spread from Andalusia to Europe via Occitania or southern France in the form of troubadour poetry.

Next to the Greeks, the Arabs are the most sophisticated lovers of human history. Everybody has sampled this tradition via the evocative and flirtatious tales of *The Arabian Nights*. Night was also the time for audacious amorous adventures. Humour, dialogue with subtle innuendo, music and mysticism, food and aesthetic pleasure, were all part of the Arabian art of love. Silk-clad veiled women and scantily dressed belly-dancers are just external clichés from this tradition. Incidentally, the use of veil and concealment illuminates the difference between Western and Arabic cultures. We see unveiling as a virtue; the Arabs see veiling as art and virtue. They love to conceal; we love to reveal.

Upper-class women in particular would surround themselves with courting musicians and poetic songsters. The love poets are numerous. 'There is nothing good in those who do not know the passion of love,' proclaimed the lyric poet called al Abbas from Basra (Ibn al-Ahnaf, the court poet of the caliph). Here we see the precursor of the troubadours. The very name troubadour possibly derives from Arabic *tarab*, meaning music. The first Occitan troubadour, William of Aquitaine (1070–*c.*1126) had perhaps more than just a warrior's contact with southern Spain. The view of love proclaimed by William is probably influenced by the tenets of the poet-philosopher Ibn Hazm (d. 1064) from Cordoba and his famous collection of poems *The Ring of the Dove*. Despite – or perhaps because of – unrequited love, Hazm celebrated eroticism in all its aspects, wanting at the same time to make love the most important thing in life, something unconditionally binding – as in romantic love. Most readers will intuitively recognize this ideal and the kinship between the heart images in Arabian art and those of the troubadours when they read poems from the two cultures of the heart. There are numerous literary precursors in Arabic poetry. The foremost poet of courtly love was perhaps Ibn Daud (d. 909), who wrote *The Book of the Flower*, an erotic anthology. He belonged to a sect also joined by the Andalusian Ibn Arabi. In Persian and Arabic love poetry the symbolism of the love of God and of a woman is often the same, and the female nature of the soul is part of the mystery of love.

The precise role played by Arabic culture, based in southern Spain, in the development of key aspects of European culture has not yet been fully acknowledged. No historian of ideas denies the mediating role of Averroës and other Arabian philosophers and scientists, but what the doctrines of the heart in Arabic culture have meant for the European heart has not been investigated. This is also the case for Sufism in general. The ways of history are often unfathomable and paradoxical. The butterfly effect also applies to history, where little strokes fell great oaks, and a single word may sow a seed that becomes an entire culture. This is particularly the case in cultures of the word such as the Islamic Arabian and the Christian European. In the same way that the Koran could not have come into existence without the Bible, Western culture would not have become what it did without Arabic culture.

Friends, though, often agree best at a distance. For over 1,000 years, there has been animosity between Christian European and Islamic Arabic culture. It was not until the seventeenth and especially the eighteenth century that the attitude of the West towards Arabic culture changed, culminating in the Romantic enthusing about Orientalism in the nineteenth century. The Koran was translated into a number of European languages, and the classics of Persian and Arabic poetry became known.

Germany's great writer, Johann Wolfgang von Goethe, played an important part in this process, with Islam portrayed as a humane and enlightened movement (cf. Mommsen 2001). Goethe made Islam, the Koran, Muhammed and the Persian writers a life-long project that was so nearly symbiotic that the writer 'does not deny the suspicion that he himself might be a Muslim'. How close and profound was Goethe's relation to Arabic culture, the Koran and Muhammed can be seen from one of the main works of his canonical writing in world literature: *West-östlicher Divan* (1818), a title that alludes to central works by the Persian-Arabian poets Rumi (*Divan-i Shams-i Tabriz*) and Hafis, Goethe's favourite, who also wrote his *Divan*. Not surprisingly, the symbol of love in Arabic and Islamic art appeals to Goethe, both the *heart* and the *rose*, which is the main motif in many classical poems of Arabic culture, including Saadi's *Rose Garden*, which Goethe knew. The inner glow of the work and the 'Seelige Sehnsucht' that he praises, the living that longs for a death in flames, that is transformed into what it shall be by dying (*Stirb und werde!*) alludes to al Hallaj's death as a martyr.

The intimate spiritual kinship with, and love of, Persian-Arabic Islamic art and culture was aptly formulated by the late Goethe (the two first verses are a direct quotation from the Koran), expressed as a talisman in *Buch des Sängers*:

God's is the Orient!
God's is the Occident!
Whether north or south, all lands
Are at peace within his hands.

Goethe's magic talisman with the desire to build a bridge between dissimilar cultures springing from the same world source is the expression of
a different attitude than the one Rudyard Kipling (historically weighed
down by the culture-imperialist credo of the Occident, *The White Man's
Burden*) expressed almost a century later in his well-known *Ballad of East
and West*: 'Oh, East is East, and West is West, and never the twain shall
meet.' Goethe's remedy to *A Clash of Civilizations* is that hearts should
open up to their common origins and speak to each other across all
political and religious, ethnic and cultural borders, for, as he rightly says:

Only when the heart opens
is the earth then beautiful.

The influence of Arabic on Western culture made itself felt in Europe
at the same rate as European voyages of discovery around 1500 laid the
foundations for world-wide colonization. The role of the Arabs as mediators and developers of the scientific heritage of Greek Antiquity was a
prerequisite for the scientific revolution and the new world view of the
Renaissance, which in turn is one of the fundamental preconditions for
the extrovert, expansive phase being entered on by European culture. The
discovery of new continents quickly changed into campaigns of conquest
and the plundering of foreign cultures. It is perhaps no coincidence that
the Arabian-influenced Spaniards were leaders in this almost shatteringly
effective wave of conquests. Nowhere does it reach a level of brutality
equal to that found in South and Central America, where Spaniards
reduce high civilizations to ruins in the space of a few years. One of the
reasons the Spaniards offered to justify their violence and plunder was the
widespread practice of human sacrifice they witnessed among the Aztecs.
To cut the heart out of people still alive the Spaniards found so cruel and
bestial that they thought it justified their razing this culture to the ground.
In 1531 the bishop of Mexico was able to declare more than 500 temples
and 20,000 idols destroyed in his diocese.

The worst thing was that almost all of Aztec literature was destroyed –
both religious and secular. To annihilate the collective memory of a
national civilization in this way raises the question of who is the more
heartless. If one measures human value in terms of ruined lives, the
answer is self-apparent, since the Aztecs had almost been exterminated by

the end of the sixteenth century. Even if epidemics and internal demoralization carried off a great number, there can be no doubt that the Christian conquistadors must bear the prime responsibility for the destruction of the Mesoamerican civilization. In our comparative perspective of cultures this raises a series of questions, since we see here an encounter between two cultures, in both of which the heart has a key position. In Christianity with its Arabic-Semitic origin, the heart is an image of suffering and love, which via love of one's neighbour represents the central Christian dogma. This is why Christians are to be tolerant towards other peoples according to the Biblical formula 'there is neither Jew nor Greek'. These moral tenets were, however, shelved in the encounter with aliens in Mexico, where the heart and sacrificial death had a different meaning and a different function than in Christian Europe.

One of the few Europeans of the time who recognized these paradoxes and, as early as the sixteenth century, raised the question of who was the more heartless, the natives of foreign climes or we Christian Europeans, was the essayist Michel de Montaigne, to whom we shall return in another chapter. He is surprisingly modern when holding up aliens as a mirror to the familiar. In his essay 'On Cannibals' he asks what is worse, to kill and then eat one's prisoners, as some Brazilian Indians did, or to mistreat and torture them until they die from their injuries, as the Spanish conquistadors did – and as his own countrymen did in a bestial manner during the civil wars of his own time.

Montaigne lived at a time when cultural influence was becoming a worldwide phenomenon, in the same way that mutual influences had long been a part of everyday life among the peoples that lived around the shores of the Mediterranean. But because this globalization (as it is called today) during the last 500 years has mainly been a matter of one-way influence from Western culture to others, Montaigne's question is as relevant as ever. No other culture puts to the test our ability and our willingness to understand others and that which is foreign as radically as does our encounter with the Aztecs and its alien nature. To what extent we will pass the test is a matter of whether we can understand the Aztec concept of the heart. This test is also one of our capacity for self-awareness and not least of calling ourselves to account – and our ability to assume something of the global responsibility of Western culture. Cultural understanding appears to be becoming increasingly important with the shrinking of the globe after the discovery of the New World. We therefore take our leave of the forefathers of our culture and our near relatives in the Middle East and the Mediterranean to make a detour to the last of the Mesoamerican civilizations.

CHAPTER 6

The Aztecs – Why So Heartless?

Of all means of elevation, human sacrifice
has always lifted and uplifted humans most.

Nietzsche

Aztec culture is the last of the Mesoamerican high cultures. It established itself in the thirteenth century and culminated in the fifteenth. The Aztecs took over elements of earlier Mesoamerican cultures that can be traced many centuries back to a time that precedes the arrival in Mexico of the Aztecs from the north. A common feature of these cultures was that they grew out of certain ceremonial sites with temples and pyramids linked to religious practices, sites that then developed into towns and centres of administration. Their religion was based on a cosmogony and a cosmology, a narrative or mythical explanation of how the world came into existence, and how our world is, with the sun and astronomical calendars determining our life on this earth. The core of their teaching is that the world is in constant motion and in constant change – that the world is fundamentally unstable. Chaos and destruction are a constant menace. In order to create and maintain order, great sacrifices have to be made by both gods and man.

The Aztecs did not only take over land from the peoples they subjected; they also adopted many of their religious ideas and gods. This particularly applied with regard to their immediate 'predecessors' – the Toltecs and the Maya. One of the main Aztec gods, Quetzalcoatl, was the central god of several of the predecessors and cults from which the Aztecs borrowed their mythical material. This feather-clad snake-god shows a different facet of Mesoamerican culture from the one Europeans know best, embodying the questioning wonder at the world being so menacing and unstable – characteristics that (without comparisons being drawn, by the way) are reminiscent of certain aspects of the wise man Odin in Norse culture. The astronomical insights of the Mesoamericans that include the magic of numbers have emerged from this questioning wonder.

Also deriving from some of their predecessors are important features of the heart culture for which the Aztecs are well known among Europeans, perhaps because of the propaganda concerning human sacrifice among the Aztecs which the conquistadors and their Christian missionaries spread to justify their own greedy plundering and mass murder when they destroyed this culture. However, the Maya, the greatest and most long-lasting of the Mesoamerican cultures, also had both blood and heart sacrifices, though it was most usual among the Maya to offer one's own blood to provide nourishment for the gods and the universe, by, among other things, making a cut in one's finger.

During the human sacrifices practised by the Aztecs, the chosen victims – normally captured warriors – were placed on the sacrificial slab at the top of the temple pyramid where, while still alive, they had their chests cut open with a flint or obsidian knife and their heart ripped out, so that, still throbbing, it could be offered to the sun-god. Women, too, could be sacrificed. According to certain sources, 80,000 humans were sacrificed in this way on a particular occasion (in 1487). Later research, however, has shown that this was unlikely. At the official opening of a new temple in the capital, Tenochtitlán, the victims were said to have stood in four rows, each of which was 4 km long. That human sacrifice had reached such large numbers at the time when the Spaniards arrived in Mexico, however, is beyond doubt. 'At a conservative estimate, almost 15,000 people were sacrificed annually in Tenochtitlán.'[1] What, then, can the Aztec human sacrifices tell us about the feelings and conceptions the Aztecs attached to the heart? The Spaniards believed that a culture that could allow such a bestial sacrificing of human beings had to be exterminated at all costs. The conquistadors destroyed most of the literature of the Aztecs, robbing them of their collective memory. Even so, some of their cultural sources survived. In addition, much mythical material was written down both by the Mexicans themselves and the Spaniards. The most well-known source on the Aztecs was written down in Aztec using the Latin alphabet by Sahugún between 1558 and 1580 – at the time of Montaigne, *nota bene*.

Both illustrations and written sources make it quite clear that the heart is of cardinal importance in the religious myths and the corresponding religious sacrificial cult. Underlying the human sacrifices is the idea of an analogy between cosmos, state and human being – a triad represented by the heart. At the centre of the cosmos is the sun (which can also be portrayed as a heart), just as Mexico with the capital Tenochtitlán was the centre of the earth, and the heart was at the centre of each human being.

In the Aztec creation myth, the world has been created and recreated a number of times after having perished because the sun went out. At the time of the Spanish conquest, the Aztecs had embarked on the fifth and last era. To begin with, everything was dark, until the gods got together and lit a fire. The myth also relates how the gods brought the sun back to life by one of them throwing himself onto the fire. Immediately afterwards, he rose above the horizon, reborn as the sun. Soon, however, its journey across the heavens came to a halt once more. It was not until the gods sacrificed themselves on the fire, providing the sun with nourishment, that it continued its path across the heavens once more. This myth is crucial to our understanding of Aztec human sacrifice. Only via sacrifice could the sun gain strength to rise every morning; this was only possible when the gods sacrificed themselves – and later by means of repeated human sacrifice.

Various explanations exist – both demographical and ecological – as to why human sacrifices were so numerous and intense among the Aztecs. Religious motives alone could not result in such comprehensive sacrifices, it is claimed. Nor do motives connected with political power explain the extent of the sacrifices, for if the religious was only a pretext, it would have been much more expedient to kill prisoners of war in another way than by this elaborate ritual. Furthermore, it was not only enemies who were sacrificed. Men, women and children from the tribe were as well. The religious ideas that underlay the sacrifices must therefore have been seen as true explanations of how the world comes into being and perishes once more. The extent of the sacrifices presumably has to do with the short intervals between the eras. In most other cultures and religions, the world is created once and for all (as in the Judaeo-Christian), or the cycles of creation and destruction take place at intervals of millions or billions of years (as in Buddhism). But the Aztec cycles were shorter and varied in nature. The era of the flame lasted no longer than twice 52 years. When it ended, the world perished. This meant that the destruction was not experienced *sub specie aeternitatis* or from a long (theoretical) time-perspective as in other cultures, but that it was always imminent. Thus it had to be actively prevented, and the sun-god needed nourishment the whole time in the form of blood and heart via sacrifice. And it necessitated the sacrifice of many people – probably more the closer the end of the world came. According to the religious and astrological analyses, the end of the world was nigh when the Spaniards arrived, the same time as the god of the morning and evening star, Quetzalcoatl, was to return from the east across the sea – a notion Cortés was not slow to make use of.

Based on the cosmic analogy of the sun as the centre of the universe, the Aztecs made the heart the centre of man, both physiologically and religiously. That there is an analogy between microcosm and macrocosm, between body and cosmos, is a conception familiar to us from other cultures. But with the Aztecs the idea that it is the heart that keeps man alive is more pervasive than in any other culture. The Aztec word for heart is derived from the verb *yollotl*, which means 'live, enliven, be born'. The heart lives, beats, is warm, and causes man to live. In Sahugún it says that 'the heart governs everything'. As long as we stick to the physiological, it is not difficult for a modern European to follow Sahugún here. An alchemist anatomist from the Renaissance could have said something similar. Another similarity with pre-modern Europe is that the Aztec language 'did not make any distinction between heart and intellect' and soul.[2] But with its divine and cosmic potential the heart in Aztec had a wider meaning than in other languages that link heart and intellect.

The place that the heart occupied in religion also explains why the Aztec could approve human sacrifice. For without it, both state and people would perish. By giving one's heart to the gods and the sun, the individual was also ensured a worthy life in the hereafter – he could even become divine and avoid eternal darkness in the underworld, the worst fate that could befall the individual. The way in which the individual died was crucial for becoming part of the divine light or the eternal darkness in the afterlife.

The heart not only occupied a central position in the idea of the origin and end of the world and the individual's possible resurrection in the hereafter. It was at the centre of human awareness and experiencing of everything that takes place here on earth and was also the main motif in Aztec literature of wisdom and the poetic depictions of life here on earth, as expressed in the ancient Aztec songs, the *Cantares Mexicanos*, as they are called in Spanish, written down anonymously in the period between 1536 and 1565 (and which must be kept separate from the religious songs that Sahugún committed to paper). The central images of this 'alternative' poetry of wisdom, which was often critical towards human sacrifice, were *flower*, *heart* and *sun*, where the form was important, since the form of poetry was also to form the individual. Human plasticity is analogous to the instability of the world, and calls for active and artistic forming, as in other aesthetic cultures such as the Egyptian.

Flowers and birds also speak especially to the heart. The song of the magnificent bird (quetzal) did not arise on the earth, and it rises to the heavens with its beautiful notes:

> With moved heart I hear it, oh singer. My thoughts rise aloft and force a path into the sky, and I sigh, full of longing. I understand him completely, the Caquan bird and the Hummingbird and what they are called up there in the sky. (Song II: 3)

When the singer sighs with longing and wishes he were a bird that can soar up into the sky, it is because he realizes that the magnificence of the bird and the sweetness of the song are of divine origin. It is the heart that realizes the connection, and the heart that is able to fly even further than the magnificent bird (quetzal) and the song can imagine. All the senses are concentrated in the rejoicing heart, with its visionary gaze which sees the omnipresent one in the sky: 'Yes, my heart looks to where you are near, at you, Ipalnemoa!' (Song ii: 5). The lovely flower, which his gleaming heart resembles, he is also going to offer to the god. Here is the basis for the analogy between the earthly, with the flower and the magnificent bird as central symbols, and the heavenly, with the sun as the original symbol of the divine and the goal that lies beyond earthly life. The flower and the sun are both mediated by the heart, man's bloody flower to which the divine sun gives life. The flower is a symbol both of earthly power and beauty and of divine presence. All this beauty reminds the heart of where it belongs. Such religious thoughts also console the war hero, even though he knows what kind of death awaits him: 'Nothing does my heart fear, there on the field of battle; I long to do by the stone knife, yes, our heart wishes death for itself in war' (xvi: 5). In such notions we find the explanation to the Aztec heart-sacrifices and perhaps the reason why they did not give rise to revolt among potential victims. Unless the songs were precisely an alternative to, or a criticism of, the sacrificial rituals. The songs repeatedly underline the connection between the song and the individual, and the song only works for the individual who has learned 'to converse with his heart'. They can, however, attain unity with the god's heart and experience that 'flowers and song' exist in everything.

That the Aztecs, by our standards, could be so heartless and literally cause people to become heart-less, is in itself an example of how relative human emotional life is. To offer the heart was to save the heart, as far as the Aztecs were concerned. For them, heart sacrifices were a condition for the heart being able to continue to beat both for the individual and for the universe, while we only see heart-death as someone perishing. That is why our culture, via its highly developed heart medicines, does everything it can to maintain life in the heart for as long as possible. That is why we are caught in our own prejudices when we assess emotional patterns and reactions in other cultures. Similarly, we do not see either that our own emotions are a function of our thoughts and conceptions, as Nietzsche with his radical cultural criticism has underlined. It is one of the basic insights of Nietzsche that conceptions and prejudices, belief and conviction determine the emotions, and that man can believe whatever it is – and thus feel whatever it is. What *we* perceive as evil can, in different climes and with different time-horizons be perceived as virtue:

Cruelty is one of the oldest festive joys of mankind. Consequently it is imagined that the gods too are refreshed and in festive mood when they are offered the spectacle of cruelty . . . : it may well be that the gods frown upon us when we are fortunate and smile upon us when we suffer – though certainly they do not feel pity! For pity is reckoned contemptible and unworthy of a strong, dreadful soul.[3]

Nietzsche writes this as an implicit criticism of Christian morality. Norwegians, for example, ought to understand what Nietzsche is talking about, if they understand their own forefathers, the Vikings, and their beliefs and cults. The Vikings were not known for being soft-hearted either, and preferred not to look on weakness with compassion. Nor was human sacrifice unknown in pre-Christian times in northern Europe. The heart ideal of the Vikings may perhaps have more in common with the Faroese or Aztecs than with the later, Christian, Europeans.

CHAPTER 7

Norse Anthropology

In many ways, the Vikings with their sacrifices, even humans, and belief in heathen gods are just as strange to us as the Egyptians and Aztecs. That is why I situate the Norse conception of the heart with those of the non-Christian and non-European civilizations, in order to illustrate how problematic it is to understand the alien and the ancient when something new has placed itself on top of the old like more recent archaeological strata, as with European Christianity upon Norse heathen gods. To make a leap from the Mesoamerican to the Norse can thus help to bring out the unfamiliar in the familiar and the familiar in the unfamiliar, making us better able to understand both ourselves and others. There is also a historical link between America and Europe that is several centuries older than Columbus. But this link between the old and the new world was not rediscovered before Norse literature was rediscovered in the new age after Columbus.

In the battle of Stiklestad (1030), King Olaf of Norway was beaten by his heathen enemies – and became a victorious martyr. In his army fought the brave Icelandic *skald* (poet) Tormod Kolbrunarskald. Every Norwegian knows the words the writer of the history of the Viking kings *Snorri Sturluson* (1178–1248) placed on Tormod Kolbrunarskald's lips at the battle, when he pulled out the arrow that had pierced his heart and saw there were strands of fat on it: 'Well has the king fed us; fat am I still about the heart-roots!' The words express certain ideals that were held high in a culture concerned with shame and honour, courage and loyalty towards the Viking chieftain until death. These qualities are what ensures the man's honourable name after death – here a name guaranteed for all posterity thanks to the pithiness of his remark. The words also say something about what kinds of emotions were held in high esteem at the time, about what the Norse heart was like. That Tormod's words became immortal is not only because they applied to the vital organ purely physically and expressed a fearless unruffledness in the face of all danger and death but because the heart was seen as the seat of courage. This is an aspect of the Norse heart that represents something distinctive and of interest in our particular context. We can find evidence of this in the Edda and in the skaldic poetry.

The heart is frequently mentioned in old Norwegian poetry. This is not so strange, perhaps, since it is this organ that, if injured, most frequently led to death on the battlefield. It is the centre of the life-force. That is why the mythical hero Sigurd Fafnisbani (the Nordic parallel to Siegfried in the Germanic *Niebelungenlied*, cf. Wagner's operas) is given the advice to eat and drink the heart and blood of the dragon Fafni when he has killed it, as this means the power and qualities that Fafni once had will be transferred to him, including the ability to interpret the song of birds. But the most distinctive thing about Norse anthropology is that the physical properties of the heart reveal whether the man is brave or a coward. The warrior and skald Egil, for example, says at one point that the heart quivered, *es skelfi . . . mér hjarta*, i.e. that courage is lacking.

A more detailed account of the brave heart is to be found in *Saga of the Foster Brothers*. In Chapter 17, it is explained why the body of the fallen Torgeir (his foster brother, by the way, is Tormod Kolbrunarskald) has his chest cut open to determine what the heart of a brave man looks like. It is to be decided whether what is believed is true: that a brave man's heart is smaller than that of a coward. The reason for it being small is said to be that it is the supply of blood that makes it big, and that it therefore is blood that causes the heart to quiver. In other words, a brave heart only contains a little blood and is therefore small, firm and cold. The result of this particular dissection is that it is decided on purely physiological grounds that Torgeir is a brave man, for his heart (according to a shorter version of the saga) is no larger than a walnut, and it is *hard*. That was why it did not quiver with fright. Torgeir is just as firm in his courage as in his heart. Yet this dissection, with everything it stands for, is more reminiscent of the ancient Egyptian heart ideal than a subsequent European one.

Similar evidence for the analogy between the physical consistency of the heart and a person's character is found in the first *Helge Saga* (the legend of another mythical hero from the migration period), where the following is said about Helge Hundingsbane:

> fearless was he/ bold for battle,
> bone-hard his heart/ within his breast. (Str. 53)

Even though these verses apparently represent an old literary tradition and not actual anatomical studies, such a passage says something about how man was perceived in Norse times. The heart is the seat of qualities that were highly valued in a warrior culture. The mind was therefore also situated in the heart. The word has to do with *hugs*, the intellect – or rather the mind. Such qualities as courage and its opposites, cowardice and faint-heartedness, did not come directly from attitudes that belong to the mind, from conscious and developed qualities, but from purely anatomical relations, according to the specialist of Norse history Klaus von See, who has examined this more closely:

> The important thing for the present argument is that the metaphors mentioned refer to the anatomical composition of the heart and that they see in its smallness, hardness and absence of blood a cause of courage – and not only a symptom of it.[1]

This conception of the heart is also confirmed by other accounts. The heart is the stage of the well-known depiction of the battle between the giant Rungne – the strongest of the giants – and the god of war and thunder Thor, whom he challenged. The reason why Rungne is the strongest of the giants – the diametric opposite of the Norse gods – is that he has a heart of stone. This quality about him is so dominating and mythically important that he is simply called Rungne with the Stone Heart. Thor naturally allows himself to be provoked by the giants – that is one of his qualities as the incarnation of an emotionally primitive being. Even though the giants are stupid, they know who perhaps is stronger and more dangerous than themselves. Thor is one such figure, though not as dangerously clever as Odin, the supreme and wise god of creation. For in addition to Thor having a hard heart (he is a tough nut in more than one sense), he also has his hammer and his belt of strength, Megingjord. Therefore the giants make careful preparations for Thor's arrival. This they do by making a huge clay giant that is nine miles high and three miles wide, which they place at the entrance to the home of the giants, Jotunheimen, in order to scare Thor. They have trouble, however, in finding a suitable heart for the clay giant. The most suitable they can find is a mare's heart. This proves fatal. For this is a large, blood-filled heart and thus not courageous. It starts quivering so violently when Thor appears on the scene that the whole giant begins to quiver, wets itself out of fear and collapses into a heap. Rungne is then an easy victim for Thor's invincible hammer.

An important feature of this Norse anthropology – one that we will also meet in other ancient cultures – is that what in our own age is regarded as psychological and relatively subjective was in pre-Christian times traced back to objective relations – in this case natural, physiological characteristics. That we are talking about forces and objective conditions that go beyond personal control and will can also be seen from ritualistic sacrifices in the Norse era. Norse culture with its belief in heathen gods was in many ways a bloody culture. During sacrifices, blood was sprinkled both on those taking part and on nearby effects, for it had a magical power.

Human sacrifice also occurred, though the influence of Christianity soon restrained this facet of heathen god worship. Even so, it is worth noting that it is mainly civilizations that have human sacrifice (while many primitive societies have cannibalism). To tear out a human heart for religious purposes is a sign of civilization. A distinction has to be made between human sacrifice and ritual killing, which is widespread in all archaic and primitive cultures. Several of the oldest sources of Norse culture tell us about human sacrifice among the Vikings and the Germanic tribes – including Arabic sources, the Roman writer Tacitus and Danish Saxo. Adam of Bremen writes about human sacrifice in Uppsala. It is non-Norse sources that offer us most insight into this special aspect of Viking belief – the Arabic, Latin and Germanic sources tell us more about their encounter with the Vikings and their religious cult. In addition there are some depictions, direct and indirect, in Norse sources.

In the worship of Norse gods, human sacrifice is in particular connected with supreme god Odin, who is the god of the hanged. Historian of religions George Dumézil, among others, has seen the fact that Odin climbs into the tree of life, Yggdrasil, and hangs himself in order to gain insight as proof that Odin is a god of Eastern origin, since his sacrificial death has shamanistic reminiscences. Sacrificial death by hanging is normally accompanied by stabbing (often with a piece of wood, a spear) to the heart, as depicted in the following lines of *Gautrek's Saga*:

> To the gods I had / to offer Vikar
> Geirtjov's killer / high in the tree
> I thrust my spear / to the prince's heart . . .

It could be that the two methods of killing are dedicated to different gods (Thor and Odin), or have separate functions:

> Double death, by strangling and stabs / blows does not have to mean more than it was a practical method, since one first empties the body of the sacrificial blood one wanted to get hold of, and then hangs the body in the sacrificial tree.[2]

In Norse culture there was a finely graded view of man, with a clear touch of intellectual rationality and mental strength. The wise Odin, for example, wonders about the world he has created. For everything is not as it should be. The Norse gods are not in possession of the truth, unlike the Christian and Jewish God, who not only has possession but *sole* possession of the sole truth, i.e. His own. 'Do you know more, or not?' the visionary prophetess in the mythical Edda-hymn *Völuspá* asks. In the Bible, there is no such question. That a *woman* is in possession of deep truths was also unthinkable in Christianity, with its high level of misogyny. In Norse society, women had considerable power – and it was a dastardly thing to lay hand on a woman.

The intellectual aspects of Norse anthropology also find expression in terms of myth in the names of Odin's two ravens, *Hugin* (the mind) and *Munin* (memory). The mind is conceived as something substantial and is the centre of man, more so than the heart. And the mind is rational. The various dimensions of which man was composed in a finely graded system were not unlike the Homeric division, as can be seen, for example, in str. 18 of the Völuspá: 'Spirit gave Odin,/ Thought gave Hönir,/ Blood gave Lodur/and warmth of life.'

Norse culture is not one of emotions. The Vikings were not humane in our modern sense of the word. This is shown not only by their susceptibility to ravaging and pillaging but also by a brutal punishment ritual – cutting the blood eagle – connected to a religious warrior cult. This was more an act of magic than a method of torture (cf. to carve runes). It is first mentioned in Snorri's stories about the king 'Harald Fairhair', where Earl Einar carves the blood eagle into the back of mysterious Halvdan after capturing him on the Orkney Islands. Snorri's account is brief and laconic:

> Then Earl Einar went over to Halvdan and carved the eagle on his back, thrusting his sword into the body at the back and, pulling down to the lower back, slicing off all the ribs. He then heaved out the lungs – such was Halvdan's fate.[3]

The lungs probably provide associations with the eagle's wings. Einar is portrayed as being vile and one-eyed, 'though cleverer than the others', since he sees that something occasionally rising and falling on an island where he has hidden could resemble either a bird or a man. One-eyed Odin springs to mind here. But it could also be that this episode is of Anglo-Saxon origin, since the Saxons were known for cutting out the hearts of their enemies. That it is the lungs that are cut out, where the spirit is located, could also indicate that Earl Einar was carrying out a magical act.

The connection between emotions and the heart, as mentioned before, comes mainly with the advent of Christianity, which shapes the conception of the heart early on in the Norse era. Many of the heart-expressions that occur in the mythical Edda and the writings of the skalds probably have a literary model that can be traced back to a Christian medieval period. We have to recall that Norse literature was written down in the twelfth and especially the thirteenth century, when literary ideals from the Continent were also making a considerable impact on Iceland. Here, we meet the heart as the seat of – and an image of – sadness and grief, joy and love. The metaphorics of the Christian heart in particular have now penetrated what might at first glance appear to be quintessentially Norwegian, as in the mythical poem *Hávamál* (Tale of the Supreme, i.e. Odin). But such a didactic poem has clear models in contemporary European literature. Klaus von See's words fittingly sum up this somewhat complex thematics. He has demonstrated that

> the metaphors and formulas that designate the heart as being the seat of bravery are to be clearly distinguished from those that ascribe emotional states such as sorrow, joy, love and goodness to the heart: The former group rests on purely anatomical and physio-logical observations and conceptions and sees in the physical nature of the heart the cause of courage or cowardice in a person (and also in an animal, by the way), whereas the latter group sees the heart as the psychological centre of a person, allowing typical human emotional states in the heart to be concentrated in the heart as the most receptive and sensitive human organ, and often there-fore referring to these affections as being wounded or as the bleeding of the heart. This presupposes on the whole an internal-ized view of man, one that does not reach the North until the arrival of Christianity and the rich biblical metaphorics of the heart.[4]

Since the metaphorics of the heart in the written Norse sources is influ-enced by Christianity to such a great extent, it becomes difficult to say that the Norwegians continue to wear a hard, pre-Christian Norse heart. The wildness of Odin's warrior-like berserks has been tamed and reinterpreted via the Christianization of the Norse area. But the basis for this con-version was long-lasting, comprehensive contact between the Vikings and large sections of what during that period was in the process of becoming a European culture. The Vikings have made their own contribution to this common culture, among other things in the form of straightforward intentionality and a dynamic will which enabled them to conquer large areas both in the British Isles and on the continent – not least in France, where the Norse chieftains in many respects were local leaders, and not only in Normandy. That these hard-hearted Vikings were to play a role in the development of social power in France, where the new heart culture was later going to flourish, is one of history's many paradoxes. But the main influence goes, even so, in the opposite direction – from Christianity to the Norse. That the Christianization of the Nordic area led to a new conception of man says something both about how easily man is formed and how strong a formative force Christianity exerted. This is particularly evident in the new metaphorics of the heart which emerges in the High Middle Ages, and which in many ways becomes a generator that forms the modern Western Man.

PART TWO

The Battle for the Western Heart

His heart in me keep him and me in one,
My heart in him his thoughts and senses guides:
He loves my heart, for once it was his own,
I cherish his because in me it bides:
My true-love hath my heart, and I have his.

Sir Philip Sidney

CHAPTER 8

The Emotional Turn in the High Middle Ages

The emergence of modern man is in many ways a battle for feelings and a battle for the personal, individual right to follow one's own heart at all levels, independently of all external authorities and the power of the Church over emotional life. In the subsequent phase, the Renaissance, this battle raises the question of what sort of being man is, whether he has been created in 'God's image' and determined once and for all by nature, as was the prevailing view far into modern times, or whether he is free to shape himself.

The fight for the right to follow one's own heart emotionally and erotically arises as a sort of counter-movement precisely in the era when the Church and Catholic Europe reach a high point at all levels – the High Middle Ages of the twelfth and thirteenth centuries, when the cathedrals with their gothic spires almost soared into the heavens. But at this point in time, the age of chivalry, people's demand to be allowed to live their extremely earthly lives of flesh and blood here and now also made itself felt. In practice this demand took the form of an intense acting out of a 'natural' and temporal passionate love. This gives the High Middle Ages a central position in the cultural history of the heart. For it is in the High Middle Ages and the age of chivalry that this history takes a new turn, one which I shall refer to as the emotional turn, and which points forward to self-sufficient modern man, who trusts in the potential for development that nature has provided for him to create himself in his own image – with unrestrained egoism as the reverse side of the coin.

This emotional turn has a number of historical premises. In the period after the year 1000, an economic boom and material growth take place that create optimism and a belief in life. The cathedrals had this as their foundation. The fortified castles with their chivalry and urban growth with a new economic elite of tradesmen and craftsmen are part and a prerequisite of these extra reserves of energy. Of decisive importance are gradual changes of mentality and new modes of thought, in short the extra reserves to think for oneself, something the upsurge in philosophy and theological thinking at the new universities also bear witness to. The increase in intellectual freedom further results in people and groups interpreting the Bible for themselves, in their own way. This gives rise to a number of alternative religious movements which the Church with its monopoly stamps as heretical and ungodly. An artistic upshot of this new era is found not only in architecture but also in figurative art. Polyphonic music broke with the monotony of the Gregorian chant. Pivotal to these changes is a new conception of woman, who now becomes the subject of the distinctive literary expressions of the new age. This new artistic expression and the new view of woman, though, were both linked to a special social order that characterizes the High Middle Ages: chivalry.

The age of chivalry represents a particular development and shaping of emotional life that the literature of chivalry promotes far outside the knightly environment. Two literary genres in particular developed and spread the new ideal of love – one of them oral and performed with songs and music, the other written – the troubadour songs and the courtly romances. These two genres and everything for which they stood have had no insignificant influence on the formation of the human heart in Europe. It is commonly held that love is invented during the twelfth century. And it was the heart that was centre-stage in knightly or courtly love, which was the ideal of the age of chivalry. That this love was just as much a social practice as an erotic one is revealed in the term itself. The word *courtly* comes from the French word for court, *la cour*, as do the words *courtesy* and *courtesan*. (The Scandinavian equivalents come from the German word *Hof*: court(yard), house and home.) This was a set of manners developed at the court and in the castle, where the knight had his position as a (secret) vassal of a lady, or as a knight of a maiden. Their feelings and their modes of expression as depicted in the romances and the songs are thus not universally human, but partly derive from a time- and culture-determined formation of emotional life within a particular social class – the aristocracy.

The age of chivalry is one of the most exaggeratedly artificial phenomena that Europe has created as a system of life and society. This manifests itself, for example, in knightly patterns of behaviour towards other knights and nobles, which were finely regulated by an unparalleled set of rules and rituals that corresponded to those between the knight and his chosen woman in the new erotic scenario. In the various different erotic depictions, however, it is difficult to distinguish between passionate, chivalrous and courtly love. What distinguishes them is, in particular, the question of whether love also has to be sexually consummated. There is a tendency for the earlier expressions of chivalrous love to have sexual consummation as their aim (thus passionate love), whereas courtly love regards the sexual consummation of love as being something that is uncourtly. This applied in particular to the later troubadour songs and certain courtly romances from the thirteenth century in which love becomes increasingly refined and Platonic. The emphasis is placed on universal ideals – on being magnanimous, compassionate and protective. The common term for these two types of erotic practice is romantic love.

Historians and historians of mentalities agree that knighthood with its ideals contributed to shaping our ideal of humanity. Violence becomes modified or gradually rejected, and beautiful words and beautiful manners gradually replace bellicose behaviour and much of the vulgar sexuality that is richly represented in the medieval period. In the thirteenth century in particular, the knight must first and foremost love his lady in his heart and rejoice in being able to do precisely (only) that. Courtly love is thus a mixture of *eros* and *agape*, of sensual and Platonic love. With the poetry of the troubadours, this ideal of love spreads like some new fashion across Europe – even to its farthest outposts.

THE TROUBADOUR SONGS

The lifestyle that belonged to the age of chivalry could also accommodate entertainment and art. It was here that the itinerant singers, the troubadours, with their lute, acquired a stage for their songs of love. The troubadour songs and *Minne* songs, as they are called within the Germanic area (from *minne*: love), flourished during the twelfth and thirteenth centuries, with the twelfth century as their zenith. It is a literary form that emerges in various countries, but that spreads over the entire continent with these itinerant poets – *vagantes*, as they were called in Latin, troubadours in the Occitan language – from west to east, from Occitania to other Romance areas via the crusades, from south to north and back. Even earlier than the German *Minne* songs and French troubadour songs are the Spanish – especially the Catalan and Andalusian – songs, which go directly back to Oriental models. The influence of the Arabian lifestyle and art are now making themselves felt. The southern French, Occitan, songs are the real troubadour songs, which are central not only in European literature but also in European intellectual life, where they represent a permanent fixture in our mentality.

The ideal for the new erotic practice that the songs depict called for the man to submit to the woman, who belongs to the nobility. *She* is often married (to another). Marriage and love are not only different, but irreconcilable. Marriage would ruin the tension that passion – and the genre – are based on. To be worthy of her love and become her worshipper, the man has to master all knightly virtues and accept all the trials to which she wishes to submit him – without granting him what he is ultimately seeking. This, then, is a forbidden love, with all that this entails in the way of duplicity and dual communication. Precisely because the goal is never achieved, suffering becomes part of – and just as great and powerful as – the passion itself.

The concept that was used when talking about courtly love was originally Provencal, *fin'amor*, which is supplemented in the late nineteenth century by the French term *amour courtoise*, courtly love, such as a person loves at court. The refined love of the troubadour songs goes to the boundary of consummation. The aim is pleasure of various kinds, despite or parallel with all the suffering that passion also entails. Erotic love is also lifted out of its procreative function. This represents an anti-Church breakthrough. The detailed codex that regulated this game of pleasure did not originate from the Church, either. Troubadour literature also represents a new erotic rhetoric. The question is whether it is eroticism that creates the literature, or the rhetoric and the literature that create the love and the passion they deal with.

From our mental perspective it is important to emphasize that this bold erotic play was implemented without any consciousness of sin and outside Christian doctrine regarding sin. The Church is without any influence here, which explains why the Church fought against the courtly culture. One of the crusades, the Albigensian Crusade (1208), was directed against the Cathars and, in particular, Occitania, where troubadour literature was cultivated. That the crusade against Provence was so violent and fierce – on 22 July 1209 about 20,000 inhabitants of the city Béziers were slaughtered – was not only because of the Cathars, who attacked all papal and high-Church pomp and power, but also because of the troubadour cult, which was conceived as being a critical lyrical form and, furthermore, was closely connected to Moslem Spain and Catalan:

> It is one of the paradoxes of the Middle Ages that while the crusades were raging there were also more hidden lines of communication between the cultures that by both parties are often portrayed as mortal enemies. In actual fact, it is perhaps in this Moslem-Christian no-man's-land that one of the hidden sources of a European art-poetry should be sought.[1]

The heart becomes the symptom, image and symbol of the new emotional ideal that the age of chivalry conveyed. This led to the development of a distinctive thematics of the heart, as in this song (after Pedersen):

> My heart would now resort to love/And freely live under its
> constraint. . . .
> I consider him a man stone-dead,/Whose heart does not offer
> love shelter.
> Better to flee from life,/Should one's nature be without love.

When love comes from a 'whole' and 'pure' heart, it can defy all social
norms, as well as the religious ones which those passionately in love sin
against. That the power of the Church over emotional life could slip at
such a central point as sexual morality says something not only about the
tensions and dissonances in the Middle Ages but also about the power of
the new poetry and the courtly romances in particular.

This epic genre is called the *romance* because it was not created in Latin
but in the 'Romance' languages people spoke. The courtly romances build
on the pre-Christian Celtic or Breton legends about King Arthur and the
Knights of the Round Table. In these *romans bretons* the Celtic heroes and
heroines are dressed in a medley of Christian symbols and emblems of the
age of chivalry in a new emotional landscape. One example of the fusion
of heathen and Christian material is the quest for the Holy Grail, which
becomes identified with the Christian chalice. By means of this Christian
veneer, erotic and sensual passion is legitimized and idealized. But this
idealization and cultivation of passion is fundamentally unchristian,
representing a breach of Christian morality. Nevertheless, it is romantic
love that gains ground as an ideal for emotional life in Europe.

In the chivalrous epics passion is cultivated, as is the case in the
'primer' of this productive genre *Tristan* (*c.* 1205–15) by Gottfried von
Strassburg. In this work, the romance of Tristan and Isolde is written
about on the basis of Thomas of Britain's version (from the 1170s) of this
well-known Celtic legend. The bodily passion that St Augustine attempted
to condemn several centuries earlier got its own back here. And Gottfried
was not the only one. Wolfram von Eschenbach wrote *Parzifal* about
another of Arthur's knights, a continuation of Chrétien de Troyes'
Perceval (from *c.* 1188). Chrétien also wrote – partly in opposition to the
erotic love of *Tristan* – the more idealized romance about *Lancelot*, which
had great contemporary appeal and forms the model of courtly love.

Chrétien's efforts are remarkable, not only in terms of the history of
literature but also that of Western mentality and culture. To explain his
inspiration, it should be noted that he was closely associated with Countess

Marie de Champagne, daughter of Eleanor of Aquitaine, from where William, the first troubadour, came. Once again, Arabic influence is at work, interacting with Celtic tradition. It was first and foremost Chrétien who established the basis for the creative legacy of Arthurian literature down through the centuries. Not only did he write the exotic novel of the heart *Cligès* (*c.* 1176), whose heroine, in order to be united with her hero, successfully uses a potion later to be used (unsuccessfully) by Shakespeare's Juliet; but with *Perceval, the Story of the Grail* Chrétien established the basis for the legend of the Grail and Holy Blood in literature up to the present day. The entire bestselling cult of *The Da Vinci Code* (2003) derives from this tradition as well as the legend concerning Christ's last days and his relationship to Mary Magdalene (cf. Otfried's *Evangelienbuch*). The magic and mystique of Arthurianism reflects Chrétien's own life and death. For he died while writing about the Holy and mysterious Grail and shortly afterwards, his home city of Troyes burnt down – his manuscript in it. The year of his death was also that of the Fall of Jerusalem, where the Knights Templar fought for glory. Nothing excites the imagination more than an incomplete or lost manuscript, a body or a corpse that disappears and secret orders. Just think of what Umberto Eco made of such a theme in *The Name of the Rose* (1980), which also derives from medieval literature, its title alluding to the most popular novel of the thirteenth century, *The Novel of the Rose*.

Perceval is the earliest recorded account of the Holy Grail, developed in the continuations of the unfinished romance, with mixed elements of mysticism and magic of the blood, of chivalry and Christianity, as the *gral* also is the cup of the last supper and the grail in which the sacred blood was collected from the wound of Jesus when he was taken down from the cross, thereby also giving the grail a function of the chalice. The point here is that there is both a cult of blood that is of Christian and secular origin in the High Middle Ages, and a parallel and intertwined cult of the heart of the same mixed origin, both traditions being continuously creative to this very day – thanks to the new, historic role played by literature in Western culture in the High Middle Ages as represented by Chrétien's works. The literally provocative power of the tradition can be illustrated by another international bestseller, *Holy Blood, Holy Grail* (1982) by Michael Baigent, Richard Leigh and Henry Lincoln, those who inspired (and later sued) Dan Brown for his bestseller. The book you now are reading is also in certain respects a response of the early twenty-first century to this very tradition, tracing the origins of the heart cult 5,000 years back in time, to the cradle of culture in Iraq, where blood has for years been flowing and hearts bursting as a result not only of the arrogance of power but also of a lack of the virtue most valued in Western culture – the art of self-reflection, *sophrosyne*, praised as divine ever since Odysseus dialogic-ally encouraged his heart to restrain the passions of his heart. In the drama of the passions, the courtly romances have played a decisive and highly ambiguous role in Western culture.

The mythical subtext and all the bonds of allegiance in the Arthurian romances can explain the fascination with naturalized passion, where the one who betrays love betrays everything, a principle that is still valid. Courtly behaviour and knightly virtues are linked to fidelity, to the great love and the noble heart on which all social and religious norms are based. In many ways the courtly romances transfer those ideals of fidelity and friendship that had developed between the knight and his lord to the relationship with the chosen woman, who was his social superior. The complex context within which the literature of chivalry emerged and the difficult social position of the knight explain many of the restrictions imposed on the lovers in this genre.

All the restrictions would seem to be lacking in *Tristan*. In Gottfried's work there is no distinction between erotic and religious love when Tristan and Isolde meet in their love cave in the depths of the forest, something between an altar and a bedroom, where everything is in the service of love:

> They fed in their grotto on nothing but love and desire . . . I mean
> pure devotion, love made sweet as balm that consoles body and
> sense so tenderly, and sustain the heart and spirit – this was their
> best nourishment. Truly, they never considered any food but that
> from which heart drew desire, the eyes delight, and which body,
> too, found agreeable.[2]

In this work, consummated love overcomes the dualism between body and soul, turning earth into heaven and paradise: 'Just what one could imagine in other countries as being necessary to be able to create a para-dise, they had here.' In this sex-fixated love paradise they need neither priest nor mass, for they have everything in nature's cathedral, where the birds sing mass for them. When desire is satisfied, the meaning of life is fulfilled and complete:

> What better food could they have for body or soul? Man was there
> with Woman, Woman there with Man. What else should they be
> needing? They had what they were meant to have, they had
> reached the goal of their desire.[3]

What is striking is not that someone could formulate such thoughts, but that they could become so widespread – so widespread that *Tristan*'s passionate creed with everything for which it stands leads to a turn in European civilization. *Tristan* is the first work since Antiquity that makes Eros an absolute value to which humanity is subject. And the heart has not only become the most prominent metaphor and seat of passion but is the centre of the force that has set the world in motion and kept everything going. Like nobody else, Gottfried induces people to adopt this cult of the heart. In the prologue alone, the heart is mentioned almost 30 times.

The age of chivalry via its ideal of love represents a kind of standardization of emotional life. With its strict rules it also shows how artificially human love life is formed and what artificial modes of expression it acquires. It is not easy to decide what is nature and what is culture, what comes from the heart and what comes from convention. When the lovers in a knightly environment swoon, for example, it is a convention or a literary cliché. Swooning because of misfortune in love is a precursor of death, as is depicted in various versions of the Tristan and Isolde epic. Both of them eventually die because of love, betrayal and sorrow.

So it is the heart that stops when love is stopped in courtly literature, often as a result of misunderstandings, intrigues, betrayal or social conventions that prevent the lovers from gaining each other. But everything is permitted for those who love, both betrayal and adultery, in the courtly romances – to a greater extent than in the troubadour lyrics. It can nevertheless be asked how whole and pure the heart is when the lovers so often get involved in a series of betrayals and deceptions. Tristan has a great deal on his conscience even according to contemporary norms. He has killed Isolde's uncle in a duel, as a minstrel he has found favour with her mother, until as a bridesman he seduces and allows himself to be seduced by the bride (admittedly as the result of a magic potion that works for three years). In the French version, he does not end up as a monk or hermit but flees to Normandy after having been revealed and finds another Isolde for himself.

There are a number of loving couples in the circle round Arthur, and infidelity is just as strong as the bond of allegiance to the king. Even his wife, Queen Guinevere, is unfaithful, taking the noble knight Lancelot as her lover. While Tristan is the passionate lover, Lancelot is the model example of courtly love. He consistently refuses to enter into a relationship with other women since he, according to the demands of the genre, loves being Guinevere's secret lover, with all the excitement and all the difficulties which that entails.

The obstacles are part of the requirements in both the genre and in romantic love, claims Swiss cultural philosopher Denis de Rougemont (1939). Where the obstacles are greatest, passion is also at its strongest. For that reason obstacles are created and the lovers often separated from each other to increase the suffering and the passionate longing to meet each other again, a cumulative spiral that only has one possible outcome – death. Tristan and Isolde do not love each other – they love love, claims de Rougemont. He claims that Tristanism has its own inner logic. Love of love conceals an even more frightful passion – a death wish. Without realizing it, the two lovers only have a single wish: to die together. The deeper roots of this death mysticism go back to the Middle East and Manichaeism and the dualistic division between light and dark, good and evil.

But one does not need to have recourse to the history of ideas to explain the inner weaknesses of the chivalrous ideal of love. The history of ideas is not unambiguous, either. Ever since Antiquity, blindly passionate love has been considered a form of madness. Now, however, this madness is turned into a norm. On the basis of plain common sense, many would say that the new form of love has a considerable number of constructional defects and distorted aims. For the infatuated knight who loves being in love actually only loves himself and cultivates his own suffering and self-pity. He has to conquer his lady in the same way as he has beaten his opponents on the field of battle. War and eroticism belong together in the age of chivalry – not only rhetorically. Romantic love has thus contributed to promoting egotistic love, the conquering and competitive mentality of our culture. That is why jealousy is also passion's attendant.

Courtly wooing was also part of a power struggle at court. The knights were as much rivals for prestige and honour as for the lady, who becomes the means and object of this rivalry. That the fight has been moved from the battlefield into court is part of the humanization of society and part of the general trend for the external to be made internal. But the fight and the battle metaphorics live on. The knight loves to conquer and win the noble lady and literally have her as a feather in his cap – or her silken band, knotted as a symbol on his helmet or his lance.

The new view of eroticism could not have acquired such great impact had it not been underpinned by a more profound motivational factor, one anchored in Christianity. The link between religion and eroticism intensified both the suffering and the passion.

EROTICISM AND RELIGION: ABÉLARD AND HÉLOÏSE

In a strange way, certain inherent traits of Christianity and Church institutions form the foundation of romantic love. The sublime gothic churches with their spires can stand as a symbol of the ardour that filled and fuelled the human mind at this time. For the religious ardour that led man to strive upwards towards the divine was the same as that which drove crusaders towards the Holy Land in wave upon wave in the twelfth and thirteenth century, inspired by the pope and the Church with the promise of financial and spiritual reward – a mixture that tends to make the recipient more cursed than blessed according to the teachings of Christ. And knights with red crosses on their chests led the crusades. With the sacred conviction that 'This is God's will', the West as a bloc, for a period of almost 200 years, waged war for the first time in history against the 'infidel' Muslims, who were often slaughtered in what was nothing less than a blood-bath – and who responded in kind.

The red cross stands for suffering, as do blood and the heart in courtly literature. It is a strange coincidence that at the same time as the troubadours are praising erotic passion, religious suffering is also being emphasized and cultivated. In the High Middle Ages, a reinterpretation of Christ on the cross is taking place. Earlier, Jesus was mainly depicted as the victorious and living Jesus; now to an increasing extent he is portrayed as the dying and suffering Jesus. There is no end to the torments and suffering that can be extracted from images of Christ on the cross in the High Middle Ages, until, in the fourteenth century, there are no holds barred in the passionate portrayals of suffering. Thus do erotic and religious passion meet in suffering – and thus can religion and eroticism have a synergic effect on each other. Just how permeated the High Middle Ages were by passion with all its emblems and symbols can also be seen from the religious writings. Love was in the air.

It is hardly surprising that many of the images and expressions, metaphors and symbols that were used by lovers in the age of chivalry were transferred to the love of Jesus. For that reason, Christ's heart is more and more frequently mentioned towards the end of the Middle Ages, when a direct link is made between his heart and his suffering and salvation. This leads to a direct adoration of Christ's heart and later to an actual cult, for which there was a strong following in Protestant countries, linked to its own theology of the heart, *theologia cordis*, in the seventeenth century in particular, when Johan Arndt was not without a say in the matter. It is possible to trace the motif of the heart as a symbol of the loving and suffering Christ back to the fourteenth century in Germany. As part of this cult of Christ's heart, the flaming heart also arises, set directly on fire by Jesus and his love. The first depiction of the flaming heart appears about 1500, becoming a widespread image during the Baroque period and in the eighteenth century. In both Protestant and Catholic countries, the symbol of Christ's heart was extremely widespread in the first centuries after the Middle Ages. It was a favourite motif on innumerable altarpieces, paintings and illustrations. Running parallel to this is a separate tradition with iconographic depictions of the Virgin Mary's heart, often shown transfixed by arrows and surrounded by a wreath of blossoms. Occasionally, it too was a flaming heart that lit a corresponding glow in the congregation. Nowadays, such a passionate practice of Christianity is euphemistically referred to as charismatic. The charismatic layman movement of today is the most successful of all Christian persuasions, with roots stretching back to the very oldest of Christian congregations. But this worship of the heart did not begin until the age of chivalry in the High Middle Ages.

It is in fact a Christian work from the early medieval period that links eroticism and religion, passion and suffering. The unfortunate rhyme of heart with pain – *Herz/Schmerz* – also dates from this work. The rhyme was first used by a monk from Alsace, Otfried von Weissenburg, in his *Evangelienbuch*, an almost unreadable 15,000 half-line epic from the mid tenth century dealing with the life of Jesus. In no other work from the early Middle Ages is there so much mention of the heart. For the first time, the heart becomes a term of endearment. Here, though, it is not primarily the hearts of Jesus, the Virgin Mary and the saints, as is the case later on in the Middle Ages and the Renaissance, but of the heart of Mary Magdalene who wept for him and lost her heart to him. Here, by the way, we meet love between a man and a woman that lies just as far from Paul as Paul does from Jesus's view of the prostitute. Since Otfried, *Herz* has rhymed with *Schmerz* in a large section of world literature.

Religious ardour – whether it resulted in great art, cathedrals or crusades – represented, from the Middle Ages onwards, an encouragement and legitimization of passion and thereby subjective emotions that include erotic passion. This emotional turn is thus not merely the result of courtly literature. For when passion is a prerequisite for faith and mercy, it is only a short step to approving erotic passion as something positive or natural as a basis for Christian love. In the Middle Ages there are fine transitions between religious and erotic passion.

The foremost representative in the High Middle Ages for religious ardour and a Christianity based on the emotions was Bernard de Clairvaux (1090–1153). As the charismatic founder of the most influential order of monks in the High Middle Ages, the Cistercians, he stands not only for the monastic virtues of obedience, faith and prayer, renunciation and chastity, piety (*pietas*) and humility (*humilitas*) inspired by the life and teachings of Christ, but also for a heartfelt intimacy as one of the sources of the new view of love in that period. Bernard's sermons are basically only about love, *caritas*. In order to receive and give love, Bernard emphasized personal religious experience and emotional empathy (*affectum*) more than intellectual cognition, since *Amor est affectio naturalis*,[4] a natural affection that is first felt in the heart, as the seat of the soul. Here, he is building on the biblical idea of the difference between the cold and the warm heart. There is no point in professing with words if one's feelings are not involved. Augustine's *cor inquietum* is reconciled by Bernard in the faith that the flow it feels comes from God and can rest in God's heart, *in corde Dei*. Bernard also excludes the possibility of a person with a cold heart, one unable to love, being in a position to understand God's word. Subsequently he preaches a theology of the heart, where the complementary nature of *cor caritatis* and *caritas cordis* is an earthly, *anthropological* condition for divine love.

Protestant northern Europe was also, via Luther, influenced by this theology of the heart and the prime access of the emotions to faith and salvation, something the comprehensive metaphorics of the heart in the treasury of hymns written in the seventeenth and eighteenth century are an expression of. In one and the same breath, Luther also claims that the intellect is warm. Bernard also presented the meeting between the soul and Christ as one between bride and bridegroom, who become one in the love of the heart. The emblematics of the bride we will come across again both in mystical-alchemical literature and in Protestant hymns.

Bernard lived as he taught. And he taught with an incandescent charisma – some would say fanaticism – that was irresistible for most of those who experienced him. In ascetic renunciation and piety Bernard repeatedly went beyond the physical boundaries of the body and never spared himself when the good cause was in need of an ardent spokesman. His missionary zeal also shows, however, how badly things can go wrong when religious ardour forms the basis for political activism, for Bernard was the mastermind behind the second crusade. He convinced European princes and kings to wage war against the infidel Muslims, a crusade that ended in destruction and ruin, also for Bernard personally. He did, however, win a different crusade – against his contemporary colleague Abélard who, on the basis of Bernard's criticism, was sentenced as a heretic.

All these passionate sources of the emotional turn in the High Middle Ages meet in a sense in the life-story of the scholar and theologian, the knight's son Abélard (1079–1142), as expressed in his autobiography *Historia calamitatum* (The Story of My Misfortunes). This work links religious and erotic love. Here the conflict between the Knight and the Monk, the singer with his lute and the scholar with his book, between *cupiditas* and *caritas*, is enacted in one and the same person – as an expression of the modern internalization of the composite nature of love.

Abélard was one of the foremost thinkers and rhetoricians of the first half of the twelfth century. He was, moreover, already a well-known lyrical poet when, at the age of 38, he caught sight of the beautiful, gifted Héloïse

(1099–1164), niece of Canon Fulbert of Paris, and saw that 'she had all the desirable attributes the lover seeks'. Abélard took Héloïse as his mistress in the home of her uncle who, so to speak, gave him a free hand as her private tutor – without realizing by what sort of desire the man was driven. But when Héloïse became pregnant, Abélard did not behave in particularly noble fashion – rather in what was a conventional church fashion – and had her sent off to his sister in Brittany. She stayed there until she had borne their child. Under pressure from the incensed uncle, Abélard offered to marry her. Héloïse initially declined – out of love for him, so as not to bring him into dishonour and spoil his career, or to prevent him from carrying out his duties as a learned scholar. Abélard suffered dishonour even so – and definitively as a man – as Fulbert took a frightful revenge for himself and his niece for having been dishonoured. One night, some men took Abélard by surprise in his bedroom and castrated him. After that, the eunuch went into a monastery with his shame. A career in the church was formally forbidden for a eunuch. At the same time Héloïse was sent to a nunnery, where she ended up becoming the abbess.

We know this love story from both sides, since Abélard wrote it down several years later in his autobiography, which Héloïse happened to come by. When she read it, she plucked up courage and wrote to Abélard, after ten years of silence, though he had not taken a single initiative in trying to contact her during all those years. This led to an exchange of letters that is one of the best known in world literature. The autobiographical and anti-authoritarian confessions of Abélard and Héloïse, both in terms of genre and emotions, are a continuation of Augustine's *Confessiones* 750 years earlier – but with a reverse assessment of the body and emotional life. In her letters Héloïse declares her lasting love, while also explaining her reasons for not having wanted to marry Abélard in a true romantic spirit. She would rather be his mistress in full and total love, for in marriage coercion would replace love. And she remained true to those motives throughout her entire life at the nunnery, where she lived more on her love of Abélard than her love of God.

In her letters to Abélard Héloïse sums up the various aspects of love: passion, suffering and compassion. Sorrow and pain at present misfortune is no less than the happiness of love they once shared. Nor does she refrain in her letters from accusing Abélard of having betrayed love. In well-chosen words, the abbess berates the seducer who misused his supreme gifts as a teacher, singer and poet towards an innocent child (as did Tristan with his lyre towards Isolde), asking:

> Tell me, I say, if you can, or I will say what I feel and what everyone suspects: desire rather than friendship drew you to me, lust rather

than love. So when desire ceased, whatever you were manifesting for its sake likewise vanished.[5]

It is a double tragedy for Héloïse, for she has not entered a nunnery out of piety or love of God, but out of love of Abélard. She therefore does not expect any reward in the hereafter for her life at the nunnery:

> When little more than a girl I took the hard vows of a nun, not from piety but at your command. If I merit nothing from thee, how vain I deem my labour! I can expect no reward from God, as I have done nothing from love of Him . . . God knows, at your command I would have followed or preceded you to fiery places. For my heart is not with me, but with thee.[6]

This attitude represents the great turning-point in the High Middle Ages. Utterly consciously, Héloïse places physical, human and secular love higher than a love of God. Hardly strange, then, that she was an ideal in the Romantic period. Rousseau felt so attracted by her love story that he wrote *La nouvelle Héloïse* about the elevated, self-sacrificing Héloïse in 1761. There is thus a direct line from the emotional ideal of Romanticism and the religious and secular age of chivalry, represented by Héloïse's love story, which was almost as well known at the time as the slightly later Tristan stories. The exchange of letters between the two, though, once more raises the question of the chicken and the egg: Is it the writing that is concealed behind their love, or love that is concealed behind their writing?

Héloïse has subsequently become a symbolic figure that demonstrates how the West understands true love when it is something more than erotic passion and sexual desire: sacrificing oneself in word and deed for another human being of flesh and blood. Her counterpart, the theologian Abélard, is abstract and theoretical in his declaration of love, which is a cover for his self-righteous and self-centred attitude. Thanks to her cast of mind, Héloïse is nevertheless able to hope for salvation – from a human point of view. Héloïse defies both the man's egoism and double betrayal, the condemning attitude of the Church and Christianity towards personal physical love, which for her is in fact the goal. That is how we interpret her. Her own age, however, viewed her differently. Many believe that her letters are forgeries, written by a cleric who wants to depict Héloïse as a dire warning of what may happen to anyone who turns his gaze away from God and does not give Him his heart. In that case, it is one of history's paradoxes – and a triumph of ethics of the human disposition – that posterity has interpreted the letters in a way directly opposed to the conscious intention of the sender.

In word and deed, with her entire attitude, Héloïse abolishes the dualism between body and soul that otherwise characterizes medieval thought, a dualism that Abélard also challenges with his nominalist-inspired theology – to the extent that he *was* a nominalist and not more of a conceptualist. Nominalism was a theological-philosophical tendency in the High Middle Ages which believed that concepts and ideas originated on the basis of and as general characteristics of concrete single phenomena in the world which exist prior to concepts, and not vice versa, which the universalists had as their point of departure. This led Abélard to upgrade the sensory world of objects. But he also upgraded the conceptual world – and that is the most strikingly modern thing about him – by claiming that concepts originate in our reason and capacity for abstraction in itself, and do not exist in a direct relationship of correspondence with the world of objects (or a divine origin). For this, he was found guilty of heresy, a sentence that ruined his health and indirectly took his life, even if he avoided being burnt at the stake. In that sense both Abélard and Héloïse died for a concretely lived life in the here and now. In death they were reunited in that their earthly remains were placed in the same coffin in a Paris cemetery in the nineteenth century.

The story of Abélard and Héloïse represents not only the emotional turn that takes place in the High Middle Ages but also a challenging of the omnipotence of the Church, pointing forward towards the concept of the free individual who does not recognize any other gods than common sense, personal experience and the consciousness one gains for oneself via one's reflections, senses and experiences. The fidelity of Abélard and especially Héloïse to the voice of the heart bears witness to a courage that came to characterize European intellectual life in the time ahead: the courage to follow one's personal conviction and the voice of the heart, even if this flies in the face of tradition and all forms of authority. And this emancipation and duty to think for oneself begins with the emotions.

Also new is the fact that Abélard in his theological writings anticipated Luther, placing the purpose or intention as what underlies moral acts and assessments. This leads to emphasis being placed on the state of mind in which an action is carried out to determine whether the intention is good or not. Discovering one's own cast of mind calls for self-awareness, to examine one's own motives and what one's heart feels. As eloquent as it is attractive, Abélard's ethics also has the classic title *Know thyself.*

Abélard and Héloïse represent the religious or Christian counterpart to the troubadour literature that reached a high point in their century. Abélard was himself both a great troubadour *and* hymn writer. What these two movements represent explains both the emotional turn and how it could result in a particular ideal of love that will be dominant in an entire culture for the rest of the millennium. On this basis we can seek to sum up the new European heart.

We have emphasized the naturalization of love in Tristanism. The lovers are doing something that is 'natural', they 'are following their heart'. This heart, however, is in no way a natural but an artificial creation – a metaphor and a symbol. Romantic love stands quite simply for the triumph of art over nature. It is a result of the metamorphosis the heart undergoes in the medieval period.

In the Middle Ages the heart becomes divided and man acquires two hearts. In Greek Antiquity man had several hearts with different names and qualities. What they had in common was that all were experienced as being concrete and physical. In the Middle Ages the symbolic heart gradually separates off from the physical. Heart and love become one, but not in the sense that heart and courage belong to each other. The heart is not the organ of love in a physical sense but a symbol and a synonym for love. Love is not bound by the heartbeat. It belongs to the non-physical heart with which it is identical and is, then, an artificial or specifically literary product. When love and eroticism are called *heart*, they are released from taboo and become less offensive for many people, enabling them to speak more freely about it. This was an advantage not only for singers but for lovers.

Behind this metaphorization of the heart there lies an older cult of the heart based on the magic power of the heart and blood. To enter into a blood fellowship by mixing blood was a variant of the heart-magic that placed the parties under an absolute obligation until death. The oath of allegiance, when the knight fell on one knee in front of his lady and swore allegiance to her with his hand on his heart, replaces an older ritual exchange of hearts where his heart was to beat within her breast and hers within his, so that what the one felt the other did likewise – as Héloïse did towards Abélard. But the idea of the exchange of hearts survived as an expression for mutual love. When Tristan and Isolde have to part after a night of love in secret, Isolde exclaims: 'My body remains here, you take my heart with you'.[7] This concept that the hearts of the lovers become one in perfect love is found in both religious and secular literature. The Church also promotes the ideal of the inseparable marriage, the hearts of the faithful marriage partners becoming one, *duo in corde uno*. This concept has been inspired by Bernard's understanding of the meeting between the soul and Jesus as one between bride and bridegroom, who become one in love.

One of the romances by Chrétien de Troyes, *Cligès*, has to do with precisely this exchange of hearts, and contains long discussions as to what it means to give one's heart to another person. Emotions and reflecting on emotions thus provide a new approach to a knowledge of human nature. The ritual exchange of hearts is also an expression of empathy. In the age of chivalry, this exchange – really an expression for a fusing of hearts – could be mediated ritually or symbolically by a kiss. The kiss sealed the fusion of the hearts, making the knight particularly susceptible to his lady's emotions, which he felt and answered as if his own. It is here that the new literature and courtly love come in, making the heart the symbol of (sensual) love. The narrow, erotic interpretation the kiss has nowadays becomes easier to understand when we know it has its origins in romantic love, as illustrated in the following representative verse from the time of Richard the Lionheart:

> Soft caresses can well sweeten/heartache and distress,
> But our lips should they be meeting/mean my certain death,
> Sorrow only brought the kiss/healing only she can give
> I will die lest with a new one/she my lips enflame.

As a rule, the kiss was the first and last bodily contact the knight had with his lady. The rest was courtship and art. In this sublimation it is reasonable that love itself, with the heart as its metaphor, becomes the prime motif for art. In this the heart was supplemented by a whole series of increasingly finely graded images and allegorical forms. Of these the flower and the rose were foremost. Love also gains other metaphorical attributes, poetic birds such as the nightingale and the lark, but primarily the rose – as reflected in the title of the popular thirteenth-century work *Le Roman de la Rose* (*The Novel of the Rose*). Once again, there is an echo of Arab influence, with the rose as the prime attribute of the heart.

Le Roman de la Rose is really an erotic manual that presents courtly love allegorically, written by Guillaume de Lorris in the years 1230–45. The book depicts the obstacles a young man comes across when he forces an entry into garden of love to pluck the beautiful rose (young woman) who is in the process of coming into full flower. The young man is not allowed to pluck his rose: 'Only look, but do not touch' is the message of this unfinished text. But when Jean de Meung wrote the second part of the book a decisive generation later, in the years 1270–85, the young man is allowed to pluck his rose. It is also worth noting that love has now moved outside the castle and into a garden where 'Nature' and 'Genesis' (the original, i.e. the 'right') reign. Now once more it is the natural, cosmic powers that reign, as in Antiquity, in accordance with the new insights that were being disseminated via the newly established universities, especially in Paris. The goal for love is no longer a married woman either, but a beautiful young woman that the young man can marry.

This latter version of the *Roman de la Rose* represents a strong attack on both Christian love and courtly love with its hypocrisy, affected jealousy and false courtship, provoked insanity and harmful suppression of natural love. Against all this, the author argues in favour of 'true' love, with friendship and respect between the two who love each other. And sexuality is not sinful either, but natural. God and nature are united once more.

Of particular interest from our point of view is the fact that Amor with his arrows now re-appears, precisely as an allegorical expression of passion. And now the arrow is pointing straight at the heart – in order to set it blissfully aglow – whether the fire be erotic or religious. That various different types of arrows make their appearance in the *Roman de la Rose* does not invalidate this principle. Thus the symbolism of the heart becomes complete. Around 1300 the synthesis of human and divine love reaches a new high-water mark in the new Italian writing, in *dolce stil nuovo*, where Dante is the supreme master (cf. *Purgatory*, XXIV: 52–7). For him too the noble heart, *cor gentil*, is the source of both love and inspiration.

When pictorial art flourishes once more, culminating in the oil paintings of the Renaissance, the heart and other motifs are there – not least the naked body – for the presentation of the new man. It is in the High Middle Ages and the Renaissance that our European hearts are really formed. When Martin Luther wants to choose a seal as proof of his true identity, he confirms his identity as a child of his time via his images: he chooses a cross in a gleaming heart (sun analogy) let into a rose-flower. All in one! Our identity lies in our images and symbols. For man is a being of symbols who lives in a universe of symbols. Thus it is impossible to separate our image of the universe and our universe of images. The heart is identical with the images we have of it at any given time.

With Romanticism, the symbolism of the heart becomes complete, corresponding to modern emotional life, which becomes naturalized at the same pace as the images become perceived as expressions for something given. The actual relation, which is anti-romantic, is forgotten: it is images and symbols that, once created, also shape our emotional life. It is precisely this which is the magical thing about language, and artificial symbolic language, it creates what it names. Words become magic formulae. Images and symbols create a code that makes it possible to transmit love and emotions at the same time as these emotions are shaped by precisely these symbols. But without the code most of these emotions would not have existed, according to German philosopher Niklas Luhmann.[8]

The oldest culture of the heart is that of the ancient Egyptians, where the properties of the heart determined whether the deceased could rise from the dead in a paradise beyond this life. The most widespread symbol of the heart was the *scarabee*, which is found in a vast range of forms, from stone and precious metal to this beautiful mosaic from the grave of Tutankhamun.

This vase image of the bound Prometheus from the 6th century BC is an early expression of what the heart (more accurately the liver at that time) symbolizes. According to the myth, it was Prometheus who created humankind, teaching it many arts and imparting knowledge. He also gave it fire, having stolen this from the Olympian gods. As a punishment, he was bound to a rock in the Caucasus, where a vulture (the eagle of Zeus) pecked at his heart/liver. There was no end to his suffering, for every night the wound healed, which the vulture could then peck away at again the following day. Knowledge, punishment and suffering were thus intertwined in this myth cycle, something we also recognize from the biblical myth of the Fall.

The Greeks were aware that erotic love had several dimensions or levels, from the animal to the divine, without this realization – as in Christianity – leading to a downgrading of eroticism, here illustrated by Aphrodite together with the small, flying figure of Eros and the wild Pan, the principal representative of animal desires. Sculpture from *c.* 100 BC.

Aztec sacrifice of the heart on a temple pyramid, a drawing of the 16th century. The Aztecs tore the hearts out of thousands of young men as sacrifices to the sun god. The Spanish conquistadors reacted with a brutality rarely rivalled in human history.

The Aztecs were not unique in performing heart sacrifices. They inherited both gods and heart sacrifice from the Mayas and their conquered predecessors. Here in a drawing from the Toltec period, a bound prisoner of war is having his heart cut out with a flint knife.

Are we really able to understand the emotions of those who sacrificed to the warlike Thor and Freyr, the god of crops, and gave human sacrifices to Odin, the god of the dead. When we compare these gods from Norse mythology with contemporary pictures of Christ and later ones from the age of chivalry in the medieval period, we can sense we are dealing with two completely different pictures of humanity and the world.

In all mysticism the heart is the medium for the divine. In Islam and Sufism, the transformation of the heart is a prerequisite for becoming part of the divine. That the divine force and flow of the heart is something objective, lit by a spirit that comes over a person, is expressed in this picture of the flowering heart from religious Arabic art.

It is commonly held that love was invented during the age of chivalry in the High Middle Ages, first as a literary motif, with the heart as symbol, in the literature of the troubadours. During the age of chivalry, the written romance and the troubadour songs could both release love and replace the physical conquest of woman, weapon in hand, by refined behaviour and courting.

The heart was the image used in the High Middle Ages to signify that two persons shared the same feelings for each other. Two who loved each other could therefore give each other their heart in a ritual exchange, as portrayed in the courtly romance *Cligès* by Chrétien de Troyes, and in this book illustration from the 13th century.

Detail from Leonardo da Vinci, *Leda and the Swan*, 1510, oil on canvas. One of the most sensual pictures of the Renaissance. Few Renaissance artists can rival Leonardo in uniting the concretely sensual with the sublime. By means of his allegorical figures, he suggests what the theme is all about, with the erect and insistent neck and warmly embracing wing of the courting swan indicating what love between a man and a woman is. Here, sexuality is not conveyed as sinful (even though we are dealing with infidelity and seduction) but as something divine and as the quintessence of the joys of life. The picture refers to the myth of the seducer Zeus, who in the guise of a swan rises out of the water and embraces the bathing Leda (the goddess of nymphs), beautiful wife of the Spartan king Tyndareos. Thus the divinely beautiful Helen is conceived. She is so erotically attractive that – even though so fateful – it is beyond all morality to seduce her, as the Trojan prince Paris does.

Allegory of Venus, Cupid, Insanity and Time (*c*. 1546, oil on canvas) by Agnolo Bronzino illustrates the leap in form and content from Greek via Roman Antiquity to the Renaissance. In the Renaissance, love is depicted more intimately, sensually and anthropomorphically than in Antiquity. Here pleasure is centre-stage in a different way than in Antiquity, while the realistically sensual aspect becomes ambiguous because of the aesthetic stylization and the loaded allegorical context, which includes a reminder that everything goes the way of the flesh, by the linking of passion and insanity, time and death.

Passion, suffering and compassion. This oil painting by Pieter Paul Rubens, *The Descent from the Cross* from 1616–17, brings out with strong, expressive means the various aspects of Christian love. The realism is so powerful that it almost overshadows the allegorical depiction of the sacrament. The picture shows that blood originally had the place the heart gradually acquired in much Christian emblematics. Blood is also able in a more spectacular and dramatic way to illustrate suffering and affliction as a necessary aspect of both love and passion. These dissimilar aspects of love are illustrated by the persons who loved Jesus best – all having physical contact with him and almost drinking his blood (the sacrament). His mother stands for compassion. Mary Magdalene, in her richly coloured clothes, stands for erotic love and is kissing the hand of the one she loves. The artist has given her a strikingly central position, with bright colours that contrast with Jesus. The third person, the mediator John whom Jesus loved, represent the love Socrates called *philia*, friendship.

Augustine by Bartolomé Esteban Murillo (1618–82), oil on canvas. The picture reveals what transformations the heart has been through since Antiquity. Here, Amor with his arrows is portrayed as the child Jesus, as a follower of Mary as Eros is of Aphrodite. Amor's arrows do not point at the heart in Antiquity. It is only in the High Middle Ages, the Renaissance and, in particular, the Baroque that this becomes a favourite motif, for example Bernini's sculpture the *Ecstasy of St Theresa*, who is transported after having been struck in the heart by an arrow from Christ as angel/Amor.

In the Baroque period, Christian blood symbolism literally bursts its banks. Symbolism of blood and heart peaks in Gian Lorenzo Bernini's art. Less well known than Bernini's *Ecstasy of St Theresa* is this oil painting *The Blood of Christ* from 1699, made by François Spierre after a corresponding drawing by Bernini. The pious Bernini believed that he could literally have his sins washed away and be cleansed in a sea of Christ's blood.

The Jesuits cultivated the heart as an image of divine love, suffering and salvation, as depicted in this spectacular picture, *The Worship of Christ's Holy Heart with St Ignatius Loyola and Aloysius Gonzaga* by José de Páez (1720–90), oil on canvas. It must be one of the paradoxes of history that this example of the Spanish cultivation of the symbol of the Christian heart was painted in Mexico, where the heart was to bleed in profusion in one way or the other before, during and after the conquests of the Spanish conquistadors in the 16th century.

In the 1890s, Edvard Munch (1863–1944) was one of the first European artists to give an expressionistic, modernist image of complex human nature, split between the forces of light and darkness, between life-giving and irrational and destructive passions. He also theoretically formulated a view of humanity with different centres of desire, with the heart at the centre as an image of the emotions. An artistic expression of this 'theory' is *The Separation* (1896), where the bloody hand becomes an image of the heart and all it represents emotionally and erotically. The picture is a counterpart to Henry Holliday's 'harmonious' picture of Dante (from 1883), who takes his hand to his pounding heart on the one occasion he meets the pure, white Beatrice in the street in Florence.

Henri Matisse: 'Icarus', illustration from *Jazz* (1947). With simple strokes, this brilliant artist shows that everything in human life has to do with the heart. The print (after a paper cutout) alludes to the myth of Icarus who, inspired by the glow of the heart and his own creativeness, rises up towards the divine. From pride at being able to defeat the forces of gravity by means of his artificial wings of wax, he rises yet higher, but comes too close to the sun and falls when his wings melt. But this picture is not called 'The Fall of Icarus', merely *Icarus*. It was made during the Second World War, but is just as topical now in today's insane wars, and the sun has been replaced by stars that remind one most of exploding grenades that strike the heart. The glowing heart is a bleeding, suffering heart. Icarus is a martyr of the infringement of power and human misrule, of what Nietzsche calls spirits of gravity which kill creative forces and cause everything good to fall.

In folk art, too, the heart is one of the most widespread symbols. Here a belt buckle with fine filigree work placed on an apron band from a traditional woman's costume from Telemark, Norway. The short collar from a man's costume is from Bø in Telemark, from 1830.

Along with this metaphorization of the heart and the development of the language of the heart in the medieval period there is an upgrading of the senses. Philosophy (via nominalism), the growth of science and art all contributed to giving the sensual its rightful place in human life – once again contrary to the Church's assessment of the sensual. In troubadour literature it is subjective feelings and the senses that both reveal and open up for love. And it is, in particular, sight – the sight of the handsome, courageous knight in his courtly behaviour and the refined, beautiful maiden – that lights the erotic glow and longing in the noble heart. Even in translation the first lines of a song by the great troubadour Guiraut de Borneilh (1138–c. 1200) bring out the new role of the sense of sight.[9]

> So, through the eyes love attains the heart:
> For the eyes are the scouts of the heart
> And the eyes go reconnoitring
> For what it would please the heart to possess.

A new world opens up for those who dare defy the Church's condemnation of the sensual, a world of wonderful sights and exciting smells, of gracious bodies with soft forms, warm bodies and arms that long to embrace each other and share the burning glow with each other. It was this longing for the corporeal and sensually seductive love that was released by the troubadour literature. This release often led out into the temple of nature, away from the stifled and stifling rooms of the religious institutions. Once again, the age of chivalry anticipates Romanticism, with its worship of paradise-like Nature. In nature's groves there are soft couches for love trysts beneath sheltering branches and a wide, open sky. During this period, *al fresco* takes on a new meaning, one that explains some of the popularity of the *Tristan* romance and the song 'Unter den Linden' by the greatest German troubadour Walter von der Vogelweide (c. 1170–1230).

Courtly love not only functions as a liberation of emotional energy but also of power of expression. This process of emancipation points forwards towards the Enlightenment and, in particular, Romanticism. The emotional turn in the age of chivalry is a precondition for the expressivist turn of Romanticism, which claims that man only really comes into being when he expresses himself and, especially, his feelings. In that sense, there is a direct line from the troubadour songs via the Romantic period to our own age, to the Hippie movement of the 1960s and flower power with its slogan 'Make love, not war', which challenges all fundamentalism that threatens eternal bodily torment in hell or promises the self-named

martyrs and 'true believers' an eternal life in some fictive place. In troubadour literature and courtly literature in the twelfth and thirteenth century
there is only one world and one happiness, the one the lovers experience
here and now.

But this love ideal is so total and thus totalitarian that it does not
always offer room for other images next to it. By depicting this culturally
determined passion as something natural, eternal and unchanging, however, it is raised above all debate and given pride of place before all other
images and forms of love. The one who has nature on his side has always
the competitive edge – this applies not only in evolution but also in
rhetoric. Tristanism's insistence on being natural is the background for
the success it has enjoyed in our cultural circles, contrary to the teaching
of the Church of self-restraint.

What Christianity and religions represent in practice in their system-
atized power can be seen from the counter-reactions that met the popular
and emotional emancipatory movements of the Middle Ages: the Inquisition, heresy and condemnation to eternal torment. Dissidents and
'unbelievers' are always persecuted – in the name of the 'True God', as
injustice and misuse of power always invokes when calling on God and
morality. 'Holy' war and witch trials are always directed against those who
have a different view of the body and a different view of heaven and hell
(while life here on earth is overlooked). Fundamentalists, power-seekers and
moralists are always against laughter. That is why freedom – and truth –
always has to do with the release of the body and of laughter. Official
Christianity never found an equal balance between body and soul and
never managed to release the laughter that liberates the body in the
Homeric *asbestos gelos*. Solemnity prevails. This applies not least in relation to homosexuality, which the Church has condemned from the High
Middle Ages and since the Reformation, at the same time as the Church's
struggle to combat the lusts of the flesh via the establishing of closed institutions, monasteries and nunneries came to promote homosexuality in
Europe. This could even take place with ecclesiastical blessing. St Aelred
of Rivaulx praised homosexuality as a way of investigating divine love.[10]
And Richard the Lionheart was neither less pious nor warlike because of
his homosexual tendencies.

STORIES OF EVERYDAY LOVE

The ideal love of the age of chivalry was absolutely heterosexual and so
contributed to the cultivation of virtues that were exclusively male and
female. Trivial erotic love is another story. Chivalrous friendship

between men was not always all that chivalrous in sexual matters. And single-gender chaste life among men in monasteries was not always all that virtuous. It is one of history's paradoxes that the same Church that condemns homosexuality actually helps to create it with its closed institutions. This unofficial story not only provides food for thought, morally and culturally speaking, but is also a reminder that perhaps there is not anything 'natural' about human erotic love and that moralism does not serve morality. Unless one should say that medieval homosexuality demonstrates what happens when the natural body is suppressed and is denied what is its right. This can be seen from the Church's own archives, from the wealth of material that was collected about people, including their sex lives, by the Inquisition over a period of several centuries.

One of the classics of the history of mentalities is Emmanuel le Roy Ladurie's *Montaillou: Cathars and Catholics in a French Village, 1294–1324* (1975). Ladurie has first-hand sources about the village of Montaillou in the Pyrenees, namely the protocols of the inquisitor Jacques Fournier, who later became pope in Avignon, where he also took his protocols. The reason for the Inquisition in Montaillou was the heresy of the Cathars, a variant of the Albigensian heresy. The Cathars were influenced by Greek Manichaeism and believed in the transmigration of souls. Their teaching was strictly dualistic, since they viewed the visible world as a form of decay and the work of the devil. A paradoxical side-effect of this view was that it did not matter much what one's attitude was towards sensual, earthly life, including the sexual. There are certain such heretical interpretations to be found in Montaillou. So Fournier carries out a judicial interrogation of the inhabitants of the village, concerning their everyday lives in matters great and small – not least their sex lives.

What Fournier can report about love life in Montaillou diverged radically from official medieval morality. It also diverged from the high-tension love ideal of courtly literature, which had left its mark. In Montaillou we encounter trivial stories of everyday love – with all its virtues and vices. Here, love came down to earth, where people live their earthly lives in a pragmatic compromise between the demands of the body and the dogmatic demands of the Church. Sex life in Montaillou was by no means a taboo subject, and a large number of the inhabitants were sexually active across the official norms, before and outside marriage in one way or another, late or early, in the middle of the day rather than the middle of the night, with relatives as well as with young girls before marriage. And among the clergy, homosexuality – sodomy as Fournier calls it – was widespread. The biggest womanizer, the *bayle* of the village was its priest, Pierre Clergue, who was influenced by the heresy.

One of the women heard by the inquisitor, Grazide Rives, was a relative of this Pierre. With her mother's silent consent, he seduced Grazide when she was 14–15 years old. According to Grazide's own explanation it had not been rape. She explains herself how things had been:

> Afterwards [after the defloration in the barn during the harvesting] he continued to know me carnally until the following January . . . It happened chiefly during the daytime. After that, in January, the priest gave me as wife to my late husband, Pierre Lizier; and after he had thus given me to this man, the priest continued to know me carnally, frequently, during the remaining four years of my husband's life. My husband knew about it, and was consenting. (158)

What is interesting from our point of view is how Grazide experiences this sinful life with a man she does *not* love, where she makes herself guilty of incest, according to the norms of the time, and infidelity, etc. Without having read any courtly literature, which was widespread at the time, she uses words in her court hearing that are reminiscent of courtly literature:

> She employs the same tone as the *Brévaire d'amour* and the *Flamenca*: 'A lady who sleeps with a true lover is purified of all sins . . . the joy of love makes the act innocent, for it proceeds from a pure heart.' She went further: *With Pierre Clergue, I liked it. And so it could not displease God. It was not a sin.* (159)

According to Ladurie, it is not first and foremost courtly literature that explains why she does not know guilt but her background in Occitan culture, where there was a considerable degree of sexual tolerance. Only when desire was lacking on her part would sexual intercourse with the priest be a sin. It was the joint desire to consummate their passion that guaranteed that the relationship was innocent.

The case of Grazide shows that human hearts and emotional life are culturally defined in form and function. When Grazide, on the basis of common Christian norms, can make the dramatic assertion that she did not sin with Pierre but acted from a pure heart, it simply shows how relative emotional life is. Grazide's heart would seem to be a function not merely of her sexual desire and lust but also of her cultural background.

Homosexuality is a striking example that neither is something natural nor eternally unchanging for the cultural being *homo sapiens*. For in the village of Montaillou as elsewhere in rural areas homosexuality was not widespread. In the High Middle Ages it was an urban phenomenon, specially linked to and created in the religious institutions:

Fournier's register is categorical on one point: whatever the origins of the young person concerned, sodomy meant the city. Arnaud claimed that *in Pamiers there are over a thousand people infected with sodomy . . .* So much for the town. In the Occitan village, the range of cultural behaviour was less varied, and rural homosexuality was not a problem (147, 149).

One homosexual in Montaillou was Arnaud de Verniolles, a subdeacon and Minorite monk who had been excluded from the order for having infringed the rules. It was the son of a knight, with whom he had shared a bed for several weeks at a school in Pamiers, who was the direct cause of Arnaud having become homosexual. This experience had activated a latent tendency, sufficient for Arnaud to become an active but not notorious homosexual, one who with great success seduced youths between 16 and 18 years of age. This did not always take place in chivalrous fashion. 'It took place on a dungheap (there was one in nearly every courtyard in Pamiers, as in Montaillou)' (147).

Arnaud's culturally determined homosexual desire is not particularly heartfelt, nor is it at a more profound emotional level. He did not experience any love in his homosexual relationships, despite his literal knowledge of it through, for instance, Ovid and the tolerance he encountered as a homosexual. In his testimony he says practically nothing about what he felt for his friends. There Christianity had set a definitive boundary.

The case of Arnaud shows that officially acceptable love opens up only two views of homosexuality: perversity (and crime) or primitive desire, both of which were a sin in the Middle Ages. It also seems as if Arnaud himself sees his sexual inclination as being a personal deficiency. That would explain why he apparently does not harbour any of the feelings that would have been 'natural' in such a relationship in the present day. Arnaud defies official Christian morality just as much as Grazide. But her motivation for her acts is more in line with the erotic ideas of the age of chivalry: when both parties gain joy from the erotic contact, it cannot be a sin. Both Arnaud and Grazide and many like them did what they felt like doing, as people have always done. But when this subjective desire can be used as a general justification of something that officially is viewed as a sin, it shows that a new age has arrived. Europe is entering an era where the personal subject acquires a completely different status than previously. Without such a subjectivism and the right to think for oneself independently of all authorities neither the scientific revolution nor the Renaissance would have been possible. At the same time, however, the old continues to exist. Europe is and remains a Christian culture. These tensions between the old and the new were especially obvious in the dualism that seems to survive all eras and turns in European culture. The Renaissance is not an exception. There, dualism and the new subjective thinking would seem to reinforce each other.

CHAPTER 9

The New Subject

The greatest intelligence and the warmest heart
cannot co-exist in one and the same person.
Nietzsche

It is frequently said that modern man is a product of the Renaissance. And this is of course true if one takes art, philosophy and the scientific and technical revolution as one's point of departure. A new outward, expansive attitude towards life asserts itself, one which leads to Europeans discovering the rest of the world, conquering and destroying other civilizations. But the prerequisites for this lie in the High Middle Ages and the emotional turn. And behind them, in turn, lies Augustine, who set the whole process in motion.

The most important result of Augustine's life and work from a history of mentalities perspective is a psychological internalization of the forces that the human mind knows it is exposed to. It takes several hundred years, however, before the mentality that Augustine represents makes its mark in terms of culture. In many ways he is isolated in his understanding of the inner, mental life of his age. This means that the process of self-awareness with emphasis on the inner life that we have been following from Odysseus via Socrates and Plato to Augustine goes underground for several centuries before re-emerging in the period after 1050. Then, the emphasis is once more on the inner life, with repentance (*contritio*) a key mental concept.

The Christian culture of confession accelerates during the twelfth and thirteenth century. In 1215, the Church decrees that everyone must go to private confession at least once a year. Medieval man, because of confession, was obliged to say 'I' and 'my' the whole time: it is *my* fault (*mea culpa*), my sinful thoughts call for an acknowledgment of 'myself' all the way if I am to be able to gain peace and redemption for *my* soul, etc. This places focus on the inner self and creates a new subjective self-understanding and increased individualization of the Western mentality.

The central perspective in painting that emerges in the fifteenth century is an illustrative example of the new way of seeing and perceiving the world. The new linear conception of time, with the carrot dangling ahead, pulls in the same direction, making it possible for the individual from his present-time perspective to realize that things have not always been as they are now, and that the future does not have to mean apocalyptic annihilation and a Day of Judgement but may mean greater material and mental happiness here on this earth. Not that medieval man thought in terms of historical and personal development – that only arrived in full strength with Romanticism and Hegel. But inherent in linear time is the idea of progressive development. Most of what is new in modernity is, paradoxically enough, a product of Christianity as a mode of thinking and being: focus on the individual soul, selfacknowledgement – even in the form of self-confession and consciousness of sin – and the linear perception of time as a basis for rational planning are all Christian ideas.

In the Middle Ages concepts of personal and individual guilt became a central idea in Western culture, which is a culture of guilt and not of shame (as were the Greek, Norse and Arabic). Collective guilt is not part of our legal system. Our entire way of viewing responsibility, morality and integrity comes from the Christian Middle Ages. Guilt is the secular or common variant of what Christianity refers to as sin. Since all sin in Christianity must be acknowledged and confessed, this places an enormous load on the process of self-consciousness. Self-awareness becomes quite simply a part of ethics, as expressed in such a wise, fine way in the subtitle of Abélard's ethics: *Know thyself.* For God sees everything. Perhaps we can fool our fellow humans, secular powers and the legal system, but not God – and not ourselves (even though that is precisely what we do, according to Freud, when consciousness of the self makes demands that are too great).

Historical changes normally take a long time, especially those that have to do with human mentality. They are often rather like diseases that have a long incubation period. The seed has been sown, a potential latent, just waiting for the right conditions to unfold when the time is ripe. That is what happens in the Renaissance when the forces that had been gathered during the High Middle Ages unfold in expansive, self-assertive acts at all cultural levels. The implosion of inwardly directed medieval energy has reached a limit of pressure and now explodes. Everything is turned inside out. In the long term, this leads to a fragmentation or even dissolution of the soul in a Christian sense.

Despite a new understanding of the body and brain resulting from anatomical research, the Renaissance is also a culture of the heart. More than that, the Renaissance opens up a new understanding of the heart, since it was anatomy with the dissection of the human body that was a pioneer discipline in the scientific revolution. Initially, however, these anatomical insights lead to an intensification of the opposition between body and soul rather than to a resolution of the dualism.

DESCARTES AND THE DUALISM OF BODY AND SOUL

Ever since Plato, all reflection concerning man has had either the *soul* or the *body* as its point of departure. Furthermore, it seems as if all those who take the soul with its rationality as their starting point are dualists, whereas those who start with the body are not. This also applies to the Renaissance and the two key spokesmen to be presented here, the philosopher René Descartes (1596–1650), who was a dualist, and the body-oriented essayist Michel de Montaigne, who was not. We begin with the former, since he represents the philosophical tendency that 'won' in terms of the history of ideas, while Montaigne in a two-fold sense represents the undercurrent of intellectual history, one that goes from Homer and the cynic Diogenes in the barrel to the popular carnival culture of the Middle Ages and the first short-story writer, Boccaccio, the grotesque realist Rabelais and the essayist Montaigne in the Renaissance.

A possible starting point for the analysis of dualism can be the close connection between the soul and the heart, where the soul is conventionally placed in a live human being. But when that being dies, popular belief imagines that the soul leaves the body in order to try to reach the other life, a life beyond this world with our earthly nature of flesh and blood. This idea of two universes is the Christian basis for the dualism that operates in Western culture. Christianity not only established a dualism between the other world and this world, between the spirit and the body of the senses, but also between good and evil, represented by the symbolic absolutes 'God' and 'Satan'. Such a fundamentalist understanding of Evil has led to much evil – in the name of Good. The different variants of dualism have led Westerners into many dilemmas, not only in terms of the history of ideas but also in politics, practical pedagogy and existential ethics. So dualism is still a real challenge, not least because this mode of thinking still maintains a strong hold on medicine, science and technology – even though practically no one would defend dualism theoretically or philosophically nowadays.

That medicine, after Dr Barnard's first heart transplantation in 1967, is actually capable of transplanting a heart from one human being to another, tells us something about how we perceive the heart. The transplantation of a heart from somebody else makes it impossible to place the human soul in the heart. Knowing that the heart is a muscle that pumps blood round the body is not unimportant as regards how we view the emotional heart. It is one of the great paradoxes of Western culture how dualism survives the scientific revolution of the Renaissance – and long after the Renaissance continues to dominate our self-conception. This has something to do with the defining power of language and with what is required to establish alternative definitions and images. The medical history of the heart is in itself a good example of this.

In the Renaissance, dualism is scientifically strengthened by Galileo's physics of the universe, which Descartes – and later Kant, based on Newton – legitimizes philosophically. René Descartes is important in this context because instead of doing away with dualism after the scientific revolution he attempts to reconcile Christianity with the new science by means of explanations that are scientifically and philosophically valid. He succeeds to the extent that through him dualism enjoys a new lease of life – *post mortem*, so to speak – thanks to its being linked to Christianity. Descartes distinguishes between science (i.e. natural science) and religion. He does this by connecting the exclusively human ability to think (*res cogitans*) to the soul as what makes it fundamentally different from the body, which can only be understood scientifically as nature and matter (*res extensa*).

Just how important this distinction is can be illustrated by Descartes' conception of the body as a mechanical clock. When the concrete body becomes inferior and is reduced to mechanical matter, thought is pushed in the direction of pure abstraction. Correspondingly, the modern subject according to Descartes is to be defined as having self-consciousness and a rational ability to reflect, as expressed in his axiom: *Cogito ergo sum – I think, therefore I exist*. This marks the great watershed in the self-image of Western individuals, one that deeply affects us. The strong focus on the self-sufficient *ego* in various forms dates from this point, as do words for consciousness and self-consciousness. The English philosopher John Locke uses consciousness for the first time in its modern sense in 1689. The entire philosophical tradition since Descartes has to deal with the idea of man as having a rational self-consciousness, *cogito*, German *Selbstbewusstsein*. All this expresses the fact that the Westerner now sees the world from the inside.

But Descartes himself is not unambiguous in his dualism between body and soul, subject and object, consciousness and matter. It is still one of the great curiosities of the history of ideas how Descartes, contrary to his own dualism, declares that the connection and interaction he could actually see existed between body and thought (via a small gland in the brain, *glandula pinealis*). It is also a paradox that the father of the self-conscious subject of modern rationality can also be seen as the father of modern emotionalism because of his great work on the passions, *Les passions de l'Âme* (The Passions of the Soul), of 1649. The title is worth a study in itself, as it demonstrates the dilemma of dualism. *The Passions of the Soul* gives the impression that emotions are something that impassion the otherwise rational soul, almost 'animating' it with something irrational. Consequently the task of reason will be to oppose the emotions that are making the soul passive and receptive to the non-rational sensations. Values – since they not are objective – are also rejected by Descartes as something inferior that confuse rational reason.

The heart does not gain any central place in Descartes' categorization of the passions, i.e. the emotions, since the (spiritual) passions in his interpretation belong to the rational soul. So the heart is presented in physiological terms as a generator of heat that maintains warmth in the brain as well as in the body. Descartes' view of the heart, though he respectfully refers to 'Harvey's opinion concerning the circulation of the blood', still has elements of Galen. He is thus able to assert,

> that while we live there is a continual heat in our heart, which is a species of fire that the venous blood maintains in it, and that this fire is the bodily principle of all the movements of our members . . . It is also this alone that gives the blood its motion, and make it flow ceaselessly with great rapidity in all the arteries and veins, by means of which it carries the heat it acquires in the heart to all other parts of the body, and serves as their sustenance.[1]

Since the spiritual emotions belong to the soul, animals do not have such emotions, since they lack a soul (rational consciousness). They can therefore be dissected even when alive. For pain – like joy – is something only experienced by beings with a soul. Other sensations and feelings come from the 'animal spirits' of body and function in a practical (mechanical) way, but they only mean something if perceived mentally. The dilemma of dualism can also be illustrated via the heart-brain relations in Descartes, asserting that 'in all the body the soul can have no other place than this gland' in the brain, where he places the soul's ability to think, in line with the anatomy of the Renaissance, where the brain is very much part of the body.

The distinction between emotions and thoughts remains unclear in anthropology in the century after Descartes. For the soul, which he sees as having the ability to reason, had previously been traditionally placed in the region of the heart, and was as such integrated in emotional life. This is expressed in the well-known statement by Pascal, Descartes' younger contemporary: 'The heart has its reasons, which reason knows not of' ('Le cœur a ses raisons, que la raison ne connaît point'). Pascal, by the way, was spokesman for a mystically oriented *theologia cordis* that gave the heart the ability to know God. Descartes, however, laconically states that the opinion of those who think the soul receives it passions in the heart, is not worth considering. Medically speaking, he is way ahead of his time when he claims that 'it is easy to observe that this alteration [passion] is felt in the heart only by the mediation of a little nerve descending to it from the brain'.[2] Luther, however, was in line with Pascal when he emphasizes that reason is hot, not cold as rationalists have always claimed.

The important – and in my opinion correct – thing about Descartes' concept of the soul from a present-day perspective is that he links the soul to our use of reason and our conscious choices. The pre-Cartesian concept of the soul sees it as something substantial, almost on a par with the heart. The soul, though, is not a bodily organ, rather the expression of personal integrity that comes as a result of our thoughts and our consciousness, our attitudes and actions. When these cohere to form an integrity where theory and practice correspond, we also get an integrity in a moral and personal sense. A stab of pain to the heart registers a break in the integrity we otherwise experience when over time we live in accordance with our deepest thoughts and attitudes. So Descartes is right when he links the soul to conscious thought, for the soul is our own work and responsibility. In focusing on the capacity to think as a subjective venture and the basis of a person's existence there is also implicitly a normative demand to make use of this capacity: *Think for yourself!* In making such appeal, Descartes is part of the anti-authoritarian project that the Renaissance represented, with a quite exceptional release of creative forces in many countries.

In many ways, Descartes appears on the scene *post factum* and puts things into place, since he explains epistemologically or methodologically what has already taken place – in the High Middle Ages and in the Renaissance. Others who break free of Christian dogma in the Renaissance and contribute to establishing a modern image of man – on other premises than Descartes – are Pico della Mirandola and, especially, Montaigne. Both are important from our perspective, because they are the foremost spokesmen in the Renaissance of the tradition of self-expression.

CHAPTER 10

Montaigne: Man is his Own Work

It is bad enough to powder the face
if one is not to powder the heart also.
Michel de Montaigne

In the Renaissance, the Sophist theory of the instability of man also enjoyed a renaissance, culminating in homage to the self-made man. When the geocentric view of the world that the Catholic Church defended collapsed, so did the theocentric view of man, with man making himself creator in an anthropocentric universe. This is precisely what the well-known and papally condemned speech by Pico della Mirandola (1463–1494) deals with. *De dignitate hominis* (On Human Dignity) talks about creating oneself in one's own image. Just as the Renaissance engineer was to reform outer nature by developing the technical aids for doing so, man was to form his own nature. In his speech Pico claimed that even if God has created man, he has created him undetermined, without any special form or function, and not assigned him any particular place in the world. Nor is there anything that holds man back from determining his nature for himself, using the free will he has been given.

Alongside Pico, Michel de Montaigne (1533–1592) is the central name in the Renaissance tradition of self-expression, following in the footsteps of the Sophists. Montaigne is important in this context because he reflects on man's nature without getting caught in the closed systems of theology and theory, relying instead on personal experiences, not least those with his own body, and on written sources from Antiquity, which also had as their point of departure what man had discovered when trusting in his own nature.

Montaigne was very much a Renaissance man, and he competes with Descartes for the title of founder of the modern subject. No one, though, can rival him as the founder of the essay genre on the basis of his three-volume work *Essais*, published in 1580 and 1588. His view of man cannot be detached from the *way* in which he wrote. Montaigne is one of the first to recognize that form and content are one. This observation in itself – that content is not given prior to or independently of form – is a death-blow to the belief that man has a given being.

The genre of the essay derives its name from the method that underlies Montaigne's self-reflections. When he writes, he abandons himself to the spontaneous idea and to chance and coincidence, allowing his thought to follow his free associations. That is how he carries out his tries and attempts – *essais* in French. And the goal Montaigne set himself with his essays was to find out who he was: 'This is purely the essay [trial] of my natural faculties, and not at all of the acquired ones . . . These are my fancies, by witch I try to give knowledge not of things, but of myself'.[1] The experimental principle that underlies Montaigne's informal attempts opens up another view of man than, for example, the formal-methodological view of Descartes, and later Kant.

The exceptional discovery Montaigne makes when attempting to find out who he is, is that the perceptions he formulates via his essayistic drafts also shape him as a person. The writing and the product of the writing form the writer. Much suggests that Montaigne begins his essayistic project of self-discovery with a classic conception that man's being is something solidly or essentially given (identical with himself) that can be apprehended via linguistic clarification and defining of concepts. But whenever he thinks he has captured the nature of man in language and found an adequate expression for it he discovers that it slips through his fingers in the actual process of formulation. He cannot clutch what is human within his grasp. The nature of language is such that each linguistic definition contains within it an opposite, which in turn opens up the indefinable in man that now has to be defined – and so on *ad infinitum*. For existence is change and movement away from that which is fixed; 'and being consists in movement and action'.[2] 'Our life is nothing but movement'.[3] This understanding, that everything is movement, is, according to Jean Starobinski's presentation in *Montaigne en mouvement* (1982),[4] the very basis of the new identity for which Montaigne is seeking. The motion that exists in everything human means that everything is change and subject to the law of transformation. In order to avoid the personal instability this involves Montaigne writes his essays. In writing, he can fix on paper something that cannot be pinned down in life as it is lived, and reconcile the opposites in dynamic patterns. That is, at any rate, what he believes to start with.

The constant motion of everything human demolishes constants to such an extent that habit, for better or worse, is the most stable thing Montaigne is capable of finding. It keeps the fleeting heart in balance in the face of all opposing impulses. But since habit is relative and culturally determined it can never become a fixed norm that regulates human emotional reactions and individuality – not until habit, by means of practice and sensible reflection, becomes an integral part of one's nature. Montaigne deduces this from his ideals, Socrates and Cato, who die without losing their composure. 'We see in the souls of these two persons . . . so perfect a habituation to virtue that it has passed into their nature'.[5] Habit and virtue, developed by repeated attempts, become the nature of the soul. With this emphasis on habit, social law, *nomos*, Montaigne, not completely unsurprisingly, comes back to a view of man found in Sophism, which in Antiquity defended what was culture-related and constructed against the universal and natural (*physis*). As an antidote to this Sophist relativism, Montaigne the pragmatist stresses the development of discernment and judgment.

It is only apparently so that nature in man represents anything constant. For each time he approaches the natural, it transpires that it has already been formed, that pure human nature does not exist. He goes so far as to say that there is no trace whatsoever of universal nature in man. He therefore draws the paradoxical conclusion that man must learn the natural from, for example, animals. For people have distorted nature with so much reasoning and reflection that it has become changing and specific for each and everyone and has lost its own unchanging and universal form; 'that fine human reason butts in everywhere, domineering and commanding, muddling and confusing the face of things in accordance with its vanity and inconsistency. Nothing is ours any more; what I call ours is a product of art', Montaigne concludes, quoting Cicero.[6] Via reason, man can contradict the universal and manipulate the naturally given so that it becomes something specific to himself.

Montaigne is one of the first in Western culture to emphasize that this second nature of man (conscious reason and will) is not true being but mere appearance and that this appearance is not a degenerated form or something unauthentic, but in actual fact is man's true being. In this, he anticipates Nietzsche. The mask is the face. An insoluble paradox in the process of human formation is that as soon as the individual seems to have found his form, the form turns against itself and reveals itself as appearance. This becomes especially clear in the linguistically formulated process of cognition, which for Montaigne is the most fundamental process of formation. At the same moment as we determine and define ourselves, we become our own work. But it is only an apparent work, since all works are artificial and can be replaced by other ones: 'What I chiefly portray is my cogitations, a shapeless subject that does not lend itself to expression in actions. It is all I can do to couch my thoughts in this airy medium of words'.7 Man only becomes real as a work that can be communicated in language. But as a being that has language, man becomes ambiguous and turns against his own expression. Via communication he compromises himself, so to speak, as a consistent being. But there are no other alternatives, as man creates works and can only show himself through the work and in the work. For that reason, Montaigne's essays are something more than a literary genre.

To counteract this instability, Montaigne emphasizes upbringing and education, since the first forming of the individual takes place in childhood as a result of parental rearing. He also has an original angle on parental love for their children: They are their work, not so much biologically as culturally. Parents have formed their children and formed their conditions for subsequently forming themselves. He is unsentimentally realistic without being cynical when he compares parents' love of their well-formed children with the craftsman's love of his work of art. For man *is* his own work is his strikingly modern conclusion: 'Wherefore each man in some sort exists in his work'.8 Man's assignment here in life is thus to form himself as a work of art: 'I have put all my efforts into forming my life. That is my trade and my work'.9 In this, Montaigne anticipates Herder and the expressivism of Romanticism, as well as Nietzsche's radical theory of self-creation.

Compared with a traditional view of man, with a belief in an inner core of being, Montaigne's finds are meagre: the inner core to which he constantly turns his gaze is empty. A lack in the perceiver and what is perceived. There is thus nothing at the centre of this inner void. Montaigne never talks about what he finds in the inner realm to which he has turned his gaze. The true ego withdraws the further his introspection seems to take him. It resists all objectivizing: 'the more I frequent myself and know myself, the more my deformity astonishes me, and the less I understand myself'.10 Here we see demonstrated the distance between classical and modern man. For Montaigne, the ego is both present in himself and yet, in some indefinable sense, also absent. Man seems to be at the mercy of the many masks with which reality and language equip him. Betrayal of the true ego is everywhere. Each unmasking creates a new mask. In this game of masks it is the body and the corporeal that offer stability and individuality to Montaigne's unstable individual.

THE TEXT OF THE BODY AND THE BODY OF THE TEXT

Montaigne would appear to be influenced to remarkably little extent by the condemnatory attitude of the medieval Christian Church towards the physical body. This has partly to do with the fact that his models are to be found in Antiquity and Graeco-Roman culture of the body. He develops his conception of the body by writing about his own (he does so very frequently) – especially his many bodily ailments. He has the rare ability to write about his illnesses and his frail body without becoming embarrassingly personal, despite traces of both hypochondria and narcissism. This has to do with his phenomenological view, which is able to lend a voice to his bodily parts and the body's own experiences, a voice that goes beyond that of the private individual. The way in which Montaigne approaches his body becomes at the same time a demonstration of his literary and scientific method, contrasting sharply with that of contemporary medical science. His view of this science is presented in his longest essay – his apology for Raymond Sebond.

Montaigne insists that his body is his own and individual, and being individual, it can never become general or universal. He always talks about 'my body', not about something general that can be subject to the universal laws of natural science. Individuals are the only ones to know their own bodies. Personality and personal identity *are* the body. And no part of the body is inferior or a lesser part of the body than any other. Each and every part of his body makes him what he is to an equal extent. Such a view of the body anticipates Nietzsche's philosophy concerning the body and the philosophical anthropology of the twentieth century which emphasized that the body perceives.

To know oneself, which is Montaigne' real aim, is to know oneself as a bodily existence. The classical metaphysical ideal (mind) is turned around to the classical physical, i.e. the corporeal: 'I study myself more than any other subject. That is my metaphysics, that is my physics'.[11] Physics becomes metaphysics, and vice versa. The cosmos of the body is the macrocosm in miniature. Cognition of the world is thus the same as sensing and sensing *through* one's body. Not until he knows his own body by sensing it will he know the world – whereas philosophers and scientists often misrepresent the senses with their abstract reasoning. Montaigne, then, shifts the perspective from capacity and factual knowledge to *sensing* – from the abstract to the concrete and sensory. It was perhaps Montaigne's implicit *sentio ergo sum* (I sense, therefore I exist) that provoked Descartes to launch his *cogito ergo sum*. For Montaigne, rational reasoning is subordinate to sensory emotion and he only evaluates himself on the basis of real sense impressions, not general concepts. Nor does he wish to separate the mental (the abilities of the mind) from the physical, which he knows best. 'But as for bodily health, no one can furnish more useful experience than I, who present it pure, not at all corrupted or altered by art or theorizing'.[12]

It is not only in terms of epistemology and anthropology that Montaigne gives the body pride of place – he also does so in terms of aesthetics. Unlike modern science, which empties the body of the psychological, he wishes to give back to the body the poetic function it has in man's self-awareness and self-determination. The sensory body is the metaphysical repertoire that makes it possible for us all to express our feelings and thoughts. Montaigne's project of writing can basically be reduced to a unifying formula that is called chiasm: The text of the body is reborn as the body of the text in the essayistic metamorphosis. To express the body is really to return to the source, since it is possible to express so many things – possibly everything that can be said – via the body, according to Starobinski's conception of Montaigne.

Not everything goes the way of the flesh that goes the way of the body, however. All the 'essays' of Montaigne can be read as drafts and projections of his own body, exfoliations and excretions of bodily awareness. He is almost Rabelaisian in his excretory metaphysics: 'Here you have, a little more decently, some excrements of an aged mind, now hard, now loose, and always undigested'.[13] But, without help from the intellect, the excretions of the body could not have assumed as attractive a form as his essays represent. That is why Montaigne also praises the mutual services that body and mind offer each other, stressing that it is necessary to process both simultaneously. And that is why he rejects dualism: 'we do wrong to tear apart a living man'.[14] That life in all its multiplicity – anthropological as well as existential – is based on mutual services is, in my opinion, one of the most attractive ideas in Montaigne's work. He seldom thinks in terms of *either or*, but in terms of *both and* – plus a little extra. Life is based on complementary relations that interact and mutually make each other and the new man possible.

It is impossible to talk about human emotions without referring to the parts of the body that house them, and the human movements they set in motion. Technically speaking, they are images one uses about the emotions, often metonyms – a type of image where a part represents the whole, or the part of the body represents what that part houses or transmits – as the parts of the body functioned for Homeric man. Which is what the heart does. And then it transpires – and this is just one of Montaigne's exceptional discoveries – that the words and images he uses to talk about his body react on the body and the body's sensations and feelings. When language has gained body via the language of the body, it reacts on the body, forming the emotions that the body can house and express. Language, especially that of art, releases emotions that are connected to the body and that set the body in motion in a way that in the next turn becomes the task of language to grasp and control, to canalize and form via new linguistic moves, concepts and images, and so on. You can call it dialectics or mutual services if you like. Both language and emotions are constantly changing streams. Images are just as polysemantic as emotions are fluid. The inter-action between the language of the heart and the heart of language, how-ever, is constant.

But that is not all. The body is something more fundamental than language and emotions. The body comes before language. A body is something we all share, since we all have a bodily existence and experience the world through our senses. We meet as bodies and experience each other as bodies. The body always forestalls us and reveals who we are. Just as speech does in language. For speech always has a voice and the mood of speech always colours its literal as well as its figurative meaning.

EROS AND THANATOS: *ARS MORIENDI*

The greatest challenge for the essayist might seem to be how, using lan-guage as a tool, he can come to grips with physical passion and sexuality. Sexual arousal is not all that easy to capture in and via language, not only because it is a natural force beyond reason but also because traditionally it is a taboo subject in culture. Montaigne breaks with this taboo, and talks frankly about what everyone is thinking but no one is talking about, espe-cially in Chapter 5 of Book III, in the essay 'On some [erotic] verses of Virgil'. Montaigne is able to talk/write so vividly about sexuality because, among other reasons, the erotic fire in the sick old man (in his forties!) is in the process of being extinguished by the cold, as he phrases it. But it flares up again at several levels in this essay, either as a recollection or in revolt against the loss of the greatest pleasure in life, in the hope of being allowed one last time more or less directly to experience the force that keeps life going (so Eros is not completely extinguished).

Erotic longing also becomes a linguistic dilemma for Montaigne in the conflict between saying and doing. First of all, words are poor consolation for the loss of consummated erotic love. But this poor man's consolation, words, is transformed by the nobleman by means of a *tour de force* into the key to love. For sexuality is itself language. Montaigne compares sexu-ality with a forbidden book, whose very prohibition makes it all the more attractive. Everyone wants to get hold of and read such a book. And everyone has access to it. For love is the hidden language, an inner script; it is the silent words whose imprint is within us all. But it is only the divine muses and the highest form of poetry that can express this force. Poetry is love's best weapon, and vice versa. Fantasy and fiction give us the full value of love. This is a central point in Montaigne: language is not only able to release love but also give it an extra value it does not possess by nature:

> But from what I understand of it, the powers and worth of this god [Eros] are more alive and animated in the painting of poetry than in their own reality, *And verses have their fingers to excite* (Juvenal). Poetry reproduces an indefinable mood that is more amorous than love itself.[15]

Via his phenomenological account of the arsenal of the body, Montaigne is able to demonstrate that language can release both natural impulses and new thoughts. And no one would deny that erotic depictions can arouse fantasies and notions, that poetry has 'itchy fingers'. This, to resort to a cheap example, is the anthropological basis of the entire porn industry. But via art man can sublimate and prolong sensual enjoyment by placing sensation in aesthetic enjoyment. Eros becomes aesthetics, comedy and play.

The best-known example in world literature of what fateful consequences itchy fingers can have is in *The Divine Comedy*. Among the very first people Dante meets in *Inferno*, doomed to eternal damnation in hell because of their sins, is a pair of lovers who have allowed themselves to be seduced by the literary depiction of love. That is at any rate the explanation the beautiful Francesca da Rimini gives of why she and her lover, her brother-in-law Paolo, have ended up in sin and hell. They had sat alone together reading *Lancelot du Lac*. All had gone well until they came to the account of the meeting between Queen Guinevere and the knight who was secretly in love with her, depicted in perhaps the best-known scene from the Comedy (Song v: 127–38), from *Hell*:

> One day, / For our delight we read of Lancelot,
> How him love thrall'd. Alone we were, and no
> Suspicion near us. Oft-times by that reading
> Our eyes were drawn together, and the hue
> Fled from our alter'd cheek. But at one point
> Alone we fell. When of that smile we read,
> The wished smile so rapturously kiss'd
> By one so deep in love, then he, who ne'er
> From me shall separate, at once my lips
> All trembling kiss'd. The book and writer both
> Were love's purveyors. In its leaves that day
> We read no more.

That Francesca blames the poet and the book and retells the courtly epic incorrectly in order to justify herself does not invalidate the point being made here, that poetry and eroticism are closely interconnected. The literary depiction of passion can function as an erotic catalyst, can couple and seduce with its itchy and exciting fingers, as was the case with Héloïse and Abélard. The poet and singer Abélard had already roused her feelings and used the books as an excuse for a continuation: 'So when we had opened our books, more words ensued about love than reading, kisses were more frequent than sentences. More often were hands guided to her breasts than to the books.'

That words in Montaigne's essays can become body or flesh is not a religious or a metaphysical thought but an anthropological triviality. Language is despite everything not able to provide an exhaustive picture of love; it covers more than it uncovers; that is why eroticized language increases the urge to uncover more and more of the love it is covering. The power of language to incarnate and sexualize cannot, according to Montaigne, be separated from the surplus of meaning that, like an aura, surrounds each word. This aura can almost bridge the gap he nearly always sees between word ('merely air') and object. He makes nature artificial at the same rate as he naturalizes art. Montaigne alternates between praising sublime love poetry (e.g. Virgil and Ovid) and insisting on the desire having pride of place in love life: 'Now then, leaving books aside and speaking more materially and simply, I find after all that love is nothing else but the thirst for sexual enjoyment in a desired object, and Venus nothing else but the pleasure of discharging our vessels'.[16]

Once again, the gap between nature and art appears, only for yet another attempt to be made to bridge it with words. Love and passion cannot be held fast; all that remains is just the memory in poetic enjoyment. Essential nature has to give way to appearance. Outer form, that of the poet and essayist, becomes the essential and most real. But mental life also withers away if the body is not involved and can vitalize the language – and vice versa. Living language incites the senses and suffuses things metaphorically; it is what gives thought flesh and blood, what rouses and stimulates the erotic urge, so that Eros is richer when expressed in terms of language than when not. Such linguistic stimulation enlivens both body and mind, in Montaigne's opinion. The analogy is a bodily stimulus in the form of being touched by a person dear to one – something that also re-echoes in the heart of the individual. For Montaigne, it is the heart – not the brain as for his successor Descartes – that is the centre of man. And the heart is a bodily phenomenon and the carrier of symptoms of man's feelings and passions.

Montaigne views the body as the house in which he dwells. But this house would appear to have empty rooms. Trying to grasp one's inner being is like clutching at water: 'for the more he squeezes and presses what by its nature flows all over, the more he will lose what he was trying to hold and grasp'.[17] It is the body, not something internal and abstract, that gives him identity. The concrete and sensual in Montaigne's language about the body conjure up the idea and the experience of something real inside that re-emerges in what he refers to as 'the airy body of speech'. Inner (mental) life does not perhaps have any other existence than what it acquires in terms of language. But the existence that language gives to the inner life is, for Montaigne, highly ambiguous. The most concrete aspect of the inner life is the energy that the exploring subject invests in his own self-examination – with a certain self-awareness as a result. As a true essayist, Montaigne encircles what is essential, demarcating it via what is unessential. The unessential, or the appearance, circumscribes the essential, that never can be grasped.

That our inner being is empty perhaps explains why the sceptic Montaigne writes his essays in order to practise *dying*. Compared with his contemporaries, his view of death is original. The Renaissance carnivalist Rabelais, for example, presents death as a social phenomenon where the individual is absorbed into the supra-individual, while the Christian Pascal sees individual salvation from an eternal perspective, with the dying person abandoning himself to something absolute and transcendent. Montaigne adopts a paradoxical intermediate position, where death is staged as an exclusively immanent individual work of social importance for the dead person. To die beautifully and with honour makes death absolutely individual and transcending. But to manage to take such a step beyond life, there must be integrity between life and teaching. 'He who would teach men to die would teach them to live'.[18] To die is to free oneself from all ties in the world via a spontaneous, free falling-in, into the unknown. 'He who has learned how to die has unlearned to be a slave. Knowing how to die frees us from all subjection and constraint'.[19] The last idea is the mind's spontaneous falling-out – out of the body, dissolving into everything and nothing. Death is the last 'essay', prepared for by all the previous ones: 'I leave it to death to test the fruit of my studies. We shall see then whether my reasoning come from my mouth or from my heart'.[20] At the edge of life language falls short. To talk oneself out of it is impossible, or rather the last great *tour de force* of life – with a word of power that neutralizes all power. Then the heart's last mental function takes over. At the point of death, language – via speech and all conceivable expressions of thought – has already done its job and formed the mind, so it can detach itself from the body and become insubstantial. He has quite a high opinion of his ability to save himself: 'Never did a man prepare to leave the world more utterly and completely, nor detach himself from it more universally, than I propose to do'.[21]

The heart is the organ of life. But mentally it is for Montaigne a function of the mind and via its reactions reveals what sort of moral qualities the individual has. The person who has practised suppressing the spontaneous expressions of the heart (consciousness and conscience), is in a bad way when it comes to death. For then it is too late to practise spontaneity and fidelity to the heart. Thinking in terms of means and ends is doomed. For no one can cheat death – in the last scene of the comedy pretence is out of the question. Unconditionally one has to be oneself. And if one is, this is not least reflected in the language one speaks:

> But in the last scene, between death and ourselves, there is no more pretending; we must talk plain French, we must show what there is that is good and clean at the bottom of the pot: '*At last true words surge up from deep within our breast . . .*' That is why all the other actions of our life must be tried and tested by this last act. It is the master day, the day that is judge of all the others.[22]

Death is the last essay – the last draft, the completion of a beautiful soul as pure form. Death becomes the crowning glory of the masterpiece, the supreme *work* that life ought to be for Montaigne.

> The goal of our career is death. It is the necessary object of our aim. If it frightens us, how is it possible to go a step forward without feverishness? The remedy of the common herd is not to think about it. But from what brutish stupidity can come so gross a blindness![23]

To die is both a transitive (active) and intransitive (passive) verb for Montaigne. Until and into death Montaigne conducts the irreconcilable dialectic between action and reflection, between grasping something actively and being grasped passively – the very heartbeat of life. On the one hand, life is what is given us, what is inside us prior to all conscious action. On the other hand, life is also action and *the work* above all other works, an aim that surpasses all other actions and works. Even though Montaigne wrote his essays to prepare himself for dying, he is nevertheless (like his successor Nietzsche) an affirmative person until death, with the motto: 'Be who you are, be it completely, realize who you are and trust in the nature that has created you the way you are!'

The task of life is always dialectically constituted for Montaigne: one must spontaneously accept oneself and position oneself in such a way that one can just as spontaneously liberate oneself from oneself and what belongs to one. One's work of life is completed in one's phenomenal, physical death that is both heavy and light, full and empty, filled because it has been emptied of its vices. The life that Montaigne lives and depicts as he looks at it obliquely can be summed up as an alternation between opposites that complement each other: Beyond the idea of something solid that we grasp for in vain, we can grasp a fluid meaning; beyond deceptive appearance we can create a beautiful life-work; beyond the idea that life is empty and vain the perishable body rises up as the place where divergent truth reveals itself: my truth, simple but absolutely unavoidable, unique but part of universal nature, impossible to communicate but part of all human consciousness. We have lost the essential in existence, but have recovered the relative and phenomenally concrete.[24]

The form of scepticism that results from Montaigne's understanding that all that is human is relative and can be constructed in an infinite number of different ways promotes a tolerance for the one and the others that is rare in history. The age in which Montaigne lived, with its civil and religious wars, was by no means tolerant. But he and the Renaissance represented a first confrontation with absolutism and fundamentalism that gradually resulted in greater individual and political freedom and a recognition of universal human rights. The focus shifted from the religious to the anthropological.

This movement reaches a climax in European culture in the two schools of thought all of us have as our heritage, the Enlightenment and Romanticism, straddling both and with one foot in each. Which mentality speaks more to our heart is a matter of personal disposition and view of humanity. This 'battle', to express it metaphorically, is one between head and heart, between reason and emotions, between instrumental utility and aesthetic expressivity. But the conflict between a rationalistic tradition and Romanticism, with its precursors and successors, is also one of method and a way of thinking. This does not always receive much attention, but it is crucial for us today, since several of the modes of thought on which Romanticism rests – especially the analogical one practised by Montaigne and later Goethe, with roots that go back to Antiquity and the Middle Ages – have enjoyed low status in many disciplines, from the Renaissance and rationalism in the eighteenth century to positivism in the nineteenth and twentieth. This has had consequences not only for how the reasons of the heart have been perceived but whether they have been recognized at all as a source of valid knowledge.

CHAPTER 11

From the Renaissance and Alchemy to the Romantic Era

When once you lay by my heart, oh my bride,
it was as if from it flowers opened out wide:
Flowers that were living and thinking and dreaming.
. . . The sun its blood o'er the roses was streaming.
The soul from its soil in sweet bliss found release.

Henrik Wergeland

The notion of Antiquity and the Middle Ages that man is a microcosm analogous to the macrocosm of the universe lives on in the Renaissance, even in the new sciences, where that of anatomy was the leading experimental school. William Harvey (1578–1657) recognized the circulation of the blood on the basis of his experiments with animals (and also with humans). He published his pioneer work in 1628, *Movement of the Heart and Blood in Animals: An Anatomical Essay* (originally in Latin). In this work, he operates with an analogy between the sun and the heart. Just as the planets orbit the sun and are nourished by it, as is life on earth, so does the blood circulate the heart, from and back to it. In Chapter Eight he writes about 'the circular movement of the blood', after having gained inspiration from Aristotle for his thesis on the universal circulation in nature:

> We have as much right to call this movement of the blood circular as Aristotle had to say that the air and rain emulate the circular movement of the heavenly bodies . . .
>   This organ [the heart] deserves to be styled the starting point of life and the sun of our microcosm [*sol microcosmi*] just as much as the sun deserves to be styled the heart of the world [*sol mundi*]. For it is by the heart's vigorous beat that the blood is moved . . . The heart is the tutelary deity of the body, the basis of life, the source of all things, carrying out its function of nourishing, warming, and activating the body as a whole.[1]

Harvey, though, could not have made his great discovery without the mechanical view of the world. Like Galen 1,500 years earlier, he is caught in and by the metaphors that his age offers him. For it is the metaphors that make it possible to see connections and similarities. New metaphors reveal new connections and uncover new analogies. The metaphor that Harvey had and Galen lacked was the pump. In the wake of the technological revolution, Harvey was surrounded by mechanical pumps and technical drawings of them – especially the water pump for mining and fire-extinguishing. When he observed how the heart with its rhythmical movement worked with the veins as hoses, the analogy of the pump was not slow in coming to mind, based on the epistemological principle: metaphor + experiment = truth. Harvey also experimented on his body, by placing a finger on an artery, and could soon conclude that blood streamed in one direction (not returning by the same route). This paved the way for an understanding of the other heart functions, and its interaction with other organs, particularly the liver and lungs. Harvey is both mechanical and analogical in his way of thinking, in the sense that mechanics provides him with the metaphorical arsenal, or language, he needs in order to discover how the heart actually works. The consequence of this shift of metaphor is a real shift of mind-set, for there is a big difference between a mechanical pump and a divinely inspired organ that animates the rest of the body. Once again, we have a demonstration of the indissoluble link between language and heart – also when dealing with the physiological heart.

Thinking organically in terms of analogies, then, lives on in an age dominated by a mechanistic view of the world. It is based on the idea that everything interacts, and that *dog knows dog*. Thinking in terms of analogies also underlay alchemy, which came to Europe via Arabic culture, which had further developed Graeco-Hellenistic alchemy. From their comprehensive medical literature it is clear that the Arabs knew about the circulation of the blood long before Harvey. Alchemy was a kind of laboratory for interdisciplinary thinking that included science, religion and mysticism from the High Middle Ages. Gunpowder and (distilled) liquor are fruits of alchemy, which underwent a renewal during the Renaissance.

The heart-sun analogy was absolutely fundamental in alchemy. The connection between the sun and the heart recurs in a number of cultures. But we must be careful about smoothing over differences. The heart-offering, the blood-offering, is not the same in the tradition of Inanna/Ishtar, in Norse mythology, among the Aztecs or in Christianity. Form and function differ. But there are many related analogies. The analogy between the sun and the heart, as we have seen, is found throughout the history of religion and culture, from the Sumerian and ancient

Egyptian to the Aztec, and in European Jesus mysticism and alchemy at the same time.

A major figure in the alchemical tradition is Paracelsus (1493–1541), whom Goethe studied before writing *Faust*. Paracelsus is a representative of another tradition within the Church that was not always strongly dualistic. He was a universal genius. Not only was he an alchemist, but also a natural scientist, doctor and medicinal reformer, a philosopher and a theologian. He discovered, for example, that Galen's blood-letting did not work, and therefore doubted his theory of humours as well. It is little known that he was the one to introduce narcotics as pain-killers when treating patients.

Central to his holistic mode of thought is the sun-heart analogy. His teaching on the micro-macrocosm contained Aristotelian, neo-Platonic and alchemical elements. The most important parts of the body in his teaching are the heart, brain and liver – with the heart as life-centre. The human organs correspond to the planets round the sun, with the heart secretly in contact with the heart of the world: the sun. In the same way as the sun moves and gives life to the earth and the macrocosm, the heart animates the entire body, keeping it alive. At one point he writes that the brain is subordinate to the heart: 'The brain only goes to the heart, and from the heart back to its spiritual centre.'

Paracelsus is part of a tradition of Christian mysticism that had a certain position in the High Middle Ages, even though it was opposed by the Inquisition. One of the major names in this tradition was Hildegard von Bingen (1098–1179). Early in her life she had revelations of an ecstatic nature, in the form of flames that struck her brain and lit a glow within. She wrote poetry and also revived medieval music. As abbess of a nunnery she was quite independent. She had, for example, a positive view of the sensory body and nature, which were not sinful in her opinion. She believed sexual life to be holy, regarding the erect penis as a flower in praise of the Creator. She also claimed that 'the coldness of the brain' needed 'the warmth of the heart' to maintain the exposed harmony of the world of thought.

These Christian mystics were, paradoxically enough, down-to-earth thinkers and in general were very much concerned with what sorts of elements and forces were necessary in an ordered system to keep life well balanced, as a condition for creative good. For that reason they upgraded woman's status and role as being on a par with those of man; together, man and woman formed a whole. Like Hildegard, Paracelsus places the soul in the heart, which breathes in time with God's breath. Thus the heart was a double centre of life. In the same tradition as these two we have the Christian mystic Jakob Böhme (1575–1624). This perhaps best known of all Christian mystics, after Meister Eckhart (*c.* 1260–1327), often referred to the heart-sun analogy. But the thinking in terms of analogies by the Christian mystics and the alchemists was replaced by the strictly dualistic interpretation of Descartes and by mechanistic-causalistic thinking. And the Inquisition accused Meister Eckhart of heresy for his pantheist-influenced thoughts.

The path of the mystic towards *unio mystica* goes via the heart. This applies in both Islamic-Arabic and Christian-European culture. The mystic seeks the source of the revelatory light in the blazing heart, with its surrounding darkness. When he closes his eyes (*mystein* = to close one's eyes), opens his inner, visionary gaze and listens in contemplation to the voice of his heart, he – or she (Hildegard von Bingen is just one of many female mystics) – is overwhelmed by a great passion where everything coalesces in a great experience of unity. The metaphorics of the heart exceeds its psychological and ethical-existential framework: the heart is the key to ancient traditions of a religious and mystical – so-called numinous – nature. The numinous is that which goes beyond human powers of expression and understanding, something that is both fascinatingly attractive and overwhelmingly frightening, that is subject to no control, something to which the human being is abandoned.[2] As Christianity becomes weaker, the numinously divine moves out of the cathedral into Nature's great temple, forming the basis of the sublime nature-worship of Romanticism. By the end of this book the sublime will be seated in the human heart, thanks to modern cardiology.

The analogically oriented understanding of nature as well as anthropology do not function in a dualistic way either, influenced as they are by Aristotle's holism, Empedocles' teaching of the four elements, Hippocrates' humorology and Galen's temperaments. The sanguine (blood-filled) attained specially positive status in the Middle Ages, until in the Romantic period it became synonymous with violent passion, as opposed to Romantic melancholy. The idea that the blood and the heart are the centre of thought and mental life was linked in the Middle Ages to the idea of Jesus's blood, creating an unparalleled blood-magic in history – something reflected in Baroque painting.

It is one of the great paradoxes in European cultural history that the symbolism of blood and heart develops with increasing strength before and alongside Galilean-Cartesian dualism, despite the downgrading of the emotions in that tradition. It is not only religious mysticism and scientific thinking in terms of analogies that further this history of the heart. Even more important is the influence of what I have called the emotional turn in the age of chivalry, which reaches a new high point in the late Renaissance with – not least represented by Shakespeare's *Romeo and Juliet* (*c.* 1595–6) – the first modern expression of Romantic love. In fact, Shakespeare writes his first work at the same time as the publication of Montaigne's essays, and at the same time as Galileo makes his revolutionizing astronomical observations and calculations, while Descartes is still a child. Shakespeare gives the metaphorics of the heart a new content, in accordance with the new insights into man's complex psyche emerging in the new, dogma-free age.

CHAPTER 12

Shakespeare and the Heart of Darkness

But my five wits nor my five senses can
Dissuade one foolish heart from serving thee.
Who leaves, unsway'd the likeness of a man
Thy proud heart's slave and vassal wretch to be.

Shakespeare

THE HEARTBREAKER

It could well be that William Shakespeare (1564–1616) and Montaigne shaped and formed the image of the modern European to a greater extent than Descartes. While Descartes proposes a theory of man, Shakespeare shows how man is in practice. He depicts what he sees around him, that which reveals itself of good or evil in word and deed. He is the first modern depth-psychologist to reveal the complex underlying impulses and motives that govern people's attitudes and actions. For Shakespeare, it has all got to do with the heart. It reveals what makes people tick.

In his later works, he supplements Romantic Tristanism with other types of love, as in the enigmatic works *Hamlet, Macbeth* and, in particular, *King Lear* (1605–6), which can serve here to represent the Shakespearian heart. In this play, the heart is also the symptom and image of personal integrity in an ethical and existential sense. Here the heart breaks not because of erotic passion or unhappy love but because of betrayal and an uninhibited lust for power. And worse than anything else is when love and trust are betrayed. This applies in particular to the love that parents (Lear and his earl, Gloucester) have for their children (Lear for Cordelia and Gloucester for his legitimate son, Edgar) and that children have for their parents.

What sets the tragedy in motion in the opening scene of the drama is the fact that King Lear lacks critical judgement and self-knowledge, proud and self-assured as he is, and that he is unable to see through the high-sounding, hypocritical words of two of his three daughters when he asks them to tell him how much they love him, as a pledge for his donating each of them part of his kingdom. Unlike her two elder sisters, Regan and Goneril, the youngest daughter with the revealing name of Cordelia (*cor* = heart) is unable to find words for her love, as it is greater than words. The tongue is unable to bear true witness to the unconditionally faithful heart – 'I cannot heave my heart into my mouth'. She is well aware that there is a difference between heart and tongue and cannot say more that the heart can encompass. The heart knows more than words can express – and cannot be used in instrumental expression or as means in a bargain. Lear fails to understand this and, in his rage, disinherits her. The opposite is the case for the two other daughters, however, who in bombastic language proclaim their love for their father, even though they do not love him, and without Lear seeing through their deception. This lack of understanding takes him ever deeper into his frustration and madness as Goneril and Regan gradually reveal their false-heartedness.

The tension in the play becomes so great because Lear is a lovable, confidence-inspiring old man who himself loves and is loved by all those who deserve our respect in the play. To begin with, he believes that he is loved by all those closest to him. But in the first part of the play Lear fails to understand Cordelia and the others who love him, Gloucester and his son Edgar – and especially the fool and Kent. The true-, noble- and honest-hearted Earl of Kent does not succeed in getting Lear to realize his groundless rejection of Cordelia, and has to pay a high price for this. Nevertheless, he never abandons the king. He follows him incognito, disguised as the poorest, dirtiest servant, while Lear is going mad from the difficulties and misunderstandings that arise when map and terrain do not tally, and as his heirs and their accomplices gradually reveal their deception through their misuse of power.

Things fare no better for the Earl of Gloucester and his son Edgar, who is accused by his half-brother of betraying Gloucester and thus rejected by his father – who shortly afterwards is betrayed and blinded by Edmund's co-conspirators (Regan and her husband) once Edmund has become an earl. When the truth is at last revealed, and Gloucester realizes the injustice and suffering he has caused for his son Edgar (who has pretended to be mad so as to be able to serve his father incognito – just as Kent did the king), his poor heart breaks out of happiness at the outcome and grief at the injustice:

> But his flaw'd heart,
> Alack, too weak the conflict to support,

'Twixt two extremes of passion, joy and grief,
Burst smilingly (Act v, Scene iii).

King Lear's happiness is short-lived when in the final act the deception of the others is revealed, for the one deceitful daughter kills the other out of jealousy and then herself, while Cordelia is killed on the orders of the sisters' common love Edmund, subsequently mortally wounded by Edgar. When the consequences of his own errors are presented to Lear, and he himself finds Cordelia hanged, he is unable to bear both truth and fact – and his own guilt. For Cordelia dies without the guilt Lear shares in her fate being atoned for and reconciled. Her death is therefore meaningless, as Lear's life now is. For this reason, *King Lear* is a modern play, because it deals with personal guilt independently of the Christian doctrine of sin – a guilt people can call down upon themselves and be forced to bear, even though they have a good character. Character is not enough – one also has to have knowledge and insight, recognize and perceive motives and be able to foresee the consequences of one's words and deeds. All this is more than Lear can cope with, so he goes mad. His heart stops after finding Cordelia hanged. He dies without a single final word of reconciliation – he who was one of the greatest word-painters Shakespeare ever created – as a mere husk of himself. He meets his death wordless.

The character who really leads Lear into insanity is the fool, who loves his king and Cordelia and therefore reacts against Lear allowing Regan and Goneril to take control. The fool's function is to provide words of truth about the folly and madness of power. There are two fundamental questions the fool unceasingly and uncompromisingly poses to the king and us as readers/spectators: What is truth? and Who am I? These two questions have been an evolutionary force in cultural history, ever since Gilgamesh sought to find meaning after the loss of his best friend Enkidu, and Odysseus engaged in a dialogue with his own heart so as to find the way home to himself and to Ithaca. But Lear does not want to hear the truth, partly because it would place a heavier responsibility on his shoulders that he is willing to bear.

Lear also talks to his own heart, but without releasing the wisdom that lies within it. He therefore tries – like Odysseus – to calm it down so it will not break out of sorrow and suffering: 'O me, my heart! My rising heart! But, down!' is one of Lear's lines that applies to the other people who unjustly suffer loss in the play. But Lear has a special responsibility, for he has unleashed the inferno. He is also the one to make the diagnosis when the fool prods his wound, hysterical passion: 'O, how this mother swells up toward my heart!/ *Hysterica passio*, down, thou climbing sorrow,/ Thy element's below' (ii.iv). Lear is unwilling to gaze into his own inner abyss, for then he will have to see himself and others as he and the others really are, and use that knowledge. In vain does the fool attempt to make him do just that.

When Lear is finally unable to avoid the fool's pertinent questions any longer, he takes flight: 'I will forget my nature' (I.v). It is his personal tragedy that he steps back from the classic demand to know – acknowledge – himself. *Not* to accede to this divine imperative is indeed madness, and leads to madness: 'O let me not be mad, not mad, sweet heaven! . . . Keep me in temper, I would not be mad!' Lear believes wits and truth are something he himself can decide on. But the person who places himself outside truth becomes nothing and no one (as does Odysseus in his fight with the Cyclops) and a fool, as the fool knows: 'Now thou art an O without a figure; I am better than thou art now. I am a fool, thou art nothing' (I.iv). When, in the same Scene, it comes to self-knowledge the king finally has to capitulate to the fool's insistent prodding and ask himself the classic question:

> Does any here know me? Why, this is not Lear.
> Does Lear walk thus, speak thus? Where are his eyes?
> Either his notion weakens, or his discernings are
> lethargied – Ha! sleeping or waking? Sure 'tis not
> so. Who is it that can tell me who I am?

The fool, along with those who knew him before he lost his mind, is one of those who can answer: *Lear's shadow.* He is only a shadow of himself.

One of the enigmatic characters in *King Lear* is the doubly false Edmund. Power is his sole goal, and the lust for power his prime passion. He loves no one, nor does he have any capacity for love. He is a psychopath and a cynical power strategist. This charismatic psychopath seduces both Goneril and Regan as the first step of his plan to get their husbands out of his way and subsequently one of the sisters, so that he himself can become king with absolute power.

When Edmund, lying mortally wounded in the last act, sees and hears that both his mistresses have died for his sake, he exclaims: 'Yet Edmund was beloved:/The one the other poisoned for my sake,/And after slew herself' (v.iii). This leads to a change in his state of mind. He now wishes to do something good, just for once: 'Quickly send –/Be brief in it – to the castle, for my writ/Is on the life of Lear and on Cordelia;/Nay, send in time' (v.iii). It is too late, though perhaps not for Edmund. As a dramatic character he conveys something about what a human being is. And finally he does acknowledge who he is, i.e. a bastard, without just claim on earldom or throne. This means he is also able to acknowledge all Edgar accuses him of – and much more besides, but only when Edgar by the use of force has exposed him and deposed him for good. The power-seeker bows only to power.

Edmund's wickedness, according to Edgar, stems from the fear that their father, Gloucester, only sired a bastard to satisfy his sexual lust: 'The dark and vicious place where thee he got / Cost him his eyes' (v.iii). Once again, suffering is a result of passion, of the father's sexual lust and Edmund's lust for power. When he finally acknowledges who he is, he has returned to his starting point – that of the bastard. The wheel of fortune has completed its circle: 'The wheel is come full circle, I am here' (v.iii). The view of humanity that can be deduced from this and from the play is bleak: Only the person who does *not* love is capable of arriving at uncompromisingly true self-awareness, the fool would proclaim. And no one derives any help from Edmund's final truth. Nor is there any talk of saving souls in this non-Christian play about life here and now. By demonstrating how pointless Edmund's change of heart is, Shakespeare also distances himself from a central Christian doctrine. Faith only and a change of heart cannot save anyone – reality decides.

In the cultural history of the heart, *King Lear* represents a radical challenge of most of what the heart stands for in Western culture in terms of positive values. In many ways, the play undermines the foundation of our Christian and humanistic view of mankind – its ideal, at any rate. Shakespeare shows that the ideal is hopelessly inadequate in real life when people expose their true selves. That is what Shakespeare wants to show – beyond all Christian-humanist ideals. One can view this disillusioned realism as part of the historical process we have been following from Antiquity up to his age. The entire process has provided material for the type of person Shakespeare represents – one that would not have been possible in Antiquity. That is why the foremost expert on Shakespeare, Harold Bloom calls him 'inventor of the human', because he invents something human we know exists in our own age, independent of any divine authority.[1] Before Shakespeare there were persons, Bloom claims, after him there are personalities, with a complex inner life and an ability to change. Man has hardly added a cubit to his stature since then. And the work of Freud can be perceived as an attempt to explain theoretically the complex psyche that Shakespeare has depicted in literature.

Shakespeare is the first person to present a modern, complex man who is self-sufficient, with the composite inner life we first encounter in humanism and the late Renaissance. The fathers of humanism, alongside Montaigne and Descartes, are Erasmus of Rotterdam and the reformer Martin Luther. Especially fascinating is the linking of Shakespeare with his older contemporary Montaigne, whom Shakespeare had probably read (in Florio's manuscript version, according to Bloom).[2] Nietzsche takes it for granted that Shakespeare has read Montaigne. Nietzsche himself also read Shakespeare, to whom Goethe for his part claimed to owe everything. In this sense modern man rests on the alliance Montaigne-Shakespeare-Goethe, with which Nietzsche associates himself. In Montaigne Shakespeare finds confirmation for his scepticism, which in his late masterpiece of a play would seem to end in nihilism. Both of them see man as being unstable and as fleeting as the wind. For that reason, Montaigne's and (in exceptional cases) Shakespeare's characters are able to change themselves (Hamlet does so all the time), because they not only hear the wind but also what they themselves and others say. Words too, however, are as fleeting as the wind, 'mere words' that strip inner life of everything fixed and lasting – a view of language that Montaigne shared. So 'the question is', whether inner life in *King Lear*, represented by the heart, is empty or something essential and lasting that makes man human, even if it is 'merely' a function of language and speech.

In Shakespeare's work, man's dark side prevails against all idealism. And power and desire of all kinds take the place of these ideals. Shakespeare is the first person to realize the psychology of power and the lust for power as a fundamental human driving force on a par with the sexual urge, here represented by Edmund and the sisters Regan and Goneril. For power gives a person everything, dissolves shame and bad conscience, and heaps irreparable guilt on him. Anyone surrendering to the dynamics of power is caught in a particular kind of logic. Anyone seeking power for the sake of power and prestige cannot be spontaneous and honest, but constantly thinks in terms of means and ends, hides his real plans, talks with a forked tongue, plays a double game and always thinks tactically and strategically. That is why those who love with all their heart are dangerous for such power-seekers, for they see that power is only a means for what is an end in itself: love. Suffering in *King Lear* is a result of Goneril, Regan and Edmund using their emotions to further their own power. They talk as if they love, while they actually hate those who love with all their heart. For they do not possess anything that is an end in itself, and have to reduce love to a means. They are truth's parasites, truth that is also the criterion for falseness. The unfortunate thing is that not everybody sees this. For the false is harmless only once it has been revealed.

The tragedy of *King Lear* is not only a supplement to but an alternative to the romantic heart, which suffers because of unhappy love and a passion that cannot reach its erotic goal. Erotic passion in *King Lear* is often portrayed purely as sexual lust and as the root of all evil. While romantic love upgrades sensual and erotic love in the event of Christianity,

Christian love of one's neighbour undergoes a corresponding meta-morphosis in *King Lear*, becoming a purely secular, interpersonal relationship via empathy, compassion and an intuitive respect of everything a fellow human being stands for. This love is made complete in friendship. Since this is a secular, realistic love, it also becomes an active force of knowledge, enabling us to see through the actual relations and understand that not everyone is our neighbour – as Cordelia, the fool, Edgar and Kent point out.

While romantic love is an egoistic form of love and Christian love of one's neighbour is an obligation, the deepest form of Shakespearian love is unconditional compassion and self-sacrifice, embodied by Kent and Edgar, who sacrifice everything to help those they love, not least by giving them critical counter-notions. They do not dress as beggars and poor servants in order to humble themselves in the Christian sense, but because they are noble-minded enough to forsake their social happiness and career. Their disguise is purely external and determined by the situation – a highly rational and goal-oriented way of helping those dear to them in their hour of need. Unlike romantic love, compassionate Shakespearian love cannot be limited to a sexual relationship between a man and a woman but also applies between equals, or as a spiritual affinity and a personal friendship. Classic friendship, *philia*, and absolute respect for a fellow human being is portrayed as being of supreme value in Shakespeare's masterpiece rather than pathetic romantic love.

King Lear makes topical a question that has always followed passion and love: whether love makes one blind or capable of seeing. The answer to this question is highly ambiguous in *King Lear*, shown allegorically through the relation between those who are blind and those who are seeing in the play. The paradoxical relationship between blind and seeing (or visionary) love is expressed both literally and metaphorically in the case of Gloucester. As long as he has his sight, he does not see through the fact that Edmund betrays him; he only does so when he has been blinded. One of the climaxes in the play is where the seeing but mentally blind Lear meets the blind but seeing Gloucester, who *sees it feelingly*. This upgrading of emotional awareness over intellectually cold vision points forwards to the final appeal in the last lines of the play, placed in the mouth of Edgar, to obey the weight of the sad time and 'Speak what we feel, not what we ought to say' (v.iii) – in other words, to follow the voice of the heart, as Lear does throughout the work in his own way. All his insights come from the heart. They are, Bloom concludes, with an allusion to Plotinus, 'emanations of his wholeheartedness'. This ambiguous emotionalism points forward towards Romanticism, which Shakespeare anticipates and paves the way for.

The blind person who sees, the madman who is wise, and the fool who tells the truth make Shakespeare a dramatist who defies all clichés and breaks all literary moulds, making *King Lear* about each and every one of us, because we fall into many of the same traps that Lear and Gloucester fall into and allow both the fool and the foolish to fool us. For the underlying motives, impulses and urges are many, some expressed, others hidden, some genuine, others *ersatz*. To distinguish between them and recognize other persons for what they are is impossible – as long as one is unable to recognize oneself. That is why the 'good' person ends up as the 'bad', because he is unable to interpret motives correctly. Lear judges others wrongly because he does not know himself – and Edmund does not want to be himself and therefore becomes no one, having a destructive effect on himself and others.

King Lear is a heartless and perhaps nihilistic play not simply because it portrays unhappiness and betrayal, killing, murder and death but because it questions our basic values, questions the nature of love. Not only is love unhappy in *King Lear* – love itself is actually the root of all evil! Love is not only dangerous and in vain – it is destructive. If Lear and Cordelia had not loved so dearly and uncompromisingly, the tragedy would never have happened. The more love, the greater the suffering. Love does not heal all wounds, but inflicts a mortal wound. There is no expiation or reconciliation here. In many ways, Lear confirms the harsh words of the eighteenth-century critic Samuel Johnson, 'Love is the wisdom of fools and the folly of the wise'. Love can perhaps move mountains, but it leads to death, or to living death in the case of Edgar, who is to take over the estate as England's future king. According to legend, the historical King Edgar had the task of ridding England of wolves. There is a deadly irony in that, since life has taught him one thing, that *homo homini lupus est*.

The lesson that ought to be learnt from this is that love 'is deadly dangerous' and to keep well away from it 'and all its works'. But that is impossible, since it is love that makes man human and that makes the world go round. Naivety and especially (if exposed) disillusion are *leitmotivs* in the play – a disillusion that seems to end in hopelessness and nihilism. Hope dies with Cordelia. That brings us to the thematic ground zero of the play, the true heartlessness – personally, morally and existentially.

'I CANNOT HEAVE MY HEART INTO MY MOUTH'

King Lear raises with renewed force the moral issue of the relation between words and what words refer to. For though this is art, all who have their heart in the right place know that words move us and say something about what it means to be human, what stuff we are made of. Words tell us what this stuff is, i.e. when one is tempted to put words to something, the pre-verbal and pre-conscious shows itself for what it is. Precisely *there* is where the drama of Lear and Cordelia has its beginning, by revealing man's Achilles heel, so to speak.

What triggers off the tragedy is, then, that Cordelia feels 'I cannot heave my heart into my mouth' (the ideal for the Egyptians) and that Lear cannot understand that she is unable to do so. The heart, sensing emotionally, bears witness to the fact that there is something in man that cannot be expressed verbally – not, at any rate, in a social context where unconditional love is valued as a means to some other end. But the whole problem of expression goes even deeper, far deeper than the *shame* that is linked to calculated self-exposure of the most intimate and valuable in one's inner life. For the unnameable is one's self. So far, then, has Western man distanced himself from the Homeric. For Homer, the body was the self, *autos*, i.e. something external; for Shakespeare, it is a complex inner whole. Both complex and complicated. That is what is new, when compared to medieval man with his wholehearted soul. For the heart in itself is at this stage of development empty – it is the black hole, the eye of the hurricane, the still epicentre of the waterspout and the actual storm at the same time – a centre of force where all lines intersect, a pure function of the forces that together constitute a human being as an integrated whole. This function also represents the capacity to recognize kinship with something irreducibly all-embracing. That is why it is impossible for Cordelia to wear her heart on her sleeve and impart her love of her father as a pledge. It can only be imparted indirectly.

Lear's function throughout the play is to expose and represent and try to express indirectly what Cordelia is unable to express. He reflects everything her heart contains and represents metaphorically and mentally, morally and existentially. He thus compels us to reflect on what resides inside ourselves, what we have to acknowledge in order not to risk reducing it to a means and violating what is wordless. So *King Lear* is definitely not a nihilistic work. To put this inviolable inner life on display can be a form of prostitution. That is a central concept in Shakespeare, one we also meet in *Hamlet* when Hamlet censures himself because he 'must like a whore unpack my heart with words'. A paradox and cause of suffering in man is that what is most valuable cannot be im-parted. That is why mysticism is esoteric. That is what underlies Nietzsche's remark that 'what we find words for is already dead in our heart'.

Shakespeare portrays how killing takes place, how the worst that can happen does happen in a world of contingency. And he does so precisely with words, to avoid the worst from happening, for the worst that can happen is that we do not have words for the worst any longer, Edgar claims: 'The worst is not / So long as we can say "This is the worst"' (iv.i). The worst, then, is without words, an absence, when something is irrevocably dead in the heart and there is no longer anything to express, or when one cannot manage to express it any longer, because it has been ruined, along with oneself. The worst that can happen is still the worst. And one must be prepared for it to happen.

Everything is language, but language is not everything, one could say in the spirit of Wittgenstein. The history of the heart has to do with this dilemma, with the difference and connection between the language of the heart and the heart of language. Man is constituted in such a way that he will speak his mind, spontaneously and straight from the heart, and do so trusting that what is said will not be misused or used against the speaker. This is what all interpersonal life is about – and socially speaking it is continually impossible. It is impossible because people exist at different levels in all sorts of different ways – emotionally, intellectually, factually and in terms of knowledge. The difference between people is often acceptable among those who understand this and who respect others, even though they stand for something else than themselves. This has to do with empathy, heart and ability to transcend oneself.

There are perhaps two types of people: those who are stunted and hardened, who are devoid of empathy and turn everything into a means, and those who have empathy and compassion or imagination enough to put themselves in someone else's shoes, and who are able to abandon themselves to phenomena that are a value in themselves. In Shakespeare's work, the characters would seem to fall into these two camps, a division that makes it meaningless to distinguish between people according to moral or religious categories such as good and bad. It is a matter of level and differences in level, of psychological and anthropological categories that lie beyond all moral and religious fundamentalism. And that is roughly where we find ourselves today, left to our own devices in a self-sufficient, contingent universe where spirits of heaviness have social gravity on their side and cause many good causes to fall.

As a heartbreaker, Shakespeare is unrivalled. The heart dies, but the heart lives in and by his words and metaphors. The resounding breaking of the heart in his dramas re-echoes through subsequent periods of Western history to this very day. In many ways the late masterpieces of Shakespeare represent the watershed in our understanding of humanity. After Shakespeare it is impossible to talk about the noble heart without in the same breath mentioning the marble heart without empathy. Shakespeare's drama concerning human nature is not, however, merely a story of disillusion but also one of illumination. Like no one else, he has with his penetrating clarity lit up the heart of darkness.

It is hardly chance that Joseph Conrad (1857–1924) begins the journey of his *Heart of Darkness* on London's Thames, where the words from Shakespeare's plays waft over the river from his Globe theatre nearby. The introductory remarks by the narrator and main character Marlow[e] – (Shakespeare's and) Conrad's *alter ego* – concerning mankind and its history can also be perceived as a dialogue with and a continuation of Shakespeare's lines concerning the falls and follies of humanity. Conrad's masterpiece is in many ways paradigmatic in both psychological terms and in the history of civilizations. It was published in 1899, on the threshold of a new century, as a kind of warning as to what a century of horror the twentieth century would prove to be, with more people killed in wars, state terrors, and genocides that in any previous century in the history of mankind. The dark horizon portrayed in the introduction and final words of the work, which form a framework for the novella as well as for our lives, are in themselves a metaphorical expression of the menacing future horizon mankind is moving towards as it enters a new century:

> The offing was barred by a black bank of clouds, and the tranquil waterway leading to the uttermost ends of the earth flowed sombre under an overcast sky – seemed to lead into the heart of an immense darkness.

In retrospect, a century after Conrad published the novel, he seems to be, with his visionary sunset, a prophet, a counterpart in fiction to the critic of civilization, Oswald Spengler, who a few years later depicted degeneration in his classic historical work *The Decline of the West* (1918–22).

Conrad's work, however, is also a highly condensed allegorical description of the past and of his own age, of the apex of imperialism, the reverse side of the white man's burden, since the work portrays one of the darkest chapters in Western culture in the form of the plundering by colonial powers of the Congo's natural resources and a corresponding humiliation of the indigenous population and their society along the mighty river of the Congo. The river – which the narrator and his narrative follow – is like a main artery leading to the heart of Africa, which until then had been the last blank spot on the white man's atlas. But this blank spot actually represents an unknown darkness that explorers, headed by the journalist Henry Stanley, uncovered geographically, and that the missionary Dr David Livingstone was to 'enlighten' culturally and religiously. Joseph Conrad has a counter-image of this story of the enlightening of Africa's supposed darkness.

Marlow's journey – from London via the headquarters of the Colonial Company in Brussels of the chief exploiter King Leopold II to the inner-most Congo – is portrayed as a cohesive unveiling of what primitive motives and greed drove the colonists (cf. Adam Hochschild's shocking documentary account, *King Leopold's Ghost: A Story of Greed, Terror, and Heroism in Colonial Africa*, published in 1998). Their exploitation of Africa brought out the worst in men, with white gold – ivory – standing not only as a symbol of material lust and riches but also for power and prestige, and as a symbol of how selfishness and greed corrupt people both morally and emotionally, leading them to trample over bodies in seeking to fulfil their aims.

Conrad's great achievement is this thematic and anthropological turn in the work, from the outer (geographical and geopolitical) to the inner, personal (psychological, moral and mental), since the work changes char-acter from depicting the heart of darkness to the darkness of the heart. The true darkness exists within man, in his complex psychology and primitive motives, which see the light of day as soon as the thin veneer of culture is scraped off the mammal homo sapiens, with the (presumably) most civilized and educated, the Europeans, becoming the most primi-tive. By travelling far out geographically, he penetrates in depth psycho-logically, with Marlow himself experiencing the analogy between the journey up the Congo river and the uncovering of the motives for the hunt for ivory: 'Going up that river was like travelling back to the earliest beginnings of the world'. Running parallel with his penetrating ever deeper into man's original, primitive psyche, the primitive history of the past also emerges, as atavistic phenomena: 'here were moments when one's past came back to one'. Seen with Romantic eyes, such a journey – into prim-ordial, uncultivated nature – should lead to Paradise and a Garden of Eden in the jungle, but it ends instead in hell, in the lawless jungle where everything is allowed. Delving into man's original nature also fails to prove that man is basically good. For deep down impenetrable darkness reigns.

With his moral keynote, Conrad's journey to the interior of the dark continent appears to be an allegorical drama parallel to Dante's *Divine Comedy*. Just as Dante undertakes his underground journey to Hell at the centre of the earth, Conrad's main character undertakes a journey to the central region of the earth – and to a hell on earth. Like Dante, Marlow follows his demon, Kurtz – who had 'kicked himself loose of the earth' – to the nether regions, to the heart of darkness, a modern epiphany of inferno, where like Dante in Hell he meets his contemporary sinners, ivory hunters and careerists who must carry the curse of their guilt for all eternity, because out of greed they have sold themselves to the system: 'They wandered here and there with their absurd long staves in their hands like a lot of faithless pilgrims bewitched inside a rotten fence. The word "ivory" rang in the air, was whispered, was sighed. You would think they were praying to it'. The demon that follows Marlow to the heart of darkness – which is first portrayed as an absent shadow and then as a frightful shadow of himself – is the most proficient of all proficient tradesmen and spokesman of civilization, the legendary Mr Kurtz, now lying ill in the depths of the Congo, and whom Marlow, on the Company's orders, is to rescue from the dangerous and deadly jungle and bring home to civilized Europe.

But the man Marlow eventually finds is not the eloquent man of enlightenment but one falling to pieces at all levels, both physically and mentally, morally and personally. He finds Kurtz at the inner station, which is a mixture of an outpost and the occult village of a chief or medicine man, where the drums beat like orgiastic heartbeats in the night, in a hut surrounded by poles with skulls on them. He is feared and loved by the natives, who bring him their hunting trophies, and loved by a native woman who is the very incarnation of erotic passion and ambiguous free love, the diametric opposite of Kurtz's chaste 'Intended', who is buried alive in the sepulchral city of Brussels. She is a pale Platonic shadow of the vital negro woman and lives on the illusion of the great love and his noble character. She is only something intended. Her noble heart is a pale plaster heart, dead and anaemic. Kurtz, on the other hand, has abandoned himself to the opposite, untamed wildness and dark wilderness without restraint. Socially speaking, he is an alpha male, seeking power over other human beings, riches, desire, vanity and prestige, obscured by an 'army of metaphors', big words and empty rhetoric about Western ideals. Kurtz is the perversion of Enlightenment, freedom and development by cultivating man's primitive nature. His fall is one back to the primitive, which lies before and beneath the Western project of self-restraint. That is why Kurtz goes to pieces, split between two worlds, and is finally forced to choose between two nightmares that represent two ways of life. But he is not portrayed by Conrad and his *alter ego* Marlow as the incarnation of evil. Kurtz is no Mephistopheles, nor a Faust. The role of evil incarnate is played by the local representative of the Company, the manager of the Central Station, who instructs Marlow to fetch Kurtz at the inner station (Stanley Falls).

The manager was originally conceived as the main character of the novel, but is only thematically so in the final version, where his function is to explain what evil, the darkness of the heart, really consists in. That is why he is included here. The interesting thing is that Conrad, as an author of modernity, does not portray evil as something essential but as something functional and relational. The manager does not represent anything absolute, as a tool of Satan, who is only a mythical figure to illustrate evil. The manager is not a devil – he is only too ordinary, just a man doing his job with his whole heart and consequently serving the aims of the Company. He has only one goal in life – and mind as well – to advance up the system and become a leader, taking over Kurtz's position, returning to Europe with merits as a director. He is nothing in and by himself, only a function of his job and his own ambition and career. He represents the new elite of rationalized society that parcels out our souls, the bureaucratic way of life that the sociologist Max Weber has analysed and depicted as the very horror of modern society: 'It is horrible to think that the world could one day be filled with nothing but those little cogs, little men clinging to little jobs and striving towards bigger ones' (Weber 1960: 455). The manager of the Central Station is such a person. Talking with him is for Marlow like talking to a ghost of power and selfishness, one who never reveals his motives and plans, turning everything into tactics and strategy, being himself nothing. Marlow finds it impossible to conduct a genuine conversation with him – nor is he able to affect him personally:

> I let him run on, this papier-mâché Mephistopheles, and it seemed to me that if I tried I could poke my forefinger through him and would find nothing inside but a little loose dirt, maybe. He, don't you see, had been planning to be Assistant-Manager by and under the present man.

The marble heart of Shakespeare's evil has in modernity been replaced by a little heart of loose dirt. This is modern man, the hollow man, without any *core* or *cor*. The end of the cultural history of the heart?

Kurtz's evil is of a different – and more profound – kind. He is also a hollow man. *Heart of Darkness* is a journey to the centre not only of the continent but also to the centre of man. As with Montaigne, it transpires that this inner core is empty. But in Kurtz's case it is a question of an active emptiness. He has abandoned the core of Western values, emptied himself of moral norms, so that he represents an evil of vacancy, filled with an active, destructive energy: 'It echoed loudly within him because he was hollow at the core'. Marlow must fetch Kurtz from his outer and inner chaos by force. He attempts to engage the mortally ill man in conversation during their journey downriver back to civilization, but the man of big words and great dreams of building up the empire from scratch is no longer capable of speaking. On the edge of the abyss of his tattered soul, he is unable to provide Marlow with any explanation as to what has happened in the jungle – until he screams out his final words: 'The horror! The horror!'

These words redeem Kurtz in Marlow's eyes. For they perhaps come as close to the truth as one is able to come. What is inner is inexpressible. Beyond words. An unfathomable source of good and evil that can led to anything at all, as Kurtz himself has experienced. That is also the horror – that the horror can manifest itself at any time, anywhere and in anyone. In Marlow's eyes, Kurtz is saved by this recognition and his final desire to know himself. After having experienced the unfathomable that lies on the far side of normality, beyond everyday speech, the will exists 'to penetrate all the hearts that beat in the darkness. He had summed up – he had judged. 'The horror!' . . . It was an affirmation, a moral victory paid for by innumerable defeats, by abominable terrors, by abominable satisfactions'. That is why Marlow remains loyal to Kurtz to the last, because *he* is loyal to the supreme Western ideal: recognition and understanding.

Marlow of course is a literary figure and as such an unreliable narrator who must be interpreted as a technical vehicle in Joseph Conrad's contribution to the cultural history of the heart. For that reason, Marlow's words about the journey into darkness must be interpreted critically. It ends in Brussels, where he is to return certain relics of Kurtz to his intended. Our question is whether Marlow will remain faithful both to the knowledge he has wrested from the inner darkness and to Kurtz's last words and insight as well. It is doubtful whether he will. For Marlow is unable to tell her the truth. Instead, he chats politely with her and bows in resignation 'before that great and saving illusion that shone with an unearthly glow in the darkness, in the triumphant darkness from which I could not have defended her – from which I could not even defend myself'. And when she asks to hear Kurtz's last words so as to have 'something to live with', he does not tell her the truth, 'The horror! The horror!' but succumbs to a kind of compassion: 'The last word he pronounced was – your name'.

With this lie, Joseph Conrad uses his fictional medium, Marlow, to pronounce the sentence of guilty on mankind, which is unable to bear the burden of truth. Man is mentally not sufficiently strong to endure the enlightenment as defined by the world's foremost philosopher of the Enlightenment, Immanuel Kant, who in his article 'What is Enlightenment?' (1784) concisely states:

Enlightenment is man's emergence from his self-imposed immaturity. Immaturity is the inability to use one's reason without guidance from another. This immaturity is self-imposed when its cause lies not in lack of understanding, but in lack of resolve and courage to use it without guidance from another. Sapere Aude! [dare to know] 'Have courage to use your own reason!' – that is the motto of enlightenment.

The definition leaves no doubt as to what the failure of Marlow, on behalf of mankind, consists in. Marlow's failure to tell the truth is self-imposed, since its cause lies in lack of resolve and courage to use his own understanding. The darkness is not illuminated because the heart does not possess the courage to bear the rational illumination of it. Conrad's explanation is a psychological one, in accordance with Henrik Ibsen's well-known words from *The Wild Duck:* 'If you take away the lie of life from an average human, you take away his happiness at the same time.' Humanity has not progressed any further, according to Conrad, whose motto was 'Lying is dying!'

Viewed retrospectively from a century after Conrad expressed his disillusioned judgment on mankind, the historical evidence in its favour is overwhelming. Darkness prevails. That has also been the situation in inner Congo and neighbouring Rwanda, where 900,000 innocent civilians, most of them Tutsis, were massacred by their close relatives the Hutus during three months of 1994. By some bloody irony of history Africa's largest genocide of modern times took place in a region of the dark continent that Joseph Conrad called the heart of darkness at the same time as thousands were killed in the ethnic cleansing in the Balkans in enlightened Europe, culminating with the Srebrenica Massacre in July 1995, while the whole world looked on as inactive bystanders.

Conrad's work and journey into the darkness is constantly being repeated, both in fiction and – alas – in reality, the latter inspiring the former and vice versa, as in Francis Ford Coppola's award-winning film *Apocalypse Now* (1979), set during the Vietnam War. The film, partly based on Conrad's novella, tells the story of how Captain Willard (Marlow) travels up the river Nung with orders to track down US Army Colonel Kurtz and 'terminate' him because he has gone amok in the jungle and massacred indigenous Vietnamese. Like Kurtz in the novella, Kurtz in the film has submitted to the lawlessness of the jungle because he believes that a war can be fought successfully only if one learns to come to terms with 'horror and moral terror'. For war is inhuman. And that was how the Vietnam War was fought. To defend the West's ideal of freedom, entire villages were annihilated by napalm bombing. So Colonel Kurtz, like

Kurtz the colonist, discovers that the consequence of rejecting his humanity to live and fight like an animal is that life has become meaningless and empty. A heartless person will by the law of necessity become a hollow man – without both core and *cor* – without restraint. To stress this law of darkness Coppola makes Kurtz read T. S. Eliot's poem 'The Hollow Men'. That is the point of our present history of the heart: a person who kills his own heart will eventually end up killing other people.

The story that begins with Montaigne's scepticism, culminates with Shakespeare's heartbreak and ends with Conrad's and Coppola's total heartlessness is a history of disillusion and misanthropic distrust. It is the tradition of the evil heart from the Bible that divides the heart into good and evil. The High Middle Ages cultivated the tradition of the good and noble heart. But does it have any future in the age of modernity? Rousseau attempts to provide an answer to this question, to give the tradition of the good heart a new foundation.

CHAPTER 13

Rousseau – Philosopher of the Heart

> The logic of passion reverses the usual order of thought,
> placing the conclusion before the premise.
> Albert Camus, *The Rebel: An Essay on Man in Revolt*

The next age of the heart in the history of ideas after Shakespeare and the late Renaissance is pre-Romanticism or Sentimentalism from the mid-eighteenth century and Romanticism in the latter half of the century, with Pietism as an anticipatory transitional period.

Pietism was a revival movement at the end of the seventeenth and beginning of the eighteenth century that stressed a genuine, personal and emotionally involved Christianity as opposed to stiff Lutheran orthodoxy. Pietism was highly subjective and individualistic and, with its emotionally based belief, an important preliminary stage of Romanticism. In Pietist baroque-style hymns, especially German, there is an almost endless coinage of heart-compounds: heart-friend, heart-eye, mother-heart, heart-ground, etc. Without Pietism and the prevailing tradition of charismatic Christianity Romanticism could not have become so passionately heart-felt. Neither must it be forgotten that parallel with Romanticism a strong pietistic tradition continued to influence Protestantism and Anabaptism, also inspiring the Anglican priest John Wesley to start the Methodist movement.

In Romanticism, the heart becomes a symbol of most of what the age stands for. The period has got its name directly from the literary genre, the *romance* that the age of chivalry cultivated. The central works of pre-Romanticism, *Sturm und Drang* poetry and sentimental novels were also inspired by this tradition. The work that more than any other inspired the Romantic love ideal was directly and explicitly influenced by the age of chivalry and the best-known medieval exchange of letters, that between Abélard and Héloïse. This is Rousseau's epistolary novel from 1761, *Julie, ou La nouvelle Héloïse* ('Julie, or the New Heloise'), which with Rousseau's

191

other works occupies so central a position in the formation of modern, subjectively emotional man.

But Rousseau was not a single swallow creating on his own the Romantic summer with its stormy nights and daydreams. Rousseau was also a child of his age, one that – with England and France as pioneers – was divided between sense and sensibility, between rationalism and emotionalism, pleasure and utility. The cult of sensibility was very much in fashion from early on in the eighteenth century. One of the first modern novels, Samuel Richardson's *Pamela* from 1740, belongs to the literary genre of this period, the sentimental novel, with Laurence Sterne's *A Sentimental Journey* (1768) as the seminal novel, since the novel also creates the fashionable 'educational journey' (Grand Tour – to France and Italy). This genre was predominant in English literature right up until Jane Austen's *Pride and Prejudice* (1813), with the gothic novel as a climax, both aesthetically and emotionally, by the end of the eighteenth century. Romanticism not only unleashed repressed feelings but also creative forces that resulted in some of the finest English poetry ever written, by Byron and Shelley, Keats, Coleridge and Wordsworth. The impact of the mentality and emotionality of Romanticism on the entire Western and the present global culture cannot be overestimated.

The mid and late eighteenth century sentimental novel produced an entirely new individual, one with a new attitude towards privacy and the public. This is the bourgeois period, when feelings are reserved for intimate privacy and personal integrity, shut off from public society, often with alienation towards society as a result. However, there is also an opposite trend, as the sentimental heroines (there were mostly female protagonists) developed outgoing feelings of compassion. They suffered if they had to keep secrets and felt an urge to confess, thus becoming part of a long Christian tradition. If there is no one worthy of trust and confidence, the heroine then opens her heart to her diary, i.e. to the novel, which in this way becomes a female genre, with a predominance of female readers to the present day. Men too, though, developed their sensibility and sensitivity as reflected in and represented by Henry Mackenzie's *The Man of Feeling* (1771) – as sensibility and compassion was a precondition of love. Since this new genre of the novel is part of the public and published, a new social sentiment of compassion is formed, with the two-way open heart as medium and ideal. Though self-pity is the motivation, this open heart also feels pity, tenderness and benevolence for the sufferings of other people. Sensibility subsequently presents itself as a new barometer of social morality. A new ethics of feeling arose (though not accepted in the philosophy of ethics until then) one that differs from both the Kantian ethics of rule and duty and English utilitarianism. This contribution of sentimentalism to the Western mentality has to a great extent been over-looked or underestimated.

The cult of sensibility in England and France in the mid-eighteenth century was fitted for a person like Jean-Jacques Rousseau (1712–1778), who possessed urges for confession and passion sufficient for a whole world. Since he was never accepted socially in the intellectual and urban *beau monde*, he preferred the rural estate in a supposed harmony between outer and inner nature, landscapes that were the scenario of the sentimental heroine, his mistress. To move from the harsh realism of Shakespeare and the sceptical Montaigne to Rousseau is like entering a world where the insights into passion of his predecessors do not exist. It is like turning the clock back to some earlier period in history. But history never moves in a straight line and progressive interpretations of man's development should be approached with caution. Everyone is a child of his time, but some times have a greater tendency than others to limp and be one-eyed. This applies to a particular extent to Rousseau and sections of Romanticism.

Jean-Jacques Rousseau is a worthy candidate for the title of the single individual who has most shaped the modern Western heart. Everything in his writing has to do with the heart. It is not only the seat of the emotions and the origin of love but also the bearer of the good in an ethical and divine sense – and a symbol of all this. The innermost in man is hidden in the heart. If one is in doubt about what is right, one ought therefore to listen to the voice of one's heart, for it speaks in accordance with the law that God has inscribed in it. Rousseau places Nature above the Bible, which, after all, is only a book. It is not on some chance pages in a book that 'God's' law is to be sought but in man's own heart. Since it is God who has created Nature – including man – which thereby is good, the goal must be to follow Nature's law such as we know it within ourselves. 'God makes all things good; man meddles with them and they become evil', is the opening sentence of the First Book of *Émile; or, On Education* from 1762, Rousseau's main work. With these words, he rejects the seminal Christian doctrine of original sin (the prerequisite for the need of an external Redeemer) and falls out with the Church. If anyone is in doubt as to what is right, this is because society and civilization have poisoned the moral instinct man has by nature.

The widespread idea – still alive and kicking today – that 'the natural' is what is best, and that Nature knows best, is something modern man has to thank Rousseau for. This is a purely ideological concept that does not hold water as a serious argument as it has a logical flaw. In epistemology, the idea is therefore referred to as 'the natural fallacy'. It is a fallacy because the leap from *is* to *ought to* is illogical, i.e. one cannot go from a descriptive depiction of nature to what it is right to do. To turn Nature into a norm, a guiding principle, has left such a bloody trail behind it in European twentieth-century history that it ought to be impossible both intellectually and politically to do so. When it comes to man, nothing is natural, as man is formed by forming nature.

So there may be every reason to emphasize that it is human nature or his given being – and not physical nature out there – that Rousseau is primarily thinking of when uttering the best-known phrase attributed to him: 'Back to Nature!' Rousseau was not interested in unspoilt nature. It was simple provincial life, the countryside and country life on the estate that he regarded as being 'natural'. The goal of his adoration of nature was first and foremost 'outside Paris', whose decadent city life ruined human nature. Beautiful souls are his concern, as in the 'Preface' to *Julie, or the New Heloise* (1761): 'Nature created them [beautiful souls], social institutions ruined them.' For that reason, he wishes to create a new society that will take care of and form beautiful souls. A new view of both nature and culture is called for.

The striking thing about Rousseau is perhaps not his thoughts but that they were to have such an impact. Alongside Darwin, Marx, Freud and Einstein, there is hardly anyone who has had a greater influence on our modern attitudes than Rousseau – mostly indirectly, since few people have read his books in the original, though his own age read some of them as 'bestsellers', especially the love story *Julie; or, The New Heloise*, where he lays the foundation for Romanticism. More than any other individual, he can perhaps be called a spiritual father of the French Revolution, which broke out shortly after his death (though many opposing political movements draw on him for inspiration, and though Rousseau himself was afraid of revolution). Virtually all major contemporary writers and those immediately after him were directly and lastingly influenced by Rousseau's thoughts – from Goethe, Novalis and Hölderlin to Shelley and Byron. The emotion-based subjectivism that Rousseau represented had an emancipatory effect on art, which was now able to throw off the classical stylistic requirements and give pent-up emotions as well as subjective expressive needs free rein.

In his opposition to the Enlightenment and the technical rationality of the bourgeoisie, Rousseau is continuing the critique of reason formulated by Pascal with the well-known words 'The heart has its reasons, which reason knows not of'. This is where Rousseau's ideal of love comes in. In his view of love he is in many ways reactionary and psychologically regressive, in the sense that he returns to the ideal of the Middle Ages and the age of chivalry. He gives Tristanism a new lease of life more than 500 years after Gottfried and 150 years after Shakespeare's tragedy of Juliet.

In his love story, *Julie*, Rousseau also places the loving couple on a country estate as a contemporary counterpart to a knightly castle. But while Tristan and Isolde consummate their erotic love in outer exile, in the temple grotto, love goes into an inner exile in Rousseau. This is what is modern about him. Love in itself becomes a problem. When the loving couple, Julie and her non-noble tutor and seducer Saint-Preux, do not get each other, it is not simply because of social class differences and outer difficulties but because they themselves have so many reservations and inner hindrances, overloaded as they are with all sorts of norms and idealistic conceptions of various kinds that their desire changes direction. These mental inhibitions, of which the outer hindrances are a symbol, are a prerequisite for passion: the greater the inhibitions and barriers, the greater the pent-up need becomes, and the easier it is to retreat into dream, poetry and fabricated ideals that can never be realized in real life. And the more unattainable the ideal is, the greater the fear of trying to bring it about. The immediate surroundings of passion and desire are broken by the diverse needs to control and the fear of distance, separation and death.

The closest Saint-Preux gets to happy love is when he is allowed to enter Julie's garden after losing her – a piece of nature that she has tended and cultivated so that it appears as an image of and the fruit of her blossoming love. He now sees it as a lover many years after his infatuation, at a distance in space and time from the goal of his love. And it is here that he experiences a great happiness in his sublimated thoughts and erotic fantasies. He is able to use his powers of self-suggestion to achieve an overpowering sense of unity. This is what Romanticism is all about. The aim of romantic love is not sex but the heart. This shift tends to produce unhappy lives – but good literature.

The Romantic psyche and the psychological motives for Rousseau's sublimations can be derived from his novel-like *Confessions* (1781–8). In them he not only continues Augustine's literary and autobiographical work of the same name but just as much the Christian confessional tradition, which he secularizes by turning it inside-out, by putting his private life on show in an uncompromising, honest *and* pathetically self-justifying fashion. Augustine's heart was set on fire after having been struck by Jesus's love-arrow. Rousseau lights his own love of himself abandoned to himself after having lost practically everything and everyone – home, family and native town – after having sent all his children to a children's home, against the wishes of his faithful wife. His mother died soon after his birth; his dreamer of a father left him to try his fortune as a clock-maker in the Ottoman land of fairytales before the lad could read or write. Sensitive Rousseau knows something about the vulnerabilities of childhood – a law of consequence later sublimely formulated by Wordsworth: 'The child is the father of the man.'

Rousseau adopts a strange, intermediate position in European anthropology when it comes to whether man's being is a creature of nature or nurture. On the one hand, he claims throughout his entire oeuvre that everything will turn out well as long as man is true to his own innate nature; on the other hand, he was just as consistent in underlining that upbringing is absolutely vital in determining whether someone becomes good or bad. In *Émile*, he wants to develop the most useful of all arts: 'the art of forming a human being'. The basis for this art he presents in the First Book: 'All that we lack at birth, all that we need when we come to man's estate, is the gift of education'. As the inspiring force behind modern pedagogy and child-rearing, he can with *Émile* be called the discoverer of the child and childhood as an age in its own right, something else than adult life in miniature.

Rousseau was ahead of his time in stressing how important not only physical rearing is – in line with the motto 'A healthy mind in a healthy body' – but also how important play and motivation are for all learning and development. Over a century before Nietzsche rediscovers the body, Rousseau emphasizes how detrimental it is for children to sit still and not use their bodies: 'Do not make a child sit still when he wants to run about, nor run when he wants to be quiet. Let them run, jump, and shout to their heart's content', he writes in the Second Book of *Émile*. Nietzsche's later punch-line – 'It is a sin against the Holy Ghost to sit' – sounds almost like an echo of Rousseau's conception of the body. If one thinks of the restrictions on physical spontaneity and sensory impulsiveness applied during the educational project of the Enlightenment and the bourgeoisie precisely in the period of history when Rousseau was writing – as the critic of civilization Norbert Elias has shown in his *The Civilizing Process* (1982) – Rousseau would seem to be a truly emancipatory figure, not only when it comes to the body but also the mind, since free thought depends on a body with unfettered senses and spontaneity. 'Our first teachers in natural philosophy are our feet, hands, and eyes', he writes in the same book, 'to learn to think we must therefore exercise our limbs, our senses, and our bodily organs, which are the tools of the intellect'. And modern neurologists concur: the intellect interacts with the emotions and the body. From this angle, Rousseau participates with his view of the child in uncovering the covering of the body that began with the discovery of spirit in Greek Antiquity and that reached a high-point in the Platonic-Pauline condemnation of the corporeal-sensual in Christianity.

Rousseau's anthropology cannot be extricated from his language and his style. More than any other philosopher he demonstrates that the heart of language and the language of the heart are two sides of the same coin. For in Rousseau there is a mutual or complementary relation between the passions and the emotions he argues in favour of as the root of all good, and the language he uses concerning these sources of knowledge. Through his style he conjures up what he believes in, creates moods via figurative and pathetic language, uses his own feelings and passions as an argument for the emotions. No matter whether he is arguing in favour of the law of the heart, the goodness of Nature or God's existence, it is always based on the emotions. So life and teaching coincide in Rousseau. His entire life and oeuvre are the expression of a specially 'ardent disposition', as he phrases it in his *Confessions* (Book III):

> Two things very opposite, unite in me, and in a manner which I cannot myself conceive. My disposition is extremely ardent, my passions lively and impetuous, yet my ideas are produced slowly, with great embarrassment and after much afterthought. It might be said my heart and understanding do not belong to the same individual. A sentiment takes possession of my soul with the rapidity of lightning, but instead of illuminating, it dazzles and confounds me; I feel all, but see nothing; I am warm, but stupid; to think I must be cool . . . I know nothing from what I see, but all from what I remember, nor have I understanding except in my recollections.

This quotation more than demonstrates that the insistence on the precedence of the emotions in Romanticism has dualism as its *sine qua non*. In his attack on reason and knowledge, Rousseau is not less dualistic than the philosopher of reason, Kant – rather more so. All Rousseau's passionately involved work on passion and emotions, love and eroticism also show how problematic it is to use emotions as an argument for truth. Not simply because of circular arguments that are logically non-valid. Emotions are neither true nor false is the post-Hume position of philosophy. But emotions always involve – not only the person involved but also the one who is the subject of the involvement. That is what rhetoric is all about. For emotions speak directly to the heart and often bulldoze any capacity for objective reflection. Emotions are human, all too human, according to Nietzsche. That is why they must be evaluated critically and interpreted symptomatically. Rousseau and his writing are in themselves an example of this fact. Nevertheless, Rousseau's strength lies absolutely in his subjective capacity for sensual experiencing and empathizing, for feeling and imagining. He cultivates subjectivity in a way nobody ever has prior to him. This gives him an important place in the history of ideas and has strongly influenced our view of mankind for all posterity.

Rousseau gave back *pathos* to Europe. More than that. He also placed sympathy in its modern meaning empathy on the anthropological agenda – completely in accordance with the sentimentalism of his age, as we began this chapter by pointing out. The question, already raised by Thomas Hobbes (1588–1659), is whether human egoism can be restricted via sympathy and empathy with one's fellow man. In that respect, the French philosophers of the Enlightenment – including Rousseau – were somewhat misanthropic. But Rousseau was the only philosopher of the age who claimed – in a violent polemic with the venomous Voltaire – that human nature originally had a capacity for empathy and for reacting spontaneously to evil and the suffering of others. His point of departure is that *heart speaks to heart* – until society and theoretical education destroyed that capacity. This is the basis for his well-known definition of a philosopher (theoretician) in his first book of *Émile*: 'Such philosophers will love the Tartars to avoid loving their neighbours'. Rousseau's solution is to begin with the familiar, to learn and develop sympathy at the local level, subsequently extending it by degrees.

This ethics of 'encounter' with the Other, with its anthropological assumptions, is one aspect of Rousseau's emotionalism that has been overlooked, and perhaps places him in a new light, especially considering that empathy went, so to speak, underground with the Kantian ethics of rule and duty, right up until the present day. Empathy does not become part of the vocabulary of ethics until early in the twentieth century. Nor does Hannah Arendt emphasize the importance of the emotions and empathy in here explanation of the holocaust and *Banality of Evil* (1961). It was not until the present age (with Emmanuel Levinas's ethics of encounter with the Other) that the importance of empathy became fully accepted if one is to act spontaneously and in a morally adequate way. But Rousseau also emphasized empathy, sympathy and the importance of proximity in interpersonal relationships. Only the person who suffers or has suffered can have sympathy for others who suffer. His autobiographical writings can be read as a personal appeal for sympathy and thereby understanding and recognition. We are perhaps dealing with a particular French tradition here, from the Héloïse of the age of chivalry via Rousseau and the aesthetics of identification of his age and its tearful novels to Zola's *J'accuse!* and Levinas's *Humanism of the Other* (1995).

This, in both senses, 'sympathetic' side of Rousseau's teaching has, however, been overshadowed by his passion. Rousseau ignored the ABC of rhetoric – that pathos is only one aspect of a whole human being. Pathos has to be combined with logos, the rational or universal, and with an ethically defensible attitude, ethos. Instead, Rousseau uses his intellect to strengthen his pathos and the conceptions, associations and images related to passion in a cumulative circle. Because of this, Rousseau's one-sided way of thinking is open to criticism.

It is suffering and passion more than compassion that everybody shares. Rousseau confuses the suffering that is a consequence of life being as it is with the suffering that results from passion not attaining its egoistic aim. He cultivates unfulfilled passion instead of trying to clarify the conditions for shared existential suffering. In so doing, he is ill equipped to live in a society with others – and he blames society. Instead of identifying the creative forces in culture that actually were the condition for his own life's work, he turns his back on culture and proclaims his regressive and reactionary 'Back to Nature!' Whereas the goal, to create a civilization with freedom for all, which he writes about with such utopian enthusiasm, is to organize conditions in such a way that it enables one to move 'Forward to Culture!' That is, in fact, what Rousseau has done with his entire life and work, despite all his declaration of the opposite. He has created culture, not nature. The images and symbols Rousseau has given Western culture are by no means few. Not least, he has shaped our heart to such an extent that all of us, to a greater or lesser degree, are Romantics – whether we wish it or not. But the Romantic concept of culture is not his – it belongs to the German philosopher J. G. Herder.

CHAPTER 14

Herder and the Expressivist Turn

> My heart leaps up when I behold
> A rainbow in the sky:
> So was it when my life began;
> So is it now I am a man;
> So be it when I shall grow old,
> Or let me die!
> The Child is father of the Man;
> And I could wish my days to be
> Bound each to each by natural piety.
> Wordsworth

Romanticism is often thought of as being both anti-intellectual and anti-scientific. In actual fact, though, it is Romanticism that creates both the science of history, philology and cultural philosophy, in addition to which it uses natural philosophy as a foundation for the new anthropology of man as a being of symbols. It is the leading Romantic philosopher Johann Gottfried Herder (1744–1803) who completes the theoretical foundation for the Romantic anthropology Rousseau had laid and Goethe had built on.

Since Herder was a contemporary of Immanuel Kant (1724–1804), decreed by the history of philosophy to have been in the victor in the battle between the two, Herder has ended up in Kant's shadow. Herder's philosophy has yet to be given the credit it deserves, though in many ways it was Herder – more than Kant – who laid the foundation for the understanding of man that has become a matter of course for us today. And that makes us more Romantics than we would like to admit.

It was Herder who founded modern linguistic philosophy, with his treatise *On the Origin of Language* (1772). And it was Herder who laid the foundation of our modern understanding of man as both a historical and a cultural being that lives in a universe of artificial symbols. Language, culture and history are the basis of the anthropology developed by

200

Herder. Man has not been created in a given image with a being fixed for eternity; he becomes what he makes out of himself on the basis of his natural and historical conditions and possibilities. And how man realizes these possibilities is revealed via his *expressions* in a broad sense – via both his material and immaterial expressions, in writing and speech, art and technology, etc. Man's expressive potential thus forms the basis of the anthropology of Romanticism. The Romantic theory of expression that Herder introduced represents an *expressivist turn,* a term introduced by Charles Taylor (1975 and 1989).

Little notice has been taken of the fact that Herder – and not Kant – was the first person to call the turn taken by philosophy in the latter half of the eighteenth century *Copernican.* In 1765 the 21-year-old Herder announced a philosophical programme with anthropology at its centre (that is what Herder calls the Copernican aspect) which he adhered to for the rest of his life: 'That all philosophy, if it is to serve mankind, must be anthropology', which also includes what later came to be called 'philosophy of life'.[1]

An essential difference between Herder and Kant is that Herder never forgets that man both *is* and *has* a nature (not only reason) with an individual body that has senses and feelings that give a different and personal approach to the world to the abstract categories of reason that Kant laid his man emphasis on in order to give knowledge a universally valid basis. Where Kant seeks the universal, Herder has as his point of departure the concrete and the local, i.e. a relational culture. Herder also stresses that man, unlike the rest of physical and biological nature, is capable of defying determinism and breaking the laws that are universally valid. On the basis of this, he characterizes man as 'the first to be released in nature'. Seen from the point of view of determinist nature, man is a *being who lacks*, with weak instincts. These 'lacks' he compensates for by means of language and reason and inherited knowledge as to how to influence nature in order to survive. The invention of language (which results in culture) Herder calls man's second genesis, the first being the creation of the species *Homo sapiens.* The heart is the sensible key to both of man's natures, as expressed by Herder's contemporary avant-gardistic Romantic poet Novalis: 'Das Herz ist der Schlüssel der Welt und des Lebens' (The heart is the key to the world and life).

That Herder throughout his life attacked the abstract philosophy of reason advanced by the Enlightenment and Kant was especially due to the fact that he – ahead of his time – claimed that reason was dependent on and determined by language, experience, history and tradition. All his life, he kept insisting that reason was linguistically bound, and that language determines everything that is human:

Pure reason without language is Utopia here on earth. The same applies to the passions of the heart, all the attitudes of society. Only language has made man human, since it dammed up the tremendous flood of his effects by placing reasoned labels on them with words.[2]

By means of language, man embodies the world in language. The world is language. Therefore, Herder is able to say – and this is the crucial point he is making – that 'the passions of the heart' cannot be detached from language either. More than this: Herder makes the passions of the heart and the emotions the source and origin of language. In his own way he makes the expression 'What your heart is full of, your mouth overflows with' the anthropological basis of his theory of expression. From an evolutionary perspective, language is – so to speak – a result of emotional pressure. That applies not only to Romanticism, but to mankind.

From his very first writings, Herder has defined all life as being an 'urge and compulsion to express oneself'. This means that the 'passions of the heart' and passionate outbursts are no longer merely symptomatic stimulus-response functions but mental expressions for meaning in and with life. In this way Herder links the emotional turn to the expressivist turn. The emotional and the expressive are two sides of the same coin, impression and expression in constant alternation. At the same instant that man begins to find words for his emotions and to define them in terms of language, this definition works retroactively on the emotions and 'dams up the effects' to use Herder's own words – dams that can admittedly burst, as Freud was able to demonstrate over a century later. But these outbursts of emotions can then be apprehended and determined in terms of language, thereby restoring the control. At the centre of this process of creation, formation and re-formation is the human heart, which is elated or depressed depending on what kind of creative or destructive influence makes itself felt.

With the subjectivistically expressivist and corresponding aesthetic revolution (art is not *mimesis*, but *poiesis*), Herder (along with Kant and his Copernican turn) completes and intensifies the process that Plato began: internalization: the world is inside – the psyche is the centre of the world. The Copernican or expressivist turn that Herder represents is really a linguistic turn. But it does not make its mark scientifically and epistemologically until almost 200 years after Herder launched it. This is when Wittgenstein and his contemporaries present 'the linguistic turn', which came to alter both humanist and social sciences in the latter half of the twentieth century, with the motto: 'all is language'. This has had such an impact that all of us talk about the cultural turn, as it is now referred to, very much in the spirit of Herder, since language constitutes culture.

Romanticism is the first historical era to realize that everything is historical mediation and development, and that the real human being is a concrete individual (and not an abstract philosophical concept) who differs from every other individual. That is why each and every person constantly has to find his own form and express it, a form that can never be found once and for all, but always has to be re-formed and re-created. This development, with all its various developmental stages, Romanticism – and Goethe – saw in nature and man himself.

CHAPTER 15

Faustian Goethe

To live is to fight with demons
in heart and brain
Henrik Ibsen

Rousseau influenced the main work of the *Sturm und Drang* era – *The Sorrows of Young Werther* (1774), by Johann Wolfgang von Goethe (1749–1832). Written in epistolary novel form, this work was directly influenced by Shakespeare's *Romeo and Juliet*. Werther ends by taking his own life, not only because he cannot get his beloved Lotte but also because she does not fit into the ideal world into which he has retreated (this is, of course, Romantic love). The aim was unwavering despite Werther's escapism: the ideal of a love that is from a different world than the bourgeois and the trivial. That, too, is how the work was perceived. It spread like an epidemic at the time, becoming a cult novel, with many young people taking their own lives inspired by Werther. The cultivation of single-minded passion, of pathos, culminated in European culture in the *Sturm und Drang* period, with the heart as a symbol of great love in both an erotic and idealistic sense.

An artistic high point of Romanticism and Western culture is Goethe's *Faust*. Here Goethe picks up the thread of the late Renaissance and Shakespeare, borrowing the Faust motif from Shakespeare's older contemporary and rival Christopher Marlowe, who wrote his Faust tragedy in late 1580s. Both Mephistopheles and Faust in Goethe's great work are directly inspired by some of Shakespeare's characters. We have previously mentioned the cold-blooded Edmund in *King Lear*, who has Mephistophelean traits, and Gretchen is the erotic equivalent of Cordelia. Gretchen can be read as a function of the Romantic metaphorics of the heart and Faust as a function of the dialectic and tension between heart and brain. Gretchen's heart represents absolute love, conscience and personal integrity, all of which are tainted by Faust's betrayal. It illustrates the connection between passion and suffering, love and compassion – a *leit-motiv* throughout Goethe's writing – with the heart as the arena where desire and pain, longing and sorrow and all the forms of mental agony are enacted. Gretchen's heart also represents the soul that is saved because she has loved with a whole and pure heart, and that is therefore also able to save others – especially *the* other, the beloved. So she sums up important aspects of the Western ideal of love.

Some quotations from *Faust 1* where Gretchen pours out her troubles can illustrate what the heart stands for in Western high culture. 'My peace is gone,/My heart is sore' (*Meine Ruh' ist hin,/Mein Herz ist schwer*) is one of the refrains. Gretchen also realizes that her opposite, the evil Mephisto-pheles, has a cold heart: 'His presence chills my blood . . . That to his heart no living soul is dear . . . And still my heart doth close when he comes near'(*Seine Gegenwart bewegt mir das Blut . . . Dass er nicht mag eine Seele lieben . . . Und seine Gegenwart schnürt mir das Innre zu*). The evil person is cold and calculating, thinking only in terms of means and ends. Goethe lets emotions be the yardstick of a human being when he makes Gretchen cry out from her prison cell: 'If thou art human, feel my misery!' (*Bist du ein Mensch/so fühle meine Not*). Empathy is the prerequisite for being human, i.e. compassionate. Elsewhere in *Faust* it says: 'Feeling is all' (*Gefühl ist alles*) – words are just noise and empty air. The feelings of the heart are both the criterion for being human and the basis of existence. That is why Faust can say to Gretchen (partly as an apology for having seduced her):

> Fill thence thy heart, how large soe'er it be,
> And in the feeling when thou utterly art blest,
> Then call it, what thou wilt, –
> Call it Bliss! Heart! Love! God!

> *Erfüll davon dein Herz, so groß es ist,*
> *Und wenn du ganz in dem Gefühle selig bist,*
> *Nenn es dann, wie du willst,*
> *Nenn's Glück! Herz! Liebe! Gott!*

With his life-work as a writer, Goethe – along with such writers as Novalis, Hölderlin and, later, Rilke as well as the English Romantics – stands out as an innovator of Western metaphorics and symbolism of the heart. There are a number of reasons why the metaphors of the heart have such a convincing aesthetical and thematic effect in Goethe's writing. First and foremost this is because it is so perfectly integrated into the classical expressive power of his poetry; also because anthropologically it represents the centre of man and what life is all about. The heart becomes so satiated with polysemantic and polyphonic meaning in Goethe's writing that it goes beyond the limits of metaphorics and regains the nature of the symbol – and becomes the jewel in the crown, lighting up the work and mind from within, enlightening us concerning what it means to be a human being in the world, a symbol that also includes the reader to such an extent that it is impossible to find a place of interpretation outside the heart that reveals the symbol as a concept – completely in accordance with Goethe's own school-founding definition of the symbol.

Goethe's work is paradigmatic in the history of the heart, where the main line in Western culture since the emotional turn in the High Middle Ages represents a metaphorization of the heart and an individual internalization of the feelings and passions for which it stands. Goethe represents another line in his art, one that cannot be restricted to art, with a transition from the medieval allegory (Dante and Christian literature) to modern autonomous symbolic language, which also represents an alternative mode of cognition as regards philosophy and modern science – in accordance with his own canonical definition in two well-known aphorisms:

> Symbolism transforms the appearance into idea, the idea into an image, and in such a way that the idea in the image always remains infinitely active and unreachable and, even though expressed in all languages would yet remain inexpressible.[1]

> That is true symbolism, where the particular represents what is more universal, not as a dream or shadow but as live-instantaneous revelation of the impenetrable.[2]

With its vast depths, the heart fathoms precisely the unfathomable that can only be revealed in symbolic form, as Goethe himself does when he allows it to symbolize what it is that makes man human, beyond any idea or scientific definition.

One of Goethe's great aims is to overcome the modern cleft between the subject and the object and to let the subjective mind become part of the objective spirit, which cannot either become real without its concrete subjective manifestations: 'Just as the objective cannot find expression unless it too comes 'from the heart', so must the ultimate innermost subjective truth go to the objective in order to find form'.[3] That what comes from the heart can also be objective clashes with what most people believe nowadays. But our personal hearts acquire meaning precisely because of what the heart represents in our common culture,

and vice versa. The common treasure trove of symbols, with its references to the objective spirit, enables the subject to communicate with
other subjects about what its heart is full of. The necessary condition is
trust. All communication – as the Danish philosopher K. E. Løgstrup
has demonstrated – presupposes openness and spontaneity, and an
irreducible *trust* in our being able spontaneously to *speak out*, straight
from the heart, without what we say being used against us.[4] Trust, in
turn, is a manifestation of the given or objective love that spontaneously
and unconditionally goes from heart to heart – moving both ways with
questions and answers in an open dialogue. This condition for objective –
or intersubjective – community Goethe has formulated both in *Faust i*
and *ii*, here in *Faust i*:

> nothing can affect our hearts
> that does not have its source in feeling [the heart].

> *Denn es muß von Herzen gehen,*
> *Was auf Herzen wirken soll.*

With Goethe the heart also recovers its substantial nature as a feeling,
sensing organ that gives man integrity at all levels – inwardly and outwardly – whose regular beat coincides with that of the nature that the
pantheist-oriented Goethe felt himself to be a part of, as in *On the Lake*
(1775):

> And fresh nourishment, new blood
> I suck from a world so free;
> Nature, how gracious and how good,
>   Her breast she gives to me!

> *Und frische Nahrung, neues Blut*
> *Saug ich aus freier Welt;*
> *Wie ist Natur so hold und gut,*
>   *Die mich am Busen hält!*

Goethe's view of man and his universe of images cannot be grasped without an understanding of his view of nature, which is both the cornerstone
and stumbling-block of his thought. Unlike the Renaissance, Descartes
and his older contemporary Kant, Goethe was interested in *organic*
nature, which has to be understood according to its purpose, not its
cause. Goethe's basic idea, anticipating Darwin, was that everything is

interconnected in a continuum (cf. his *The Metamorphosis of Plants*, 1790) – from lower forms of life to higher, from the simple to the complex. With this as his foundation, he discovered the so-called intermaxillary bone in man (later referred to in anatomy as the Goethe bone), because on the basis of his fundamental idea it ought to be there, even though contemporary anatomical science rejected the idea of there being such a 'primitive' bone in man. On this basis Goethe developed the analogical method, based on the principle that like knows like, as an alternative method to science's cause-defined knowledge of nature. Man can experience light and colour as he does precisely because the eye is adapted to light. 'If the eye were not like the sun,/ it would not be able to see the sun's light' are well-known lines from his *Theory of Colours* (1810), on which he worked for more than 20 years.

In the heart of nature man meets God at the very centre of his own self, in his own heart. When the heart feels the warmth of the light, which the eye sees and mediates, the heart also has an eye – in Goethe's system of analogies between Sun and God, light and love, eye and ear, heart and wisdom. The heart's eye is central both to Goethe's anthropology and his picture of the world, which is based on a vision of the world (*Weltanschauung*) more than scientific knowledge. The divine also reveals itself to this inner gaze that obeys the heart and sees with the heart's eye of thought, whose visionary sight it is the poet's lot to communicate. The intuitive insights which the heart's eye (which the alchemists were so preoccupied with) gains via empathy and imagination are deeper than so-called scientific knowledge of the intellect. In order to fully know both the divine and oneself, man therefore has to become absorbed in his own inner self, in the depths of the heart that testify to what reason does not know, and that only sympathetic love can gain access to by living and learning. That is why Faust's eternal striving to know the world ends up with self-knowledge. The man who strove to the utmost that he 'the force may recognize/ That binds creation's inmost energies' is reflected back into his own bottomless, complex inner self in order to find in our own heart 'what the world will not provide' – assuming that the person has allowed himself to be inspired in accordance with the prayer of the *Pater profundis* in the redemption scene in *Faust II*:

> Quiet, o God, my troubled thoughts,
> and grant my needy heart Your Light!

The feeling heart and the clear brain, love and reason, are two sides of the same coin, since it is the same divine force that inspires both thought and the heart. *Cor* and *cortex* also rhyme, anthropologically speaking, in Goethe's poetic universe.

As Oswald Spengler has so precisely formulated it, *Faust* represents the infinite, the urge towards the infinite in Western culture that transcends what is close, life here and now, the reason why we Westerners are always striving – also in the negative sense of the word – always champing at the carrot ahead, always seeking to move upwards socially. We can never relax before the goal has been reached, but once it has been reached it is turned into the means towards a new goal ahead. While the solution, perhaps, is for us to sit down in quietude in order to collect our scattered thoughts (and feelings). It costs nothing. Only time, quality time – which is what the whole thing is about.

Finite Faust, however, threatens to come apart in his chasing for what cannot be caught up with ahead of him. No one can match the restlessness of his heart, which can never rest before achieving its goals. His endless striving is both his curse and his salvation. Goethe's solution and salvation, however, are not conventionally Christian. Faust is not saved because he zealously conforms to the dogma of salvation out of faith and suffering in others' stead but because he tries to save himself:

> For him whose strivings never ceases
> we can provide redemption

Goethe personally rejected Jesus's suffering on 'that wearisome wood of torment' as 'the most repulsive thing under the sun', in a letter to his friend, the composer Carl Friedrich Zelter dated 9 June 1831. It is *the other person*, Gretchen's love of Faust, that saves him. Faust's temperament, his purposefulness, seen among other things in his will to control nature and his ecologically ruinous entrepreneurism, ultimately rests in a love that is without any intention, that drive everything forward as an end in itself: 'it is all-potent love, that gives/all things their form, sustains all things'.

Faust is a creation of Goethe's restless heart. Like Augustine, Goethe seeks rest via his work, which he once referred to as 'fragments of a major confession', alluding to Augustine's *Confessiones*. If Faust can be saved (something we doubt, even though we believe in Goethe's saving power), it is because he has remained true to his transcending heart. Like Augustine, he has sought quietude in the infinite, the transcendent, while death and destruction of nature lie behind him in a failed earthly life. Maybe scared by the fantastic imaginative power of the portrayal of instrumental entrepreneurism in the character of Faust, for Goethe personally sought rest somewhere else. One of his most famous poems was written in pencil on the wall of a hunting lodge where after a long walk he had found physical and mental rest, rest after life's long journey. While Augustine believes in rest in the One, in the utopian unity with God, Goethe the pantheist in his poem *Wanderer's Night Song* (as translated by Longfellow in 1845) seeks peace of mind in the infinite Cosmos, released from everything – 'Linger awhile' – dissolved into the infinity beyond unity, free of everything and fulfilled in the void out of which everything is created:

> O'er all the hill-tops
> Is quiet now,
> In all the tree-tops
> Hearest thou
> Hardly a breath;
> The birds are asleep in the trees:
> Wait, soon like these
> Thou, too, shalt rest.

In terms of the history of science, it must be said that Goethe lost in his criticism of modern science. But in terms of epistemology, his analogical and symbolical understanding of nature has perhaps been rehabilitated by both quantum mechanics and the linguistic turn, which have taught us that our understanding of nature is linguistic and anthropomorphic, and that our images and concepts for both man and nature also form our selves and influence nature.

An objection could perhaps be raised against this linguistic position: that it is uninteresting in relation to emotional life how emotions are theoretically defined. Emotions live their own life independently of how they are categorized by the intellect. But that is not how man works. *Cognition* and *recognition* are not merely two linguistically related phenomena. What and how we sense and feel depends on our historical conditions and on how we perceive and understand various phenomena. Nor is it merely a question of heart or head, reason or feelings, but – in line with Goethe's basic view – of trying to find a reasonable and harmonious balance between them under changing conditions. Romanticism is the first period that regards man and society as historical change and development. With Romanticism and the philosopher Hegel, man moves from something essential that *is* to something functional that is becoming, from being (*sein*) to becoming (*werden*). And Goethe was well aware of the importance of this, as in *Blessed Longing* (1814):

> Never prompted to that quest:
> Die and dear rebirth!

You remain a dreary guest
On our gloomy earth.

This state of affairs intensifies sharply under Nietzsche, who claims that man has to become a new species.

CHAPTER 16

The Disenchantment and
Re-enchantment of the Heart

We have to re-learn, in order, perhaps too late,
to attain even more: to re-feel.
Nietzsche, The Dawn

You burned your way
into my heart,
You got the key
to my brain.
Bob Dylan, 'Spirit on the Water'

If Montaigne is one of the inventors of modern Western man, Friedrich Nietzsche (1844–1900) is his conqueror. He deserves this title because he crushes the Western image of man based on Christian-Platonist morality with its particular metaphysics and humanist idealism. Nietzsche wishes to replace everything that man is in our Christian-Platonist tradition by something far more basic, with its source in the body, pre-conscious life-vitality and spontaneous reason. This does not mean that Nietzsche thinks we should follow our hearts or be 'faithful to our emotions and conscience', as if heart, emotions and conscience exist independently of inherited values and moral norms. The person who follows the heart does not follow his own heart but the prejudices, sympathies and antipathies we have inherited from our parents and the whole social environment, Nietzsche claims. He repeatedly stresses that what we believe are universally valid emotions and values are historically determined and the result of far too 'good' or effective rearing. That is why he wants a re-evaluation of all values. That is why we have to re-learn in order to feel differently. Nietzsche has no other gods than those 'in *us*: our reason and our own experience'.[1]

Nietzsche says that a new type of man can and must be created, precisely because man is an open and uncompleted being. Man is unfinished in the sense that he has not yet become what he shall become. Man is 'a not yet determined animal'.[2] Within him he has the potential to become something else, and better, that has not yet been developed and realized. For that reason, Nietzsche wants to conquer man in his present unfinished and incomplete form. This is the point of departure for his 'self-expressionist theory' (*Selbstdarstellungstheorie*). Here he takes up arms against what he perceives as being an amputated image of man that has been prevalent in Western culture, focusing on man's self-consciousness and subject-identity in the tradition of Plato, Descartes, Kant and the entire Enlightenment tradition.

The tradition of self-expression – from the Sophists, Montaigne, Herder and Romanticism via Nietzsche to postmodernism – opens up fantastic possibilities of reason and art, life-vitality and heterogeneous forces that cannot be reduced to a self-identical consciousness in the development of personality. In the tradition of self-expression, the art of life is more important than the theoretical definition of self-consciousness, as the German philosopher Wilhelm Schmid has given an account of in his school-setting work on the philosophy of the art of life.[3] For when the subject has been determined as a rational self-consciousness and self-referring identity, it can be objected that it will end up by closing around itself – in its own image. Subsequently, it is difficult to entertain an idealistic conception of a self-identical subject.

> For the modern subject, who is 'a vagabond in existence', there is no return to the 'identical'. What seemed to be our 'own' and our 'origin' is, as soon as we try to 'turn back', already different and lost.[4]

The self is composed of various different sources. Man does not have any core of identity. The art of life is not self-affirmation but an attempt to reconcile opposing forces in a purposive way to form an *integrity* rather than an identity to become master in one's own house in a constructive manner.[5] That is Nietzsche's project – his life-work in a double sense. No one can rival Nietzsche in having lived his life so much as a life of thought and thought his thoughts as life. The prerequisite for being able to create his life in the way he wants is precisely that man is heterogeneous in composition and yet unfinished. He must take sole responsibility for who he is and what he has become. Everyone, more of less, thinks and reflects about his life, but Nietzsche wants to live life in such a way that he has something worth thinking about. He views 'life as an experimental arrangement for thinking, essayism as a way of life'.[6] He pulls down the Christian cross and takes instead (as a substitute for everybody) the world on his shoulders like Atlas, in order to show humanity how effortlessly easy it is to shoulder freedom and to create one's own life-work like some Promethean Titan.

In order to overcome all the inhibiting forces that extinguish the creative spark of life, Nietzsche takes the body as his starting point. He gains inspiration from Homeric man, from the time before the human body was covered and later suppressed by the Platonic-Christian tradition. With his philosophy of the body he makes a frontal attack on the dualism between body and soul that has permeated Western culture. Instead, he affiliates himself with a 'corporeal' undercurrent that has existed through-out the history of ideas, from the Dionysian cult of Antiquity until today, from Diogenes' self-chosen 'dog's life' (cynicism) in his barrel in the marketplace in Athens to the carnivalism of Rabelais and Bakhtin. Nietzsche consequently also opposes the traditional idealists, who make the body serve the soul, while the true relationship is the opposite. According to Nietzsche, the body is the great reason, while rational consciousness is the little reason.

Nietzsche puts a definitive end to the sentimentality of Romanticism. He demonstrates that emotions in themselves are nothing, simply follow-up phenomena and symptoms of something subjective or inherited that one cannot trust. He goes deeper. Instead of emotions, Nietzsche looks for the passion behind them; instead of rationality, the body that the mind is a reflection of; instead of Christian love, Eros and desire; instead of 'feeling sorry' as disguised egoism, he wants to cultivate spontaneous strength. Instead of following the heart, he follows the deep will to power and self-affirmation via the capacity for self-conquest. Nietzsche praises the realist who can withstand all the disillusionment of the false idealism and unmasking of moralism that cloak the will to power.

Nietzsche anticipates two main tendencies in anthropological reflection over the past century that have body and language (two things he felt were intimately interconnected) as their point of departure. For language can be expressed via the body in a broad sense. Both the body and language are open and unfinished and can assume innumerable forms. The body is unpredictable and spontaneous, as thought also is. Therefore, language must have a form that encourages sudden ideas, creative spontaneity, unexpected thoughts, experimental and provisional drafts – in short *essays*. On this basis, Nietzsche presents and practises an essayistic anthropology, as opposed to the Platonic-Cartesian, which is systematically enclosed in hierarchical and linear structures. In theory and practice he ends up confirming Montaigne's and Herder's expressive anthropology that 'man is his own work'.

Many of Nietzsche's ideas had an impact only a hundred years after his death. This could possibly be because Freud showed in the twentieth century just how destructive it is to suppress and make bodily urges a taboo. The critic of civilization Norbert Elias, in the spirit of Freud, has in his main work *The Civilizing Process* (published in 1939, but widely recognized only after 1969, the year it appeared in an English-language translation) given an account of how the development of modern society from the age of chivalry via the Renaissance to the Enlightenment project of the bourgeoisie has created a new type of shame and taboo of everything to do with the naked body, sex and sexuality – with irrationality and inhibitions as a consequence. The fear and anxiety that man once used to feel for nature and a menacing environment become internalized in modern times, so that people consciously or subconsciously placed restrictions in themselves out of a fear of breaking the new limits for shame. In Elias' words, a turn takes place 'from outer coercion to self-coercion' and inner disciplining.

Freud and Elias make themselves spokesmen for a determinist view where the human psyche is a product of social *mores* – parallel to Marx's idea that prevalent economic conditions will determine what kind of ideology is dominant in any given society. Michel Foucault, on the other hand, rejects the Freudian and Marxist theory of repression, *inter alia* because of his insight into how language works in general, and in the modern enlightenment project in particular. The dynamics in the historical and linguistic, the material and mental structures in which man is embedded are of such a nature that Foucault began in the 1970s to talk about the dissolution of the subject and even the death of humanity. In doing so, he is completing the line from Plato and St Paul to Augustine, Descartes and Kant. The forces that were to be controlled via rational internalization, via consciousness-raising, have not only been restricted but killed off. Individual reason is not autonomous and master in its own house. The free inner man and the subject along with it have disintegrated. What is left is desire and determining conditions. Power becomes omnipotent – as in the works of Nietzsche. Foucault's studies of humanity are characterized by a systematic exposure of the structures of power.

In the introductory volume to what was planned as a six-volume work *The History of Sexuality: The Will to Knowledge* (1976), Foucault presents both his methodological grasp of the subject as well as some of his main standpoints (cf. the chapter on Antiquity). He indirectly shows that it is impossible to understand sex life and the emotions connected with it without first understanding the way the powers – the social institutions and the individual – administrate, think, write, speak and converse about sexuality. One can, as Foucault does, go in and analyse the *discourse* that communicates sexuality and love. Discourse can be defined as a qualified and context-related way of talking and arguing – here public mention in general. Foucault consequently operates with 'putting into discourse' – analogous to staging. Nor must it be forgotten that there is never a mechanical causal relation between transforming into discourse and socio-economic relations, or between sex life and its being the subject of discourse. Historical processes are never causally determined in a linear way, but are full of discontinuous interruptions and non-simultaneous processes, leaps and paradoxes. This applies to a particular degree to the development of emotions and attitudes.

The analysis of the historical process of putting sex and sexuality into discourse reveals many paradoxes in our self-understanding. There is a deep and indissoluble irony in many emancipatory projects of the Western world, which often prove to be subtle strategies for social institutions and power-seekers. Foucault rejects the Freudian-Marxist repression hypothesis even so, particularly because it overlooks the fact that sex and sexuality are not so much repressed in the usual sense as that sex becomes the subject of staging and modern disciplinary measures of various kinds, and because the individual can often have considerable room for manoeuvre within modern discourses. And the most prominent stager or actor of discourse is the project of Enlightenment – in the service of power just as much as of the individual. For after the Renaissance, the predominant power techniques have rather been enlightening, reforming and openly interpreting than dogmatically repressive in the old style. Subsequently, there is more discipline at work than repression in modern times. To be familiar with the functions of procreation and the dangers of infection from sex, for example, and all kinds of techniques that can increase or decrease enjoyment when having sex on the basis of anatomical insights, leads to various kinds of new anxiety that are no less effective than the Church's anxiety propaganda. What we know about HIV and Aids infection today has a greater disciplinary effect than the sexual morality of the Church, even though some people could not care less – which in turn demonstrates that enlightenment has its limits. Enlightenment is not everything.

First and foremost Foucault asks not if or why we are repressed but why enlightened Westerners have so long maintained that they are repressed in a paradoxical communication that ends up precisely by confirming the urge for disciplining that was to be done away with by emancipatory discourse. His analysis of how sex has been put into discourse over the past centuries produces surprising results. The more sex is transformed into discourse (positively or negatively), the greater space it will necessarily gain in the public (and private) space of power, 'since the end of the sixteenth century, the "putting into discourse of sex," far from undergoing a process of restriction, on the contrary has been subjected to a mechanism of increasing incitement'.[7] It is not only erotic poetry that has 'itchy fingers'. The explosive transformation of sex into discourse that Foucault finds in the eighteenth century is not only verbal. The detailed confessions of erotic thoughts, words and deeds that the Church demanded, has for logically compelling reasons its empirical counterpart, which breeds promiscuous revelations of people's sex lives. The best-known examples from the eighteenth and nineteenth century are de Sade and anonymous confessions such as *My Secret Life* (*The Sex Diary of a Victorian Gentleman*, first published in Amsterdam 1884–94), where nothing is left to the imagination. Since the Renaissance and the Reformation, both the Church and secular institutions – especially parallel with the new sciences of anatomy and medicine – have put sex into discourse. Inspired and encouraged by the authorities, sex discourses have propagated unceasingly:

> A censorship of sex? There was installed rather an apparatus for producing an even greater quantity of discourse about sex, capable of functioning and taking effect in its very economy . . . Toward the beginning of the eighteenth century, there emerged a political, economic, and technical incitement to talk about sex.[8]

But personal freedom does not necessarily increase as a result of this plethora of words. As a result of this transformation into discourse, everyone – historically speaking – Christian and non-Christian, emancipated or enlightened or not, ends up in positions that have only apparently been chosen, that became the measure and yardstick of identity and become more important than love, according to Foucault: 'When a long while ago the West discovered love [cf. the emotional turn in the Middle Ages], it bestowed on it a value high enough to make death acceptable; nowadays it is sex that claims this equivalence, the highest of all'.[9]

Something similar to what occurs in the wake of the silence and speaking of the Church – and with the same historical origin – is when power and sex meet on the 'free market'. Sex becomes a commodity that is valued according to the outer standards of surface aesthetics. On this 'meat market', *Herz* does indeed rhyme with *Schmerz*, and the soul dissolves in the body's exterior. The body becomes our soul. History turns once again, now from the inner to the outer, in a *sexual turn*. Sex has always been linked to coercion, which exists even in an emancipated age such as ours – presented in illusory fashion as the freedom to choose one's own exterior, one's body, one's own sex as well as that of one's lover, sexual desire and ideals. It is not a matter of the inner urge replacing the natural urge, but that everyone is a product of his age and that the new mechanisms of power, according to Foucault, are aimed at the body and sex. 'One must not think that by saying yes to sex one is saying no to power. On the contrary, one is then following the general direction of sexuality regulations . . . The irony of this request is it causes us to believe that it is a question of our "emancipation",' is Foucault's ironic conclusion to his book.

Nothing is natural to man, not sexuality either. The human heart is also a function of a transformation into discourse of the body and sex, sexuality and emotionality, as demonstrated by Foucault's double manoeuvre. The important thing about this double manoeuvre is that the rational, scientific and aesthetic discourse is a disciplining factor that both excludes and includes, both promotes and inhibits, emancipates and enslaves. The agent in this process is speech, putting words to things and making them rational, which creates this double movement. Foucault affirms, as do other modern theories about sexuality and emotionality, a basic principle in the book you now are reading, that *the heart of language* and *the language of the heart* shape each other complementarily.

Foucault's discursive studies of power can be read as a continuation of Nietzsche's emphasis on power being a central life-principle. In his later work, Foucault also shows how adaptable the individual is in his exploitation of the discourses of power to his own advantage. This is not surprising, since individualism runs like a thread through the Western history of ideas from Antiquity to postmodernism. This focus on the individual in our culture is reflected in the title of Foucault's book about this history, *The Care of the Self*, volume III of *The History of Sexuality*. But it is just as striking that the project of the history of ideas that has development and emancipation of the individual as its aim soon becomes a means of collective enclosure of the individual in the masses. The path from individual freedom to collective behaviour goes via the emotions. It seems to be a constant feature of late modernism that the human heart becomes more and more open, and can easily be filled with any content the market, the institutional power and the discourses of the media have on offer.

The modern project of enlightenment was directed at the individual, who by the use of reason should achieve freedom and thereby contribute to further growth both mentally and materially. Foucault is not the only one to have stressed the paradoxes of this process. Max Weber has shown how the disenchantment of the world with rational means can open up for a re-enchantment using precisely rational means. The heart, too, has been the subject of such a disenchantment when its symbolism in modernity is emptied of its unfathomable historical and moral content and turned into psychological concepts and reduced to projections of something irrational and symptoms of emotions. In science, the heart is defined as a muscle with valves that pumps blood – nothing else. Science (with its hidden passions) does not ask either what our heart is telling us. The restless heart with all its worries and questions becomes objectively fossilized in the Weberian iron cage on the liberal market of a mechanical system of production and consumption. And the undeciphered, enigmatic words written in the blood tracks of a lived life on the ancient palimpsest of the heart are either erased or written over with dead letters on a stone tablet.

'For of the last stage of this cultural development, it might well be truly said: "Specialists without spirit, sensualists without heart; this nullity imagines that it has attained a level of civilization never before achieved",' is Weber's prophecy on the last page of his classic work *The Protestant Ethic and the Spirit of Capitalism* (written in 1904–5 after a journey to the USA, translated into English in 1930). When the heart is emptied in this way, it may very well transpire that the dissected and vulnerably open heart is once more filled with a passionate glow that is not held in check by a voice of conscience that says stop, and that the re-enchanted passion takes over control of the world of rational means. We want to touch this fossilized heart of abstract administrative language, and disturb it with the questions of the restless heart. Against the fossilizing disenchantment of the heart in a technical-rational world we hold up Faust's ambiguous words as a humanizing memento: 'Fill thence thy heart, so large soe'er it be,/And in the feeling when thou utterly art blest,/ Then call it, what thou wilt,–/Call it Bliss! Heart! Love! God!'

Theodor Adorno and Max Horkheimer also give an account of how rationality, *logos*, returns to *mythos* and irrationality in modernity. In their classic work *Dialectic of Enlightenment* (1947, written in their exile in the United States) they have shown how rationality in a technologically rationalized modern society is reduced to a means or instrument for interests that themselves are not subject to critical reason. Their historical example is Nazism, which made use of modern science and rational bureaucracy in order to stage the Holocaust. The other example is taken from their exile, where they met modern mass culture and the entertainment industry, which uses the highly developed techniques of industrial society and appealing advertising to deactivate critical thinking. In that way the individual becomes the subject of a hidden profit economy that fills people's hearts and heads with the daydreaming and emotional pleasure they apparently want to have – in the short term. In that sense, one could say that the two great tendencies in Western modernity, the Enlightenment and Romanticism, meet in terms of effect in modern consumerism, which has become worldwide or global at the beginning of the twenty-first century.

Colin Campbell, in his seminal work *The Romantic Ethic and the Spirit of Modern Consumerism* (1987), has given an account of some of the historical prerequisites for the modern consumer society. The title reveals that Campbell has been inspired by Weber's *The Protestant Ethic and the Spirit of Capitalism*. Just as Weber shows that the Protestant ethic, with its self-discipline and high work morale, its scrimping and saving, was a prerequisite for Capitalism, Campbell shows that the Romantic view of man and cast of thought are a prerequisite for present-day consumerism. Since both Romanticism and Protestantism are preoccupied with individual happiness or salvation, emotions become important. In the classical Romantic period, this occurred in the form of the cultivation of a great love that was unattainable, and of daydreams that – not least in nineteenth century novels – cultivate aesthetic sublimation. Campbell demonstrates how the original ideas of Romanticism, which were critical of modern society favouring tradition, undergo a transformation process from something radical and uncompromising or transcendent into something trivial. His conclusion concerning the relationship between romantic ethic and the spirit of modern consumerism is strikingly paradoxical:

> The latter, labelled self-illusory hedonism, is characterized by a longing to experience in reality those pleasures created and enjoyed in imagination, a longing which results in the ceaseless consumption of novelty. Such an outlook, with its characteristic dissatisfaction with real life and an eagerness for new experiences, lies at the heart of much conduct that is most typical of modern life, and underpins such central institutions as fashion and romantic love.[10]

For the modern consumer the new and good is always somewhere else than here and now in our trivial everyday lives. In this respect Romanticism and consumerism are merging in the same attitude. Material advance and mass production in industrial society have made its aims attainable for the great masses in an unending circle of emotional needs that must be satisfied via the consumption of the market's many different offers. Fashions, trends and constant updates of consumer commodities have their own dynamics. The more objects of fascination and pleasure the market offers, the more unsatisfying will familiar everyday life become, and the need for new experiences will be strengthened in an endless circle of stimulation.

The actuality of Campbell's analysis from our point of view is his revelation of how Romanticism is still a potent force that acts covertly, permeating many of the everyday attitudes and emotions of our age. In that sense we are all Romantics. The point of departure underlying these attitudes is, then, Romantic love which, transformed, forms a norm for all of life's relations: be true to your feelings! By making such an appeal, Romanticism promotes a belief in immediate reactions – even though everything in human life is mediated, as critical reflection has shown. By emphasizing the emotions as a decisive motivation, Romanticism presents our preferences as something natural, concealing the fact that motives are conditioned by historical and personal interests, goals and needs.

Emotions are subjective. But subjectivism is not restricted to Romanticism. Rationalism is also subjective, since we do not have any other approach to rationality than via our own reason. That is why Kant's philosophy of reason is called 'transcendental subjectivism'. His epistemological opposite, English empiricism, is subjective, too. But the basis of empiricism for subjectivism is not reason but the senses. Empiricism claims that all human knowledge is based on experience, which has sensory experience as its starting point. Since different people never experience and sense anything identically or similarly, all knowledge is deemed to be subjective. Such a point of view can just as easily lead to senses and sensations becoming the norm instead of to scepticism. Similarly, one can also end up making the individual and individual experiences and evaluations into a norm, since epistemology claims that all valid knowledge must have the subject as its starting point.

All the major schools of thought that form the basis of the Western mentality and the common cultural attitude meet in subjectivism and individualism. Christianity is oriented towards the single individual – the question is always one of individual salvation – just as Western morality and justice are. Guilt is an individual matter; collective guilt is not part of our legal system. It is always a question of the single individual. What is good for the individual is good in itself. Classical liberalism believes that everything will become good for everyone if each individual is allowed to work for his own good. Self-realization is so self-evident in our society that we do not need to argue for this very liberal ideal any longer in Western culture. Pushed to the extreme, English utilitarianism makes morality a matter of calculating what makes the greatest number of people feel good or bad (referred to as the ethics of consequence). As early as the seventeenth century Francis Bacon used this way of thinking as an argument for developing science as a technique for exploiting nature to increase material welfare. Consequently, work in a growth society is simply a means of procuring the means to enjoy life in ever-improving material welfare. To quote the Norwegian author Kjartan Fløgstad's paradoxical statement: 'we work more in order to work less'.[11] For the aim is leisure, and the aim of leisure is to enjoy life; to enjoy life is sensual well-being and experiencing something new, ever newer, in an endless round dance with sensual stimuli at all levels. This schism between work and leisure can be traced back to Romanticism, which via its many literary portrayals showed that it was impossible to realize the good within the framework and norms of society. As good Romantics we are therefore often prepared to sacrifice the common good in order to realize our own private happiness. Similarly, public space is also becoming privatized and emotionalized in a tyranny of intimacy.[12] Personal and intimate relations that belong to private life are transferred to common social and public relations, with mass media reflecting this process.

It is a standard insight within both sociology and psychology that people act rationally in the sense that they wish both inwardly and outwardly to have good reasons and acceptable motives for their attitudes and deeds (no matter how irrational they might seem to be objectively). This also applies to the attitude towards life that intimatized consumerism and the experience-fixated self-realization ideal stand for. Both Romanticism and liberalist individualism have given us good grounds and incentives for following our egoistic desires. In that sense, we are still following – in the midst of and after intimatized late modernism – the voice not only of our heart but of Romanticism as well.

All the transformations that Western symbolism of the heart has undergone in the course of time have accumulated considerable semantic capital that is at the disposal of whoever wishes to use to his own advantage the common symbolism of a whole culture, where the most personal and something universal meets. The flexibility of this universal symbolism explains why the heart can still function as a symbol for what characterizes the commercialized consumption- and diversion-oriented civilization of our age. Indeed, it could even be claimed that the heart, here at the beginning of the twenty-first century, has regained the representative space it lost after Romanticism – quantitatively at least, if not qualitatively – not least as a result of the American celebration of St Valentine that is now spreading across the Old World as well as the rest of the world in the wake of a global economy. After the heart has been disenchanted and lost its soul in the rationalization process, it is being re-enchanted during the eternal spending-spree, using the targets means of advertising.

The celebration of St Valentine goes back to late Antiquity and the legend of the Christian priest Valentine, who married young couples despite a ban imposed by Claudius Caesar. According to the legend, this cost the priest his life on 14 February 269/270 AD. With its praise of love that defies all worldly obstacles, coercion and unfreedom, the Valentine legend corresponds to the love ideal of the age of chivalry, in the wake of which the legend enjoyed a new lease of life. The custom of sending a letter to one's beloved can be traced back to England in the fifteenth century. The earliest surviving valentine dates from 1415: a poem written by Charles, Duke of Orleans to his wife. At the time, the duke was being held in the Tower of London following his capture at the Battle of Agincourt. With this allusion to the popular legend of St Valentine, who just before he died in his prison cell in Rome sent a love-letter to the jailer's love-sick daughter, signed 'Your Valentine', a new tradition is established. The custom of sending a letter to one's beloved on St Valentine's Day was taken by English emigrants to America, where in the course of the nineteenth century it was revived and gradually commercially systematized. It is no longer so popular to write cards or letters, we might prefer to say it with flowers or a book or try to buy ourselves a place in our beloved's heart with some nice gift.

In this way a Christian saint is used in a perverse way to sanctify a highly secular spending-spree and an eroticized urge to buy. The divinely inspired heart of Bernard and Luther that praised love of one's neighbour symbolizes in today's society a consumerism that only the rich part of the world can take part in and that does nobody any good. This, in a way, means we have come full circle, not only as regards the Valentine celebration, which comes originally from a heathen Roman fertility rite, but also when it comes to the symbolism of the heart, which has passed from something objectively given in Antiquity to something subjectively inner in the High Middle Ages back to something outer and external in the commercialized celebration of Valentine's Day. From having been the innermost recess of the personality, the heart has become an image of the most superficially outer: fundamentally superficial. From having been a symbol in Christianity and resurrected as such in modern art and literature, the heart has become kitsch and clichéd – at best, a dead metaphor in everyday language. It is a long way from Augustine's *cor inquietum* and Bernard's *cor caritatis* to the *cor commercial* of our time. When the creative core of culture has burnt out and civilization is only marking time, the common symbol becomes usurped, trivialized and used as a means for something else – not a celebration of something holy, but something narcissistic. And the symbolism of the heart is now consumed like everything else under consumerism. And when one can no longer talk about the heart – what then? We reply with an altered quotation from Wittgenstein: whereof one cannot speak, thereof one must 'write' – from the depths of one's heart.

So as not to fill the heart with what in many ways can be characterized as the reverse side of Western culture, it is perhaps appropriate to go behind the clichés of the St Valentine celebration and remind ourselves of what the heart originally represents in various civilizations, as conveyed in the earlier chapters, and not to forget that the heart – to use Ibn Arabi's words – is open to all forms, to all private emotions and passions, including fanatical religious and political fervour as well as an aggressive compulsion to buy and egoism. This does not mean that the heart is once more to be closed or hermeticized, since the open heart is also the condition not only for tolerance and doubt, for questioning and dialogue, but also for access to the world. Man's fundamental openness to the world is the prerequisite for his being able to pay due care to what is given to us and inscribed on the heart, as Hannah Arendt has taught us (in *The Human Condition*, 1958), in an actively caring relationship to our surroundings that simultaneously opens up new possibilities for social life. In that existentialist sense, Hannah Arendt tells us that we constantly have the possibility for a new beginning in life.

From a historical perspective, no one can claim to have given every single individual and mankind in general more new beginnings in life than modern medical science. The most recent generation of cardiac surgery has made the Bible's promise 'to make hearts new' come true – quite literally. Modern heart medicine and cardiology have also definitively determined our contemporary conception of the heart. As a science, modern cardiology is by no means trivial either – it represents the most complex and advanced of modern science.

The commercial trivialization of the heart we are witnessing in modern consumer society, represented by the celebration of St Valentine's Day, presupposes the disenchantment of the world by modern science. The disenchantment of the heart began with Harvey's discovery of the circulation of the blood and the redefinition of the heart from a source of heat to a pump. This mechanical understanding of the heart still survives in our present-day conception of the heart as a muscle that pumps blood containing oxygen round the body. Muscles, including the heart, are the subject for moulding and manipulation. Not only in bodybuilding, with anabolic steroids, but also in top athletics as well as keep-fit sports, carried out with stopwatch in hand to count the number of heartbeats per minute as a quantitative measure of how fit the body and the heart are. And if the heart is not strong enough as a muscle and does not pump sufficiently oxygen-rich blood fast enough round the body, it is stimulated by drugs to increase its performance and the blood's capacity to absorb oxygen.

Our present age focuses on the exterior body, in line with the surface aesthetics of the sex market. That is why men and women willingly undergo surgery in the Procrustean bed and have their physical bodies manipulated, have a face-lift or breast-lift, have excess flesh removed and flesh added where there is a deficiency. As a consequence and symptom of this externalization of our view of man, the breast can no longer be used as a synonym for the heart. In our present world, where vanity has become a virtue, there are very fine transitions between plastic surgery operations for health and for external aesthetic reasons. Who receives or gives a fresh organ is often just as much a question of money as of ethics, since transplants of inner organs nowadays are in the process of becoming big business. As a point of departure, however, transplants of inner organs can be considered one of the greatest triumphs in the history of medicine and science, since they save the lives of people who otherwise would face a certain death. In this history, heart transplants occupy a particularly spectacular place, one that exceeds medical history and has become part of our common cultural history and therefore a theme in this book.

That heart transplants exceed strictly medical boundaries is because the state of the heart is a direct matter of life and death, an issue that everyone has a lasting interest in. If the heart stops, life stops – as it does sooner or later for every one of us. But for a certain proportion of the population the heart has stopped earlier than for others, because of heart failure and heart diseases of various kinds: thrombosis, heart attack, high blood pressure, too high a cholesterol level, infections, angina pectoris, etc. Heart and vascular disorders are still among the most widespread diseases. For that reason, all advances within cardiology and heart medicine are the source of great public interest.

Heart pumps are no longer merely metaphors that, by means of comparison, illustrate how the heart functions. Today, for example, temporary pumps are operated into the heart itself in the event of acute heart disease (the Impella heart pump pumps 2.5 litres of blood per minute). A mechanical heart, a ventricular assist device, is implanted to help a seriously inflamed heart. When the heart has recovered, the device can be taken out after some weeks or a few months. The heart-lung machine was first used in the 1950s. The most recent landmark in cardiac surgery is the so-called beating-heart transplant, where the donor's heart is connected to a pump that both helps the excised heart to beat and at the same time pumps nutritious fluid into it during transportation to its new host. The path to successful heart transplants has, however, been a long one, not only because of resistance from the Church to dissections and experiments with God's own creation.

When Dr Christiaan Barnard (1922–2001) carried out the first successful

heart transplant in 1967, it was immediately perceived as a historic event –
and thus also a global media event and something everyone felt involved
in. There are still millions of people who can remember the name not
only of the heart surgeon but also his patient, Louis Washkansky, who
unfortunately died after 18 days – of pneumonia. But his new heart beat
strongly to the end. The drugs used to prevent the body rejecting the
new heart had weakened his resistance to infection. The same happened
with most of this first generation of heart transplants. In the 1970s,
however, a medical scientist searching in the Norwegian mountains discovered a new drug called cyclosporin. This drug helped the patient to
overcome his body's rejection of donor organs and protected him against
infection. Subsequent heart transplants were more successful. By the mid
1980s two thirds of all heart transplant patients survived for five years or
more. Today the rate of survival is even higher.

At the beginning of the twenty-first century, heart transplants have
become commonplace, limited mainly by the scarcity of donors. Available
hearts are rare because the heart deteriorates quite quickly when cooled
down by the method normally used. This has now changed radically as a
result of the above-mentioned beating-heart transplant, performed with
success for the first time in the UK in the summer of 2006. This new technique keeps the heart warm, nourished and beating since it is attached to
a specialized machine with a pump function while being transported to
its new owner, who may be hundreds of miles away. This 'beating-heart
machine' probably has the potential to help solve a chronic organ shortage
crisis. But its expected greater availability also intensifies the ethical
dilemmas heart transplants in general represent concerning the qualities
of the heart at stake.

Heart transplants demonstrate more clearly than any other phenomenon just how different our scientifically disenchanted view of humans
is from that of previous generations, when the heart was a symbol of the
individual's inviolability and as the very incarnation of divinely inspired
human soul. In the first part of this book we saw how closely different
high cultures identified the heart with the soul. In these cultures heart
transplantations could not have been executed since it would have violated
the salvation of the individual heart-soul. Nor is it completely unproblematic from a biblical Christian point of view to remove the heart from a
deceased person and place it in a foreign body. Dogmatically interpreted,
it is an act of blasphemy, since according to the Bible it is God himself
who can give man 'a new heart' (cf. Ezekiel 11: 19–20). Since Christianity
also preaches that this divine body of flesh and blood will rise again in the
world beyond, heart transplants must be problematic, since the transplanted heart cannot know in whose body it is to reside after the resurrec-

tion. Even seen with Western Romantic eyes, heart transplants are a demonic tampering with life.

In Romantic literature, from around 1800, horror scenarios of the destructive consequences of experimental science are a favourite theme. The best-known work of this genre is Mary Shelley's *Frankenstein, or The Modern Prometheus* of 1816. The work is mentioned here because the way in which Victor Frankenstein creates life – which turns out to be a monster because of its soulless heart – has direct associations with present-day organ transplants. By assembling body parts, also from dissecting rooms, Victor Frankenstein creates his new man. Present-day heart surgery can literally or in terms of literature be located in this scenario.

Few Westerners in the twenty-first century share Mary Shelley's fear of medical science – not at least when it comes to heart medicine (if we ignore the danger of the wrong type and amount of medicine being given). For our world is disenchanted. This means that we do not attach anything religious or spiritual to our bodily organs as such. We view our inner organs precisely as organs with particular functions, even though we do not perceive them only mechanically but also biologically as integral parts of an organic whole. That is why – at least in principle – via a correct diet and healthy lifestyle we try to ensure we have a good, i.e. a *strong* heart. And as if that was not enough, we resort to heart medicines and heart surgery of various kinds, each of which represents a landmark in cardiac surgery: special by-pass operations (cardiopulmonary bypass, successful from the late 1950s), pacemakers (also from the 1950s), vascular surgery, new heart valves and new arteries, surgery for valvular heart disease and coronary artery disease, and – as a last resort – heart transplants.

However, it is not unproblematic from a psychological point of view either to have a heart transplant. If the heart is not my own, who am I then? But when the body (with the aid of medicine) does not reject the heart, nor does the conscious individual. So the new heart is yet another example of just how flexible a human being is. It is simply put together out of various parts, now with newly implanted and transplanted organs too, which it constructively embodies in its new identity, which in turn is constantly changing both physiologically and psychologically, as the body's own cells are always being renewed and replaced.

Cardiology represents the reenchantment of both the human body and our world via rational scientific means. The heart specialist is our present-day medicine man, the magician who literally holds our hearts and thereby our lives in his hands and decides the question of life and death. The boundary between life and death can never be disenchanted or done away with, only shifted. Nowhere is the reenchantment of our demystified world more obvious than in brain and heart research. One has to resort to concepts from aesthetics to be able to give a satisfactory characterization of a heart transplant, namely the Sublime. According to Edmund Burke, who with his *Philosophical Enquiry into the Origin of our Ideas of the Sublime and the Beautiful* (1757) modernized this concept, the Sublime is defined as that which goes beyond what we normally can comprehend and control, that which we have to surrender to in awe and follow, independently of our will. Likewise, we always have to follow the rhythm of the heart – always go *with* and never *against* it. So in a double sense one always has to follow one's heart, experiencing through it 'the passions that build up our human soul', as depicted by William Wordsworth in *The Prelude* (1799). In this classic poetic work the heart represents the common rhythm of nature and life, of body and mind, 'Both pain and fear, until we recognize/A grandeur in the beatings of the heart' (ll. 140–41). This 'grandeur in the beatings of the heart' is itself an expression of the human sublimity that this chapter is trying to explain.

In a heart transplant, everything is subordinate to the heart and has to follow the heartbeat, the mystery of life we know in our chest and in our jugular veins. The heart does not obey any command or wish. Other muscles in the arms and legs we are able to command to do as we want, but not the heart. It beats spontaneously of its own accord, independently of our will: that is what is sublime about it. The heart-saver Christiaan Barnard, ironically enough, died of heart failure.

We know today that the brain controls our entire organism – including the functions of the heart and blood, though the heart also sends signals to the brain and produces hormones. The strange thing is that the brain works imperceptibly. Both emotions and passions are triggered by processes in the brain, but the brain itself is without feeling. And which impulses trigger off thoughts and which ones trigger off emotions is a question of high complexity for the brain, where thought and feeling mutually stimulate each other, and where everything interacts with the rest of the body beyond any form of Cartesian dualism, as explained by the neurophysiologist Antonio R. Damasio in his *Descartes' Error: Emotion, Reason, and the Human Brain* (1996). So the heart is really located in the brain.

From this perspective, the heart is 'only' a symptom. But it is a crucial symptom, for it is this symptom that our sensibility registers and reacts to. Via the heart we pick up signals that danger is imminent, signals that enable us to distinguish between good and evil so we do not become heartless. That is the story of the heart in our cultural and psychological history, *The Tell-Tale Heart* of elementary psychology and projections as told by Edgar Allan Poe in 1843. The brain, with its unfeeling grey matter, can never take the place of the red-hot heart as a symbol of what a human being is – not, at least, at the present stage of the development of *homo sapiens*. The brain is a fact, not a symptom and not a symbol, while the heart is all of this – and much more. That is why the sensibility, symptoms and symbols of the heart are not without interest; the miracle of the heart has become yet greater because of the interaction with the brain. We have a kind of physiological overview of the heart, but we will never get to the bottom of the brain. It is the great mystery – a microcosm with just as many nerve cells as there are stars in the macrocosm. This brings us to the true mystery in and of the human being: the sublime interaction between heart and head, sense and sensibility. To preserve the qualities of the heart this interaction must be organized in a functional system. The following postscript represents a draft of such a system.

Coda: The Emotional Cycle

Ah, not in vain ... did ye love to intertwine
The passions that build up our human soul ...
With life and Nature, purifying thus
The elements of feeling and of thought,
And sanctifying by such discipline
Both pain and fear, until we recognize
A grandeur in the beatings of the heart.
                    Wordsworth, *The Prelude*

The heart has occupied a unique and often spectacular place in the cultural history of humanity. In many cultures it has been the prime symbol, functioning as a kind of mediator of the wider contexts – physical and mental, natural and cosmic, religious and cultural – of human existence, with different views of the world and of humanity as a result. Everywhere, except in the case of the ancient Greeks, the mental power and symbolic significance of the heart has been crucial, as the symbol of the heart is able to gather into itself what essentially makes humans human in different parts of the world and at different times.

Despite its many different forms and functions, all images of the heart everywhere seem to have a common origin: a sensitive and warm, openly receptive and flexible heart that reacts to what happens in and around living persons. All of these experiences have given the heart certain metaphorical functions that seem to be universal. First and foremost the heart communicates the basic human emotions: love and sympathy, passion and suffering. The function of the heart is to protest vigorously when human nature and what gives individuals integrity is violated. For this reason the heart itself is seen as being full of insight and cognitive powers, to be not just a symptom and a symbol. The ethical function that the heart has explains why it has sometimes been thought of as the seat of the soul and conscience.

Language testifies to just how important the heart is in our own self-understanding and in cultural history. There is hardly any other word in all the Germanic languages that is so much a part of set expressions as the word heart. A large proportion of the metaphors of the heart in everyday language say something about personal characteristics. It is the heart that tells us what sort of a person we are dealing with. The heart, though, is also the medium of something more profound, something inexpressible that language can put us on the trail of.

If something weights on our heart, a heart-to-heart talk may relieve us of this burden. Language is all about speaking out – trusting that what we say will not be used against us. This urge to talk spontaneously, straight from the heart, trusting that others will not misuse our trust, also has to do with other irreducible phenomena of life: compassion, which causes the receiver to feel with us, and shame, which prevents him or her from violating what the speaker inevitably reveals by communicating. There is a mutual interaction between heart and language that meets in the ability to speak out about what lies within and to be spoken to from without – heart speaks to heart – a mutual relationship that conveys some third or universal quality that is of a greater and ultimately inexplicable nature. The phenomenon of shame can illustrate this. Shame is directly connected to what the heart stands for, visible physically if someone blushes as the heart swiftly pumps extra blood out into the body. This third quality, which gives the individual integrity and his life meaning, has to do with such phenomena as trust, love, shame and compassion. The heart is the bearer of these phenomena – and a symptom of them if violated. These qualities and similar ones that maintain life are referred to by the Danish philosopher K. E. Løgstrup (1905–1981) as 'sovereign manifestations of life'. If they are destroyed or ignored, anything can happen, for the heartless person has cast off all sense of shame.

The sovereign manifestations of life also explain many of the reactions of the heart. The heart is agitated and intoxicated, shakes and quivers, boils and is wrung, uplifted and inspired – or depressed, hurt or broken. The heart allows itself to be spoken to from without and within, by other people and by nature, by someone and The One, the divine and supernatural, the good, the beautiful and the true. The fact that the heart can have all these qualities and be the bearer of some kind of mediating emotional barometer for these irreducible forces is the mystery that has fascinated people throughout history and ensured the heart the central position it enjoys not only in anthropology but also in cosmology and religion in most cultures during some or several phases of their respective development. The heart is the most sensitive and receptive of all human organs. That is why the heart is referred to in a number of cultures as *listening* – it hears what is unspoken.

In most religions, the heart mediates between the terrestrial and the 'heavenly'. The notion of the superterrestrial or supernatural has acquired its symbolic representations in 'god', in the singular or plural. But the closest we come to a general truth in this matter is to accept the existence of a dimension which we call religious, that thus opens up for something divine in human life. 'God' is *totaliter aliter*, as the medieval term says – totally other and alien – and can be neither apprehended nor comprehended by words. In that case, we ought perhaps respectfully refer to her/him/it in inverted commas as 'God'. The divine is both the closest of the close, 'closer to you than your own jugular vein', as it says in the Koran, and also the most inaccessible of the unapproachable, hidden behind veil upon veil, as it also says. It is not only the basis of mysticism. It is the heart's trivial mystery to which everyone can testify when they attempt to express what they know deep down, that which cannot be uttered or communicated, as Shakespeare portrays it in *King Lear*.

Everything that the heart represents in terms of religion and psychology, emotions and eroticism is embraced by Romanticism. In Romanticism, the emotional turn is completed in the culture of emotions in which we still live today. When we as Westerners allow ourselves to be stimulated sensually in experiences and pleasures of every kind, this is completely in accordance with the trivialized spirit of Romanticism. To the extent that we live with the idea that the voice of the heart is something naturally given, or that something divine is inscribed on the heart, we can be called Romantics. And we are, too, when we place feelings and our emotional involvement above objective, rational arguments, as we do when we passionately arguing in favour of obeying reason as if it was something given. As Westerners, we have no alternative to the heart as the central symbol in our view of humanity. The brain is a fact, not a symbol. The heart is both.

The physical heart is not in itself a seat of the emotions. It is a symptom of a signal that comes from various parts of the brain – the upper and lower, frontal and rear parts of the brain, according to what type of emotion and passion we are dealing with. Emotions are also reactions – as portrayed by both Montaigne and Shakespeare – to thoughts and notions, goals and interests, expectations and despair. And emotions create new emotions. The subjective emotional reactions are proportional to the goals the individual has set himself, and with the degree to which these goals are attained, and are often inversely proportional to the degree of insight and stoical wisdom in the person concerned.

Emotions are also something our consciousness experiences, registers and adapts to – often in a vicious circle. In many ways, emotions give substance to cognition. It was interesting from an anthropological point of view that the Greeks placed thoughts in the diaphragm and the region of the heart. For there is an indissoluble interaction between the heart's emotional reactions and reason's varying degrees of insight. The symbolic-representative heart therefore becomes a mental mediator that, as cognition increases, spontaneously integrates thoughts, notions and emotions into a sensory-intelligible whole. In this way, it is the emotions mediated by the heart that give the complex human being *identity* and *integrity*. The heart states through the senses what it is like to be in the world. This is the mystery of the human heart. That is why it can be such a serious matter to act against 'the heart's inner voice', and correspondingly dangerous to allow oneself to be seduced by one's self-sufficient heart when full of nothing but wilfulness and selfishness, by the single-stringed passion that rhetoric calls *pathos*.

The heart is both a sensory organ and an image of general values of a non-corporeal nature. It is something in humans that is neither pure body nor pure acquired intelligence and experiences. Let us call it mind or common sense (*logos*). We can think anything at all, good or evil. But certain thoughts are bound by what we cannot think – and cannot think because what we do think is not what we deserve but that which emerges involuntarily, itself something we must act in accordance with if we are not to lose our integrity – which comes from the interaction between our conscience and the imperatives of the outside world. That the heart too can be the mental mediator or voice of reason that reacts when the greater integrity is violated is one of the great mysteries of human life.

On the basis of the complex interaction between the various dimensions that constitute the fluid and composite whole that a human being is, emotionality can be explained as a cycle divided into four main categories by a horizontal and an intersecting vertical axis (as illustrated by the figure *The emotional cycle*): The horizontal axis is governed by the ego (the axis of the ego). The vertical axis transcends the ego, i.e. is a transcendental axis with love of *logos* in itself as the highest goal. It represents the elevation of the intellectual into pure thought, the path of the mystic towards the heart of hearts that ends in what esoterically is incommunicable, within or beyond the conventional world of language and the society of others. The goal is the path of the free spirit, to raise oneself above the limitations of the axis of the ego and ascend into the unconditioned universal.

Each axis in this system has complementary and mutually conditioned poles, where *passion* (*pathos*) is complementary to *suffering* (which *pathos* also can be translated by), which is a necessary consequence of passion

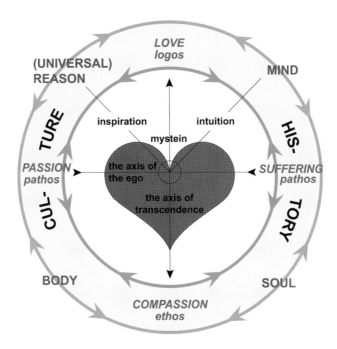

(after eventual short-lived satisfaction or disappointed expectation). Similarly, on the subject-transcending vertical axis, compassion (*sympathos*) is unavoidable for anyone who has and can experience *love*. But the compassion that is part of love goes beyond the ego-determined suffering and pain that follow despair at the lost or unachieved egoistic goal. Love is the ability to feel compassion with *the other*, i.e. empathy (from Greek *en-pathos*). The intellectual imaginative capacity or fantasy is a presupposition of being able to place oneself in somebody else's situation and to feel with that person or those persons. That is why a non-intelligent person lacks both empathy and imagination. Empathy is also the prerequisite for personal morality and an ethical disposition (*ethos*). Egoistic passion, wilfulness that insists on what it wants for itself, often goes against what is morally right in order to gain its aims. This moral right can only be mediated by what is universally true, *logos*, where reason and mind meet. The aim of the human being is to raise himself or herself above the determining logic of passion and to become part of the unlimited universal as self-development leads to dissolution of the self.

The two main axes of the emotional cycle pass right through the mediating heart, which reacts symptomatically, causally or goal-orientedly to the impulses it is exposed to from every part of composite man. The arrow or sword that runs through the heart is a conventional image or emblem of these emotional reactions. But what the emotions are an expression of must always be clarified concretely in conscious reflection and be embedded in something greater than the individual, in something universal. What normally happens, however, is that the emotions in themselves are taken to be the truth: the stronger, the truer! This is what Camus calls the reversed logic of passion.

An attempt has been made in the figure *The emotional cycle* to present the dynamics and dimensions of elementary emotional life. The term cycle emphasizes the idea that no emotion is an isolated phenomenon but that emotions are sensory reactions that have different sources in different parts of the body and intellect, soul and mind, and that interact with each other in complex social, historical and cultural processes. Language and history, including the social and cultural, are the river in which humans swim. Few emotions describe a straight linear course between two poles. The exception is single-stringed passion and desire, which follows the linear axis of egoism. The fact that emotions and passions are part of a social and historically conditioned interaction with the other main dimensions in the human being has enormous consequences for attitudes and actions. Neither is individual intelligence (which is part of universal reason) independent of the body and subjective soul. That is why we do not always manage to follow up in practice what we know to be right. For our motives become mixed, becoming grey and obscure at the critical moment. Consequently, it is also difficult to agree on aims that can serve the common good (*logos*). People are so different in their levels of insight and interests that a common understanding and agreement is often lacking. And there are more forces that pull us down than raise us up. Furthermore – and this is something that Nietzsche reminds us of – our primitive forces also want to move upwards, and 'the spirit of gravity causes all things to fall'. That is why so many good things fall to the ground, and with them often their originators.

Because of his composite structure, man is slow to change. Many of the terms referring to man in the rhetoric of Antiquity can thus still be used to describe the complex whole that man is. If images from the anthropology of Antiquity are adjusted to keep pace with a modern understanding of man's changing plasticity and historicity, it perhaps still represents the truest and most efficient anthropology. In modified form, it underlies the figure *The emotional cycle*, where the good or vicious circle of suffering has also been allocated a place.

Humans do not have a single essence or being, but a unique relational and functional universe of diverse elements, a dynamic interactive combination that biology is unable to explain, and that breaks with the continuity that otherwise prevails in nature. Only when the heart is filled with historical content via what it represents emotionally, intellectually, ethic-ally and culturally – as shown in the previous chapters – are we dealing with a complete human being. It is our historical and individual reason that fills the heart and makes it into a symbolic function of everything mental that subsequently animates the body and all our practice, as emanations of wholeheartedness, to refer to Shakespeare once again.

This irreducible wholeness of body, soul, mind and reason creates the human being, held together by the glow we feel in our heart when we live and love, when we reflect, are creative and become conscious, when we are inspired and let ourselves spontaneously be carried off by something greater than ourselves. That is the grandeur of our pulsing heartbeats. And as long as human beings are driven not by egoistic passion and instinctive self-preservation but by a love of truth and of the restless and disquieting glow of recognition at understanding one's natural and his-torical origin, life's constitutive conditions and its goals, the restless heart will continue to change as its insight grows more profound. To the extent that God's finger – as an image of the mysterious paradox of evolution and history – has touched and written on our hearts, the words inscribed there are 'Know thyself!'

References

ONE: THE WORLD OF GILGAMESH

1 These are selected verses in translation by Diane Wolkstein and Samuel N. Kramer from their *Inanna: Queen of Heaven and Earth* (New York, 1983).

TWO: ANCIENT EGYPT

1 Hellmut Brunner, *Das Hörende Herz: Kleine Schriften zur Religions- und Geistesgeschichte Ägyptens* (Freiburg and Göttingen, 1988), pp. 9–10.
2 Jan Assmann, 'Zur Geschichte des Herzens im Alten Ägypten', in G. Berkemer and G. Rappe, *Das Herz im Kulturvergleich* (Berlin, 1996), p. 149.

THREE: THE COMPLEX MAN OF ANTIQUITY

1 Keld Zeruneith, *Træhesten: Fra Odyssevs til Sokrates: En bevidsthedshistorie*, 2nd edn (Copenhagen, 2002), pp. 57–8.
2 Bruno Snell, 'Die Auffassung des Menschen bei Homer', 'Das Erwachen der Persönlichkeit in der frühgriechischen Lyrik', in *Die Entdeckung des Geistes* [1946], 4th edn (Göttingen, 1975), p. 18.
3 Kai Aalbæk-Nielsen, *Kærlighed i antikken* (Copenhagen, 1999), vol. I, p. 53.
4 Owen Barfield, *History in English Words* [1926] (London, 1954), p. 82.
5 Friedrich Nietzsche, *Die Geburt der Tragödie oder Griechentum und Pessimismus/The Birth of the Tragedy* (1870–71), in Karl Schlechta, *Friedrich Nietzsche: Werke in drei Bänden* [1954] (Darmstadt, 1997), vol. I, p. 36.
6 Friedrich Nietzsche, *Aus dem Nachlass der Achtzigerjahre*, in Schlechta, *Friedrich Nietzsche*, vol. III, p. 792.

FOUR: THE HEART IN THE BIBLE AND IN CHRISTIANITY

1 Friedrich Nietzsche, *Also sprach Zarathustra/Thus Spake Zarathustra* (Harmondsworth, 2003), vol. II, p. 457.
2 Georges Bataille (2001), p. 35.
3 Aurelius Augustinus, *Confessiones, Confessions: Books I–X*, trans. J. G. Pilkington, in *Nicene and Post-Nicene Fathers, Series One*, ed. Philip Schaff, *Volume I, St Augustine, Prolegomena, Life and Work, Confessions, Letters* (Grand Rapids, mi, 1989), bk 2, chap. 3.
4 Ibid., bk 2, chap. 4.

5 Trond Berg Eriksen, *Augustine: Det urolige hjertet* (Oslo, 2000), p. 217.
6 Peter Thielst, *Kødets lyst – tankens list: Kroppens og seksualitetens idéhistorie* (Copenhagen, 2000), p. 113.
7 Ibid., pp. 114, 116.

FIVE: ISLAM'S CULTURE OF THE HEART

1 After Annemarie Schimmel, *The Triumphal Sun: A Study of the Works of Jalaloddin Rumi* [1978] (London and The Hague, 1980).
2 Farid od Din Attar, *The Conference of the Birds: Mantiq ut-tair* (Boulder, CO, 1971), pp. 321–2.
3 Henry Corbin, *Creative Imagination in the Sufism of Ibn Arabi* [1958] (Princeton, NJ, 1969), p. 221.
4 E. H. Whinfield, ed. and trans., *Masnavi i Ma'navi: The Spiritual Couplets of Maulana Jalalu-'d'Din Muhammed i Rumi* (London, 1898) (also available at muslim-canada.org/sufi/book0rumi.html), V, 3844.
5 Ibid., II, 1157ff.
6 Ibid.

SIX: THE AZTECS – WHY SO HEARTLESS?

1 Niels Steensgård, *Verden på oppdagelsenes tid 1350–1500*, vol. VII of *Aschehougs verdenshistorie* (Oslo, 1984), p. 205.
2 G. Berkemer and G. Rappe, *Das Herz im Kulturvergleich* (Berlin, 1996), p. 25.
3 Friedrich Nietzsche, Morgenröte (1881), in Karl Schlechta, *Friedrich Nietzsch*; as *The Dawn/Daybreak: Thoughts on the Prejudices of Morality*, trans. R. J. Hollingdale (Cambridge, 1982), vol. I, p. 18.

SEVEN: NORSE ANTHROPOLOGY

1 Claus von See, *Edda, Saga, Skaldendichtung* (Heidelberg, 1981), p. 76.
2 Britt-Mari Näsström, *Blot: Tro og offer i det førkristne Norden* (Oslo, 2001), p. 55.
3 Snorri Sturluson, *Heimskringla*, chap. 31.
4 Von See, *Edda* (1981), pp. 74–5.

EIGHT: THE EMOTIONAL TURN IN THE HIGH MIDDLE AGES

1 John Pedersen, *Troubadourernes sange* (Copenhagen, 2001).
2 Gottfried von Strassburg, *Tristan: With the 'Tristran' of Thomas*, ed. A. T. Hatto (Harmondsworth 1960), pp. 262–3.
3 Ibid., p. 263.
4 Bernard de Clairvaux, *De Deligendo Deo*, VIII, 23, *On Love to God*, in *S. Bernardi Opera*, ed. Dom J. Leclercq *et al.* (Rome, 1957–), III, 138, 6.
5 Joseph Campbell, *Creative Mythology: The Masks of God* [1968] (London, 1974), p. 59.
6 Ibid.
7 Chapter 'The Voice of the Nightingale'.
8 Niklas Luhmann, *Liebe als Passion: Zur Codierung von Intimität* (1994); as *Love as Passion: The Codification of Intimacy*, trans. Jeremy Gaines and Doris L. Jones (Stanford, CA, 1998), p. 51.
9 Campbell, *Creative Mythology*, p. 177.

10 Theodore Zeldin, *An Intimate History of Humanity* (London, 1998), p. 123.

NINE: THE NEW SUBJECT

1 René Descartes, *Les Passions de l'âme* (1649), as *The Passions of the Soul*, trans. Stephen Voss (Indianapolis and Cambridge, 1995), Part I, Article 8–9.
2 Ibid., Part I, Article 33.

TEN: MONTAIGNE: MAN IS HIS OWN WORK

1 Michel de Montaigne, Essais, Book II, 10: 296.
2 Ibid., II, 8: 279).
3 Ibid., III, 13: 840).
4 Translated as *Montaigne in Motion* (Paris, 1993).
5 Montaigne, *Essais*, II, 11: 310.
6 Ibid., II, 12: 438.
7 Ibid., II, 6: 274.
8 Ibid., II, 8: 279.
9 Ibid., II, 37: 596.
10 Ibid., III, 11: 787.
11 Ibid., III, 13: 821.
12 Ibid., III, 13: 826.
13 Ibid., III, 9: 721.
14 Ibid., III, 5: 681.
15 Ibid., III, 5: 645.
16 Ibid., III, 5: 668.
17 Ibid., II, 12: 455.
18 Ibid., I, 20: 62.
19 Ibid., I, 20: 60.
20 Ibid., I, 19: 55.
21 Ibid., I, 20: 61.
22 Ibid., I, 19: 55.
23 Ibid., I, 20: 57–8.
24 After Starobinski.

ELEVEN: FROM THE RENAISSANCE AND ALCHEMY TO THE ROMANTIC ERA

1 William Harvey, *Movement of the Heart and Blood in Animals: An Anatomical Essay* [1628] (Oxford, 1957), pp. 58–9.
2 Rudolf Otto, *Das Heilige* (1917); trans. as *The Idea of the Holy* (Oxford 1958).

TWELVE: SHAKESPEARE AND THE HEART OF DARKNESS

1 Harold Bloom, *Shakespeare: The Invention of the Human* (New York, 1998).
2 Ibid., p. 739.

FOURTEEN: HERDER AND THE EXPRESSIVIST TURN

1 Johann Gottfried Herder, *Werke*, 10 vols (Frankfurt am Main, 1986–), vol. I, p. 134.
2 Ibid., vol. VI, pp. 347–8.

FIFTEEN: FAUSTIAN GOETHE

1 Johann Wolfgang von Goethe, *Maximen und Reflexionen*, Hamburger Ausgabe (HA), vol. XII (Hamburg, 1999), p. 470 (aphorism no. 1113).
2 Ibid., p. 471 (aphorism no. 314).
3 Per Øhrgaard, *Goethe: Et essay* (Copenhagen and Oslo, 1999), p. 326.
4 K. E. Løgstrup, *Norm und Spontaneitä* (Tübingen, 1989).

SIXTEEN: THE DISENCHANTMENT AND RE-ENCHANTMENT OF THE HEART

1 Friedrich Nietzsche, *Morgenröte* (1881); as *The Dawn/Daybreak: Thoughts on the Prejudices of Morality*, trans. R. J. Hollingdale (Cambridge, 1982) (aphorism 35).
2 Nietzsche, *Beyond Good and Evil*, trans. and ed. Marion Faber (Oxford, 1958) (aphorism 62).
3 Wilhelm Schmid, *Philosophie der Lebenskunst* (Frankfurt am Main, 1998).
4 Peter Sloterdijk, *Kritik der zynischen Vernunft/ Critique of Cynical Reason* (Frankfurt am Main, 1983), p. 936.
5 Cf. Ole M. Høystad, 'Identitet eller integritet?', in S. Time, *Kulturell identitet* (Bergen, 1997).
6 Rüdiger Safranski, *Nietzsche: Biographie seines Denkens/A Biography of his Way of Thinking* (Munich and Vienna, 2000), p. 16.
7 Michel Foucault, *The Will to Knowledge*, vol. 1 of *The History of Sexuality* (1976), trans. Robert Hurley (Harmondsworth, 1998), p. 12.
8 Ibid., p. 23.
9 Ibid., p. 156.
10 Joseph Campbell, *Creative Mythology: The Masks of God* [1968] (London, 1974), pp. 205–6.
11 Kjartan Fløgstad, *Fyr og flamme* (Oslo, 1980).
12 Richard Sennett, *The Fall of Public Man* (Cambridge, 1977).

Bibliography

Only sources directly or indirectly referred to are listed. Unless otherwise indicated or as can be seen from the bibliography, the translator is responsible for translations of quotations from other languages.

Aalbæk-Nielsen, Kai, *Kærlighed i antikken: 1 tidens ånd II* (Copenhagen, 1999)
—, *Kærlighed i middelalderen: 1 tidens ånd II* (Copenhagen, 1999)
Adorno, Theodor, and Max Horkheimer, *Dialektik der Aufklärung* [1944/1947], *Dialectic of Enlightenment: Philosophical Fragments*, ed. Gunzelin Schmid Noerr, trans. Edmund Jephcott (Stanford, CA, 2002)
Arendt, Hannah, *The Human Condition* (Chicago, 1958); in German, *Vita Activa oder Vom tätigen Leben* (Munich, 1981)
—, *Der Liebesbegriff bei Augustin* [1928], *Love and Saint Augustine*, ed. Joanna Vecchiarelli Scott and Judith Chelius Stark (Chicago, 1996)
—, *Eichmann in Jerusalem: A Report on the Banality of Evil*, revd. edn (Harmondsworth, 1994)
Arndt, Johan, *Den sanne kristendom* [1610] (Oslo, 1968)
Assmann, Jan, *Death and Salvation in Ancient Egypt*, trans. David Lorton, (Ithaca, NY, 2005)
—, 'Zur Geschichte des Herzens im Alten Ägypten', in G. Berkemer and G. Rappe, *Das Herz im Kulturvergleich* (Berlin, 1996)
—, *Die Erfindung des inneren Menschen*, with 'Zur Geschichte des Herzens im Alten Ägypten' (Gütersloh, 1993)
Attar, Farid od Din, *The Conference of the Birds: Mantiq ut-tair* (Boulder, CO, 1971)
Aurelius Augustinus, *Confessiones, Confessions: Books I–X*, trans. J. G. Pilkington, in *Nicene and Post-Nicene Fathers, Series One*, ed. Philip Schaff, *Volume 1, St Augustine, Prolegomena, Life and Work, Confessions, Letters* (Grand Rapids, MI, 1989)
Austen, Jane, *Pride and Prejudice* (1813)
Bæksted, Anders, *Nordiske guder og helter* (Oslo, 2002)
Baigent, Michael, Richard Leigh and Henry Lincoln, *Holy Blood, Holy Grail* [1982] (New York, 1983)
Bakhtin, Mikhail, *Rabelais and His World* [1965] (Cambridge, MA, and London, 1968)
Barfield, Owen, *History in English Words* [1926] (London, 1954)
Bataille, Georges, *L'érotisme* [1957] (Paris, 1970)
Benthien, Claudia *et al.*, eds, *Emotionalität: Zur Geschichte der Gefühle* (Cologne and Vienna, 2000)
Berkemer, Georg, and G. Rappe, eds, *Das Herz im Kulturvergleich* (Berlin, 1996)
Bernard de Clairvaux, *S. Bernardi Opera I–VII*, ed. Dom J. Leclercq *et al.* (Rome, 1957–)

Bloom, Harold, *Shakespeare: The Invention of the Human* (New York, 1998)

Böhme, Joachim, *Die Seele und das Ich im homerischen Epos* (Berlin, 1929)

Bredsdorff, Thomas, *Tristans børn: Angående digtning om kærlighed og ægteskab i den borgerlige epoke* (Copenhagen, 1982)

Brown, Dan, *The Da Vinci Code* (New York, 2003)

Brunner, Hellmut, *Das Hörende Herz: Kleine Schriften zur Religions- und Geistesgeschichte Ägyptens* (Freiburg and Göttingen, 1988)

Burke, Edmund, *A Philosophical Enquiry into the Origin of our Ideas of the Sublime and Beautiful* (1757)

Campbell, Colin, *The Romantic Ethic and the Spirit of Modern Consumerism* [1987] (Oxford, 1993)

Campbell, Joseph, *Creative Mythology: The Masks of God* [1968] (London, 1974)

Cassirer, Ernst, *An Essay on Man: An Introduction to a Philosophy of Human Culture* (New Haven, CT, 1944)

Conrad, Joseph, *Heart of Darkness*, ed. Robert Kimbrough, 3rd edn (New York and London, 1988)

Corbin, Henry, *Creative Imagination in the Sufism of Ibn Arabi* [1958] (Princeton, NJ, 1969)

Damasio, Antonio R., *Descartes' Error: Emotion, Reason and the Human Brain* (London, 1996)

Dante Alighieri, *The Divine Comedy* (New York, 1909)

Deleuze, Gilles, *Nietzsche: Et essay + filosofiske tekster* (Oslo, 1985); as *Nietzsche and Philosophy*, trans. Hugh Tomlinson (London, 1983)

Derrida, Jacques, *Of Grammatology* [1967] trans. Gayatri Chakravorty Spivak (Baltimore, MD, 1976)

Descartes, René, *Les Passions de l'âme* [1649] as *The Passions of the Soul*, trans. Stephen Voss (Indianapolis and Cambridge, 1995)

Dielz, Hermann, and Walther Kranz, *Die Fragmente der Vorsokratiker*, vol. I, 18th edn (Zurich and Hildesheim, 1992)

Duerr, Hans Peter, *Der Mythos vom Zivilisationsprozess/The Myth of the Civilizing Process*, 4 vols: *Nacktheit und Scham* [1988], *Intimität* [1990], *Obszönität und Gewalt* [1993], *Der erotische Leib* [1997] (Frankfurt am Main, 1988–97)

Dumézil, Georges, *Gods of the Ancient Northmen* (Berkeley, CA, and London 1977)

Eco, Umberto, *The Name of the Rose* [1980] (London, 1983)

Eliade, Mircea, *A History of Religious Ideas*, trans. Alf Hiltebeitel and Diane Apostolos-Cappadona, 3 vols (Chicago, IL, 1988)

Elias, Norbert, *Über den Prozess der Zivilisation* [1939], 2 vols (Frankfurt am Main, 1998–9); as *The Civilizing Process: The History of Manners*, trans. Edmund Jephcott (New York, 1982).

Eriksen, Trond Berg, *Nietzsche og det moderne* (Oslo, 1989)

—, *Augustine: Det urolige hjertet* (Oslo, 2000)

Fløgstad, Kjartan, *Fyr og flamme* (Oslo, 1980)

Foucault, Michel, *The Will to Knowledge*, vol. 1 of *The History of Sexuality* [1976], trans. Robert Hurley (Harmondsworth, 1998)

—, *The Use of Pleasure*, vol. II of *The History of Sexuality*, trans. Robert Hurley, 2nd edn (Harmondsworth, 1992)

—, *The Care of the Self*, vol. III of *The History of Sexuality* (New York, 1986)

Friedrich, Hugo, *Montaigne* (Munich, 1967)

Goethe, Johann Wolfgang von, *Faust I–II* [1808–32], in *Goethe's Collected Works*, ed. Victor Lange *et al.*, 12 vols (Princeton, NJ, 1994–5)

—, *Selected Poems*, vol. I, ed. and trans. C. Middelton *et al.* (Boston, MA, 1983)

—, *Faust II*, vol. II, ed. and trans. Stuart Atkins (Boston, MA, 1984)

—, *Faust I*, trans. Anna Swanwick, vol. XIX, part 1, ed. C. W. Eliot (New York, 1909–14)

—, *West-Östlicher Divan* (1818)

—, *Maximen und Reflexionen*, Hamburger Ausgabe (HA), vol. XII (Hamburg, 1999)

Gottfried von Strassburg, *Tristan* (Harmondsworth, 1960)

Grube, Nikolai, ed., *Maya: Divine Kings of the Rain Forest* (Cologne, 2000)

Gundelach, Kristen, *Luth og Skalmeie: Fransk poesi fra Middelalderen* (Kristiania, 1920)

Hagen, Rainer, and Rose-Marie Hagen, *Egypt: People. Gods. Pharaohs* (Cologne, 2002)

Harvey, William, *Movement of the Heart and Blood in Animals: An Anatomical Essay* [1628] (Oxford, 1957)

Heinimann, Felix, *Nomos und Physis: Herkunft und Bedeutung einer Antithese im griechischen Denken des 5. Jahrhunderts* (Basel, 1945)

Herder, Johann Gottfried, *Werke*, 10 vols (Frankfurt am Main, 1986–)

—, *Über den Ursprung der Sprache/On the Origin of Language* [1772], in *Werke*, vol. I.

Hochschild, Adam, *King Leopold's Ghost: A Story of Greed, Terror and Heroism in Colonial Africa* (Boston, MA, 1999)

Holberg, Ludvig, *Jeppe paa Bierget* [1722]; as *Jeppe on the Hill; or, The Transformed Peasant*, trans. Waldemar C. Westergaard and Martin B. Ruud (Grand Forks, ND, 1906)

Homer, *The Iliad*, trans. A. T. Murray, 2 vols (Cambridge, MA, and London, 1965–7)

—, *The Odyssey*, trans. A. T. Murray (Cambridge, MA, and London, 1976–80)

Hornung, Erik, trans., *Das Totenbuch der Ägypter* (Zurich and Munich, n. d.)

Høystad, Ole M., 'Identitet eller integritet?', in S. Time, *Kulturell identitet* (Bergen, 1997)

Kant, Immanuel, *Anthropologie in pragmatischer Hinsicht* [1800], vol. VI of *Immanuel Kant: Werke in sechs Bände*, ed. Wilhelm Weischedel (Darmstadt, 1983)

—, *An Answer to the Question: What is Enlightenment?* (Köningsberg, 1784)

Krag, Claus, *Vikingtid og rikssamling, 800–1130* (Oslo, 1995)

Kutscher, Gerdt, ed., *Altaztekische Gesänge* (Stuttgart, 1957)

Langen, August, *Der Wortschatz des deutschen Pietismus* (Tübingen, 1954)

Le Roy Ladurie, Emmanuel, *Montaillou: Cathars and Catholics in a French Village, 1294–1324* [1975], trans. Barbara Bray (London 1978)

Levinas, Emmanuel, *Humanism of the Other* [1995], trans. Nidra Poller (Chicago, IL, 2003)

Løgstrup, K. E., *Den etiske fordring* [1954]; as *The Ethical Demand* (Notre Dame, IN, 1997)

—, *System og symbol* (Copenhagen, 1982)

—, *Ophav og omgivelse* (Copenhagen, 1984)

—, *Norm und Spontaneität* (Tübingen, 1989)

Lovejoy, Arthur O., *The Great Chain of Being: A Study of the History of an Idea* [1936] (New York, 2005)

Luhmann, Niklas, *Liebe als Passion: Zur Codierung von Intimität* [1994], as *Love as Passion: The Codification of Intimacy*, trans. Jeremy Gaines and Doris L. Jones (Stanford, CA, 1998)

Mackenzie, Henry, *The Man of Feeling* (1771)

Mauss, Marcel, *Soziologie und Anthropologie. Band II: Gabentausch, Todesvorstellungen, Körpertechniken* (Frankfurt am Main, 1978)

Mommsen, Katarina, *Goethe und der Islam* (Frankfurt am Main, 2001)

Montaigne, *Essais I–III* (1580–88); as *The Complete Essays of Montaigne*, trans. Donald M. Frame (Stanford, CA, 1992)

Morus (Richard Lewinsohn), *Eine Weltgeschichte des Herzens* (Hamburg, 1959)

Nager, Frank, *Das Herz als Symbol* (Basel, 1993)

Näsström, Britt-Mari, *Blot: Tro og offer i det førkristne Norden* (Oslo, 2001)

Nestle, W., *Vom Mythos zum Logos: Die Selbstentfaltung des griechischen Denkens bei Homer bis auf die Sophistik und Sokrates* (Stuttgart, 1940)

Nietzsche, Friedrich, *Friedrich Nietzsche: Werke*, ed. Karl Schlechta, 3 vols [1954] (Darmstadt, 1997)

—, *Die Geburt der Tragödie oder Griechentum und Pessimismus/The Birth of the Tragedy* [1870–71], vol. I in Schlechta, *Friedrich Nietzsche: Werke*

—, *Aus dem Nachlass der Achtzigerjahre*, vol. III in Schlechta, *Friedrich Nietzsche: Werke*

—, *Morgenröte* [1881], vol. I in Schlechta, *Friedrich Nietzsche*; as *The Dawn/Daybreak: Thoughts on the Prejudices of Morality*, trans. R. J. Hollingdale (Cambridge, 1982)

—, *Jenseits von Gut und Böse* [1886], vol. II in Schlechta, *Friedrich Nietzsche*; as *Beyond Good and Evil*, trans. and ed. Marion Faber (Oxford, 1998)

—, *Also sprach Zarathustra/Thus Spoke Zarathustra* (Harmondsworth, 2003)

Nygren, Anders, *Den kristna kärlekstanken/The Christian Concept of Love* [1930–56], cf. his *Agape and Eros* (Philadelphia, 1953)

Øhrgaard, Per, *Goethe: Et essay* (Copenhagen and Oslo, 1999)

Olsen, Michel, 'Medeltiden mellan myt och förnuft', *Res Publica*, 11, topic booklet on 'Mentalitethistoria' (Stockholm, 1988)

Ong, Walter J., *Orality and Literacy: The Technologizing of the Word* (London and New York, 1982)

Otto, Rudolf, *Das Heilige* [1917]; as *The Idea of the Holy: An Inquiry into the Non-Rational Factor in the Idea of the Divine and its Relation to the Rational*, trans. John W. Harvey (Oxford, 1958)

Pedersen, John, *Troubadourernes sange* (Copenhagen, 2001)

Pico della Mirandola, Giovanni, *De Dignitate Homini* [1486]; as *Oration on the Dignity of Man*, trans. A. Robert Caponigri (Chicago, 1956)

Plato, *Phaidon, Phaidros, Timaios, Symposion, Politeia*, in *Platon: Werke* (Darmstadt, 1990)

—, *Symposium*, trans. Benjamin Jowett [1871] (Oxford, 1920)

Poe, Edgar Allan, 'The Tell-Tale Heart' [1843], in *The Tell-Tale Heart and other Writings* (New York, 1982)

Rappe, Guido, *Archaische Leiberfahrungen: Der Leib in der frühgriechischen Philosophie und in aussereuropäischen Kulturen* (Berlin, 1995)

—, and Georg Berkemer, *Herz im Kulturvergleich* (Berlin, 1996)

Richardson, Samuel, *Pamela* (1740)

de Rougemont, Denis, *L'amour et l'Occident* [1939]; as *Love in the Western World*, trans. Montgomery Belgion, revd. edn (Princeton, NJ, 1995)

Rousseau, Jean-Jacques, *Julie; ou, la nouvelle Héloïse* [1759–61]; as *Julie; or, The New Heloise*, trans. Judith H. McDowell (University Park, PA, 1989)

—, *Émile; ou, de l'éducation* [1762]; as *Emile; or, On Education*, trans. with intro. Allan Bloom (New York, 1979)

—, *Confessions of Jean-Jacques Rousseau* [1770–82], trans. Angela Scholar (Oxford, 2000); also available at etext.library.adelaide.edu.au/r/rousseau transl. W. Conyngham Mallory (eBooks@Adelaide, 2005)

—, *Rêveries du promeneur solitaire* [1782], as *Reveries of a Solitary Walker*, trans. Peter France (London, 1980)

Safranski, Rüdiger, *Nietzsche: Biographie seines Denkens/ A Biography of his Way of Thinking* (Munich and Vienna, 2000)

Schimmel, Annemarie, *Mystical Dimensions of Islam* (Chapel Hill, NC, 1975)

—, *And Muhammed is His Messenger: The Veneration of the Prophet in Islamic Piety* (Chapel Hill, NC, 1985)

—, *The Triumphal Sun: A Study of the Works of Jalaloddin Rumi* [1978] (London and The

Hague, 1980)

Schmid, Wilhelm, *Philosophie der Lebenskunst* (Frankfurt am Main, 1998)

Schmitz, Hermann, *System der Philosophie*, vol. ii/1, *Der Leib* (Bonn, 1965)

—, 'Die Verwaltung der Gefühle', in *Emotionalität: Zur Geschichte der Gefühle*, ed. Claudia Benthien *et al.* (Cologne and Vienna, 2000)

—, 'Leibliche Quellen der Herzmetaphorik', in G. Rappe *et al.*, *Herz im Kulturvergleich* (Berlin, 1996)

Schmölders, Claudia, ed., *Die Erfindung der Liebe: Berühmte Zeugnisse aus drei Jahrtausenden* (Munich, 1996)

See, Claus von, *Edda, Saga, Skaldendichtung* (Heidelberg, 1981)

Seifert, Josef, *Das Leib-Seele Problem* (Darmstadt, 1989)

Sennett, Richard, *The Fall of Public Man* (Cambridge, 1977)

Shakespeare, William, *King Lear* [1606–8], ed. R. A. Foakes (Walton-on-Thames, 1997)

Shelley, Mary, *Frankenstein; or, The Modern Prometheus* (1816)

Shupak, N., 'Some idioms Connected with the Concept of "Heart" in Egypt and the Bible', in *Pharaonic Egypt*, ed. Sarah Israelit-Groll (Jerusalem, 1985)

Sloterdijk, Peter, *Kritik der zynischen Vernunft/ Critique of Cynical Reason* (Frankfurt am Main, 1983)

Snell, Bruno, 'Die Auffassung des Menschen bei Homer', 'Das Erwachen der Persönlichkeit in der frühgriechischen Lyrik', in *Die Entdeckung des Geistes* [1946], 4th edn (Göttingen, 1975)

—, *Besprechung von Böhmes Buch 'Die Seele und das Ich im homerischen Epos'*, *Gnomon*, 7 (1931)

Spengler, Oswald, *Untergang des Abendlandes/ The Decline of the West* [1918–22] (Munich, 1988)

Starobinski, Jean, *Montaigne en mouvement* (Paris, 1982–93)

Steensgård, Niels, *Verden på oppdagelsenes tid 1350–1500*, vol. vii of *Aschehougs verdens-historie* (Oslo, 1984)

Sterne, Lawrence, *A Sentimental Journey Through France and Italy* (1768)

Taylor, Charles, *Hegel* (Cambridge, 1975)

—, *Sources of the Self: The Making of Modern Identity* (Cambridge, 1989–92)

Thielst, Peter, *Kødets lyst – tankens list: Kroppens og seksualitetens idéhistorie* (Copenhagen, 2000)

Thomae, Karl, *Das Herz im Umkreis des Denkens* (Biberach an der Riss, 1969)

Undset, Sigrid, *Fortællinger om kong Arthur og ridderne av Det runde bord/Tales of King Arthur and the Knights of the Round Table* (Kristiania, 1915)

Vaughan-Lee, Llewllyn, *Transformation des Herzens: Die Lehren der Sufis* (Frankfurt am Main, 1999)

Vogt, Christian, *Überlegung und Entscheidung: Studien zur Selbstauffassung des Menschen bei Homer* (Berlin, 1931)

Vonessen, Franz, 'Das Herz in der Naturphilosophie', in Karl Thomae, *Das Herz im Umkreis des Denkens* (Biberach an der Riss, 1969)

Weber, Max, *The Protestant Ethic and the Spirit of Capitalism*, trans. Talcott Parsons [1930] (New York, 1958)

—, *Max Weber: An Intellectual Portrait*, by Reinhard Bendix [with Weber 1909] (New York, 1960)

Westaby, Stephen (with Cecil Bosher), *Landmarks in Cardiac Surgery* (Oxford, 1998)

Whinfield, E. H., ed. and trans., *Masnavi i Ma'navi: The Spiritual Couplets of Maulana Jalalu-'d'Din Muhammed i Rumi* (London, 1898) (also available at muslim-canada.org/sufi/bookorumi.html)

Williams, Bernard, *Shame and Necessity* (Berkeley, CA, and London, 1993)

Wolff, Hans Walter, 'Das "Herz" im Alten Testament', in *Menschliches: Vier Reden* (Munich, 1971)

Wolkstein, Diane, and Samuel Noah Kramer, *Inanna: Queen of Heaven and Earth: Her Stories and Hymns from Sumer* (New York and Cambridge, 1983)

Wordsworth, William, *The Prelude* [1799] (London, 1851)

Zeldin, Theodore, *An Intimate History of Humanity* (London, 1998)

Zeruneith, Keld, *Træhesten: Fra Odyssevs til Sokrates: En bevidsthedshistorie*, 2nd edn (Copenhagen, 2002)

Photo Acknowledgements

The author and publishers wish to express their thanks to the below sources of illustrative material and/or permission to reproduce it (some locations of artworks are also given below):

Galleria Borghese, Rome: p. 136; graphic by Trond A. Lerstang: p. 234; Mayer Collection, Denver: p. 141; Munch Museum, Oslo: p. 142; Musée des Beaux Arts, Lille: p. 138; Museo Gregoriano Etrusco, Vatican City, Rome: p. 130; Museo di Roma, Rome: p. 140; National Gallery, London: p. 137; National Museum, Athens: p. 131; Norwegian Folk Museum, Oslo: p. 144.

Index